IN SEARCH OF THE
TALENTED TENTH

IN SEARCH OF THE
TALENTED TENTH

*Howard University Public Intellectuals
and the Dilemmas of Race, 1926–1970*

Zachery R. Williams

University of Missouri Press   Columbia

Library of Congress Cataloging-in-Publication Data

Williams, Zachery R.
  In search of the talented tenth : Howard University public intellectuals and the dilemmas of race, 1926-1970 / Zachery R. Williams.
     p. cm.
  Includes bibliographical references and index.
  ISBN 978-0-8262-2323-4 (paperback : alk. paper)

  1. Howard University—History—20th century. 2. Howard University—Faculty—History—20th century. 3. African American scholars—History--20th century. 4. African American intellectuals—History—20th century. I. Title.
  LC2851.H82W55 2009
  378.753—dc22

                                                                    2009028225

Designer: Stephanie Foley

Typefaces: Giovanni and Palatino

I DEDICATE THIS BOOK
TO BLACK PUBLIC INTELLECTUALS AND SCHOLAR ACTIVISTS,
PAST, PRESENT, AND FUTURE

CONTENTS

ACKNOWLEDGMENTS

S O MUCH GOES INTO PRODUCING A BOOK. There are so many whom I have to thank for their support, encouragement, and generosity over the six years I have labored to complete this work. There are not enough pages to offer proper thanks, and if I omit anyone's name, please chalk it up to my head and not my heart. First, I would like to thank God for sustaining me in good times and bad, as this project moved from stage to stage. This project has taught me the meaning and value of faith.

I am grateful to the legacy left by members of the Howard University intellectual community, past and present. I still remember reading Howard historian Dr. Michael Winston's "Through the Back Door: Academic Racism and the Negro Scholar in Historical Perspective," while I was a freshman at Clemson University. I never will forget that day in the library, for it changed my life. My prayer is that this work does justice to that powerful legacy. I hope that relatives of Howard public intellectuals, students, alumni, faculty, and staff will find great value in it.

This book is a revision of my dissertation. I am sincerely grateful for the guidance of my dissertation committee, my outstanding adviser Don Nieman, Lillian Ashcraft-Eason, Rachel Buff, and Apollos Nwauwa, and to Liette Gidlow, who guided my first internship excursion to Washington, D.C., to begin research on the project. Don, I will always carry with me your example as a superb scholar and dedicated mentor. You are the best. Together, Mama Lillian and the late Dr. Djisovi Eason inspired me and other colleagues in ways that are hard to express. Special thanks go to former BGSU president and current president of Howard University, Dr. Sidney A. Ribeau, for providing a great example of transformative leadership for me during my graduate years. To each of you, I am forever grateful. You believed in me when no one else did. Collectively, my experience at Bowling Green taught me a deep appreciation for the role of community in producing scholarship. Thank you, thank you, thank you.

I must thank my dear colleagues with the Africana Cultures and Policy

Studies Institute, many of whom were in graduate school with me at Bowling Green State University. I could not have completed this work without the support of Tim Lake, Babacar M'Baye, Lyndell Robinson, Robert Smith, and Seneca Vaught.

To intellectual mentors and colleagues who have encouraged me along this journey, I am grateful to each of you. There are too many to name, but I must give special thanks to Davarian Baldwin, Harold Cheatham, V. P. Franklin, Darlene Clark Hine, Janelle Hobson, Peniel Joseph, Robin D. G. Kelley, Manning Marable, Jeffrey Ogbar, James B. Stewart, Reginald Hildebrand, and Rosalyn Terborg-Penn, who at different stages of this project motivated me by their wisdom and professional example.

I would also like to offer sincere gratitude to my undergraduate mentor at Clemson University, Henry Lewis Suggs, a former Howard professor, who through his example and expertise concerning the black press encouraged me to become a historian of the African American experience. I will always remember and celebrate the lessons learned from the one I consider to be among the finest historians in this nation. Thank you, Doc, for everything.

No book of this scope could come about without the support of an expert research and archival staff. This book would not be what it is without the guidance, support, friendship, and brilliance of the staff of Howard University's Moorland-Spingarn Research Center. I am grateful to Joellen Bashir, director of the manuscript division, Tewodros Abebe, Richard Jenkins, Dr. Ida Jones, Dr. Clifford Muse, and Donna Wells, for all of you made this work possible.

I would like to express gratitude to the University of Akron, especially every colleague in the history department. Each of you has supported me since my arrival. I appreciate your wisdom regarding the publishing process and navigation of the academy. I am also grateful for receiving a research grant in the summer of 2006. Thanks go to Dean Tanya Saunders of Ithaca College's Division of Interdisciplinary Studies, former provost Peter Bardaglio, and many others, for your support in the early revision stages of this work.

I must thank all of the staff at the University of Missouri Press. First, my sincere gratitude goes to former editor-in-chief Beverly Jarrett, who believed in this project from the start. In my humble opinion there is no finer, more professional, and caring editor around. This book is a reality because of her. Beverly, thank you for believing in this work. I am also very grateful to editor John Brenner, interim director Dwight Browne, and editor Sara Davis, for guiding this book through production. I would like especially to thank copyeditor Pippa Letsky for her brilliance and expertise in pushing me to make the book even better.

Thanks go also to Mrs. Shani Trege, who served as an expert copyeditor for this manuscript in its early stages. Shani is tremendously skilled and made my work on this manuscript so much easier.

I am grateful to Mount Pilgrim Missionary Baptist Church, Saint Luke Community Church, Mount Zion of Oakwood Village, and Olivet Institutional Baptist Church for your prayers and belief in me. I am especially grateful to my spiritual and intellectual pastor mentors, Rev. Dr. Raymond G. Bishop Jr., Rev. Dr. James H. Evans Jr., Rev. Dr. Larry Macon Sr., Rev. Dr. Marvin McMickle, Rev. Dr. Otis Moss Jr., Rev. Dr. William Myers, and Rev. James J. Robinson. Your wisdom, insight, and example have sustained me through difficult times.

Last, but not least, I thank my entire family. I am forever grateful to my family in South Carolina and to my extended family across the country. It takes a village to sustain a scholar. I would not be who I am today without each one of you. Thank you Mama, Dad, Grandma, Aunt, Uncle, and others. We did it! This book is as much yours as it is mine. And I am immensely grateful to my brilliant, darling wife, Kesha, who has stood by me every step of the way, from dissertation to publication, inspiring me to never give up. You are my muse and my soulmate. Words cannot express how much I love you and thank you for believing in me. Also, I would like to thank my precious two-year-old daughter Zion Olivet, for her intellectual energy, curiosity in books, and for her creative inspiration. Zion, Daddy loves you too. This book is a reminder that with God all things are possible.

IN SEARCH OF THE
TALENTED TENTH

INTRODUCTION

A T THE CENTER OF THIS STUDY is the formation of one prominent—
perhaps the most active and influential—African American intellectual community, one that originated and operated in the era of
racial segregation. From 1926 to 1970, Howard University in Washington, D.C., represented the center of black intellectual life, and its scholars
in various ways were heirs to the legacy of W. E. B. Du Bois's "talented
tenth."[1] Many members of this predominantly black collective functioned
as scholar activists, acting as important public intellectuals, laying the
foundations for the disciplines of black and Africana studies in the United
States, and affecting various aspects of public policy.

By definition, a public intellectual is an educated individual who
engages the people on public issues and whose thought and work influence, define, and transform those issues in the public sphere. Most see
academics as being the primary group of public intellectuals. However,
many academics bristle at the idea that they might be associated with the
term, which in some contemporary cases takes on the meaning of a media-
hungry, nonserious public thinker or figure.[2] We must also make a distinction between a mainstream public intellectual, with origins in the model of
the French salon or other Western intellectuals, and black public intellectuals. In the United States, the term "public intellectual" dates to the public
stance of French writer Emile Zola during the infamous Dreyfus affair,
and to the work of the New York Intellectuals, a group of predominantly
Jewish American writers and literary critics based in New York City in
the mid–twentieth century who advocated left-wing politics.[3] Black public
intellectuals, by contrast, are shaped by the struggles and triumphs of the
black experience and are committed to engage that public and the larger
public on issues of importance to the black community.

There has existed for the last twenty years a debate about the proper role
and function of the public intellectual, especially the black public intellectual. For many, Du Bois serves as the standard of what a black public

1

intellectual should be, often possessing a doctorate and being engaged in society as a scholar activist, influencing social change. According to black feminist scholar Patricia Hill Collins, most notable among black public intellectuals are W. E. B. Du Bois and Ida B. Wells. Collins draws a direct distinction between past black public intellectuals and those operating in our contemporary society. Collins argues that today, "Black public intellectuals have unprecedented access to the media, but no longer have daily contact with African American communities. A few (mostly men) have become academic and media superstars, which helps sustain the illusion that American society is 'color blind.'" Taking Du Bois as her starting point, Collins contextualizes Du Bois's "stature as a black intellectual," as providing "an important starting point for sketching out how the placement of African American intellectuals in the context of Jim Crow segregation and current color-blind racism, shapes black thought." For Collins, Du Bois's proclivity for consistently traversing "academic and activist settings in the context of racial segregation" provides a model prototype for black public intellectual life. Collins notes that such "movement shaped the questions, themes, and direction of his scholarship," noting Du Bois's inability to achieve the type of intellectual comfort common for elite black public intellectuals.[4]

Houston Baker, literary scholar and former student of Howard English professor Sterling A. Brown, takes to task both Ivy League and neoconservative black public intellectuals, examining their writings, speeches, books, and public behavior, contrasting their impact to that of Martin Luther King Jr., who, he argues, serves as the proper example of black public intellectual life. Baker asserts current black public intellectuals have betrayed the legacy of Du Bois, King, and others, who championed black rights while promoting racial activism. Baker sees avocation of neoconservative positions and policies, on the one hand, and immersion into a sound-bite culture of celebrity on the other hand, as being equally deleterious to black advancement in twenty-first-century America. To be fair to all generations of black public intellectuals, no black intellectual is above responsibility and accountability for his or her relationship and role vis-à-vis the black community. Also, all black intellectuals have, to some degree, been constrained by the politics of academia past or present, which seeks to delimit and marginalize black intellectuals and their work, regardless of their training, political philosophy, or station in life.[5]

It is necessary to take together the concepts of the talented tenth and the black public intellectual and view them in the same sentence. I argue that even before we deal with the current community of black public intellectuals, we need to revisit their more immediate intellectual predecessors, those who form the crux of this story, the Howard public intellectual community. Far too often, the media have bypassed the evident links with the Howard community, preferring to trace their direct intellectual roots and origins of current black public intellectuals to groups such as the New York Intellectuals. In my estimation, Howard set the standard for black public intellectual life, showcasing brilliant black women and men, following in the footsteps of Du Bois as race women and men, as scholar activists intent on advancing the cause of the race in a world couched in terms of Jim Crow segregation, blatant sexism, and global imperialism, colonization, and apartheid.

In fact, part of the impetus for this book on the Howard University public intellectual community derives from this discussion, and the book is important within the discussion for two reasons. The first is that Howard public intellectuals were indeed members of Du Bois's talented tenth. In fact many members of the community—Alain Locke, Ralph Bunche, E. Franklin Frazier, Rayford Logan, Abram Harris, for example— were to some degree students of Du Bois, following in his intellectual footsteps, and taking their lead from his life example and career. Others had some professional relationship with him, were somehow influenced by him, or, as Carter G. Woodson, sparred with him over certain projects. There were a number among the Howard group who criticized Du Bois for advancing positions devoid of deeper class critiques.

Too often, our postmodern society exhibits a tendency to pigeonhole prominent intellectuals and leaders in boxes that they themselves transcended. James Cone, in his comparative examination of black nationalist and integrationist intellectual lineages (through the personages of Martin Luther King Jr. and Malcolm X) cautions us to pay close attention to the entire life span of such intellectuals, and to avoid the tendency to dehistoricize them from the entirety of their lives, in order to fit them into contemporary political categories. Cone, instead, argues for the usage of specific situational contexts as a barometer to determine the efficacy of actions taken by certain leaders in African American intellectual history, noting that positions taken may in fact evolve and diverge, based on the particular circumstances in which the leaders find themselves.[6]

The second reason this book is important within the above discussion is that Howard men and women intellectuals—successes, flaws, faults, and all—continue to epitomize the standard of what a black public intellectual should be. Based in the nation's capital and the world's policy center, at one of the most preeminent institutions of higher learning for African Americans, members of the Howard University scholarly community were steeped in a rich black public intellectual tradition that garnered and maintained for that institution the reputation as the Capstone of Negro

Education. These scholars advanced the public intellectual model, engaging the national and global black public around many of the salient issues of the day, namely, Jim Crow segregation, civil rights, decolonization, and women's rights. In their scholarship and intellectual activism, not only did they seek mere understanding and illumination of social phenomena and problems, they also boldly proposed innovative prescriptions, designed to counteract systemic local, national, and international challenges confronting Black America, the nation at large, and the world.

Although perhaps nonmonolithic, highly opinionated, and imperfect to a fault, Howard scholars forged meaningful personal and professional networks, cemented in and by varying degrees of community, which enabled them substantially to impact social change and demonstrate the capacity to inform public policy in the local, national, and international black public. As women and men highly trained in the life of the mind, Howard scholars functioned as public intellectuals, well before contemporary language and postmodern representation legitimated, popularized, and distinguished that role. I argue that Howard scholars represented more of a definite model of what a public intellectual was, is, and should be.

Operating as what could be called in today's terminology a de facto prototypical Black Africana studies policy institute, Howard professors creatively combined aspects of the public intellectual and that of the academic intellectual to produce the scholar activist, who individually and collectively popularized and pioneered original and unique forms of Negro studies, black studies, African American public history, African studies, Africana studies, and Africana policy studies, following in the scholar activist tradition of the venerable W. E. B. Du Bois and Carter G. Woodson. In some ways these race men and women were simultaneously before their time, products of their times, and situated right in time. Using commentaries in the black press, articles, speeches, books, and other forms of expression such as poetry as public vehicles, they advanced a paradigm shift in thinking about race and culture, even as they struggled to hammer out any definitive school of thought on these matters and others.[7]

The concentration of black intellectuals at Howard was not accidental. It was a direct consequence of the racial segregation policy that prevailed in American higher education and society during the nineteenth and twentieth centuries. Since most black scholars of this period—no matter how brilliant—were barred from admission to white institutions and relegated to serving on the faculties at black universities, such a community of scholars was possible. Segregation, however, was not the sole reason for such a gathering of black minds. There was also the vision of Howard University's first black president, Mordecai Wyatt Johnson, who assumed the presidency in 1926 and held tenaciously to building the greatest concentration of black scholars at any one institution of higher learning, encouraging them to use their talents to address the critical issues confronting black Americans everywhere.

This book falls within the older historiographical school of African American history, where African American intellectuals and issues of community formation were emphasized. Major themes pursued by this school of thought included the evolution and dilemmas of African American intellectuals in twentieth-century academia, the avenues through which they formed communities and networks, and the manner in which their scholarship and activity influenced social change and the policy process. Classic works in this school include "Through the Back Door," by Michael Winston; *Black Intellectuals*, by William M. Banks; *The American Negro Academy*, by Alfred Moss; and *Rising Wind*, by Brenda Gayle Plummer. In addition, biographies and works about specific intellectuals shed significant light on the challenges faced by African Americans called to a career in the development of the mind, including *Ralph Bunche*, by Charles Henry; *Carter G. Woodson*, by Jacqueline Goggin; *Rayford W. Logan*, by Kenneth Janken; *Groundwork: Charles Hamilton Houston*, by Genna Rae McNeil; *E. Franklin Frazier Reconsidered*, by Anthony Platt; and *Negro Thought in America*, by August Meier.[8]

Although these works help to illustrate twentieth-century black intellectual life, few (with the exception of those by Winston, Goggin, and Moss) focus on intellectual communities in an academic setting. Winston lays out the idea that the intellectuals at Howard during this time constituted the leading black intellectual community of the twentieth century. To date, however, no study has been conducted that examines in critical detail the activities and interactions of this community of scholars. One of the goals of this study is to illuminate both the very real accomplishments of the black intellectuals embodying the Howard community and also the dilemmas they faced.

From the outset I envisioned a multidimensional approach to the history of this Howard University intellectual community. In many ways, this is both a social and an intellectual history, which incorporates also an institutional history of the university itself. I explore, as Earl Thorpe suggests in the title of his book, the mind and activity of the Negro scholar. In a fashion similar to the approach followed by Nell Painter in her work on Sojourner Truth, I intend to emphasize how personal and professional realms dovetailed in the lives of black scholars in the Howard community. I demonstrate how racial segregation and its internalization greatly impacted the personal lives of the Howard intellectuals. I argue that the dual aspects of racism complicated both personal and professional relationships between the Howard intellectuals and scholars beyond Howard, both black and white, thus affecting overall life choices (including professional and personal decisions) and reinforcing the "double consciousness" that Du Bois accurately defined. This initial exploration into the evolution of the twentieth-century black intellectual in America will contribute to the growing body of literature on black intellectual thought.[9]

Focusing on the Howard group, this study also examines the formation and maintenance of black intellectual communities within both a segregated and an integrated setting and will offer a brief comparison and contrast of black intellectual life in both eras. This aspect of the study allows us to examine the strengths and the weaknesses of the Howard community and to illustrate both the instances of collegiality and those where the politics of race in a segregated environment had a deleterious effect upon the community. I analyze the efforts of black scholars at Howard to influence and create black think tanks and institutes. I argue that this community of scholars functioned as a prototype for the black studies institute, in general, and helped lay foundations for the disciplines of black and Africana studies, especially establishing a nascent Africana/black policy studies discipline.

Africana studies demonstrates an evolving discipline that examines the global African and African diasporan experience in an integrated manner, connecting academic and scholarly excellence to social responsibility and transformation. It originated as a de facto discipline during the heyday of the Howard public intellectuals (the 1930s, 1940s, and 1950s), coming into existence first as "Negro studies," though not yet as a formal area of study within the academy. During the Black Power movement, with the student takeovers of the late 1960s, Dr. James Turner originally coined the term "Africana Studies," and this then emerged as a separate discipline, alongside other disciplinary-related derivations of the global black experience, namely, black studies and pan African studies.[10]

Africana policy studies (the engagement of Africana studies with policy studies) is a vehicle for developing, critiquing, and analyzing public policy that specifically affects Africana peoples globally. The Howard public intellectuals of the "policy research nucleus" were pioneers in this instance. As with Negro studies, Africana policy studies once existed, in nascent form, during the era of the Howard intellectual community. Now Africana policy studies is taking on a more formal character in the academy, with the introduction of the discipline Africana cultures and policy studies.[11]

In looking at the evolution of the American Negro or African American scholars in a historical context, I also examine their influence on the current generation of public black intellectuals. The Howard intellectuals included important figures such as Sterling Brown, William Leo

Hansberry, Benjamin Mays, and Howard Thurman, who had a tremendous impact on their students—among them important figures such as John Henrik Clarke, Martin Luther King Jr., Jesse Jackson, and Cornel West—and helped influence future generations of scholars. Toward the end of their careers, many Howard intellectuals, like poet and cultural critic Sterling Brown, maintained correspondence with current black public intellectuals such as Henry Louis Gates Jr., creating real links between intellectuals at Howard during this time and the current crop of public black intellectuals like the "Dream Team" at Harvard.[12] Historian Paula Giddings, for example, reflected admiringly on the impact that Sterling Brown had on her as a Howard University student in the years 1965–1969 and as editor of Howard University Press from 1971 to 1973. Philosopher of religion Cornel West, lauding Brown as "a genius" who "at his best produced a whole generation of folk," commented that he was inspired by Brown's role as "a cosmopolitan intellectual who had a sense of calling, not just a career." West further highlighted Brown's possession of "a sense of vocation, not just a profession," adding later "that Sterling Brown was the first major intellectual in America to discern, detect, depict, and defend a democratic mode of the tragicomic" or "a tragicomic conception of being human under conditions of modern democracy created in the doings and sufferings of victims of American democracy."[13]

In Chapter One I lay out the beginnings of the intellectual tradition at Howard University, a tradition that established the university as the "Capstone of Negro Education." I look at the foundation established by figures such as Alexander Crummell, Kelly Miller, and Carter G. Woodson. I look at the student strikes that swept through black colleges in the 1920s, which paralleled the emergence of the New Negro movement, and at how these controversial events contributed to the removal of the last white president, J. Stanley Durkee, and the eventual appointment of the university's first black president in 1926, Mordecai Wyatt Johnson.

Chapter Two examines the relationship between Mordecai Johnson and the scholars he assembled at Howard, beginning in 1926. It highlights significant aspects of his inauguration speech, where he drew attention to the impressive black intellectual tradition at Howard. I explore the complicated personality of this important and complex man, and the unpublished autobiographical account he wrote of assuming the presidency at Howard. This chapter examines the various types of relationships Johnson established with members of the Howard collective, from 1926 to the end of his presidency in 1960, including both those scholars who respected and admired him and those who questioned his legitimacy and capability as chief administrator of Howard.

In Chapter Three I analyze the on-campus activities and interactions among members of the Howard intellectual community. I illustrate the various types of personal and professional relationships that Howard intellectuals formed with one another during what has been termed Howard's "Golden Years" (from 1926 to roughly 1970, though the length and timing of this period are under debate). The study will evidence instances of collegiality and mutual cooperation as well as conflict and animosity. Through the lens of the Howard scholars that comprised this community, the chapter will also provide significant insight into the evolution and challenges of black scholars from a historical perspective.

Although this book does not seek to theorize gendered aspects of black intellectual life, it does attempt to engender the examination of black public intellectual life, using the Howard University intellectual community as a model. The intentional inclusion of discussions concerning black women public intellectuals seeks to mirror the critical work done by historians of black women's history such as Bettye Collier-Thomas, Pero Dagbovie, Stephanie Evans, Sharon Harley, Darlene Clark Hine, Rosalyn Terborg-Penn, Francille Rusan Wilson, among countless others. Black intellectual history, once interpreted solely through the lens of very generalized and uncritical black male perspectives, is now heavily influenced by the critical interrogation of black women's history and studies scholars, many of which are mentioned.[14]

Chapter Four examines Howard intellectuals as black public scholar activists operating within the global black public sphere of that time, which was very different from the present-day black public sphere, where black intellectuals have a larger and integrated audience. The Howard community during this period from 1926 to 1970 was dynamic in the context of a segregated and colonized world. Howard scholars formed relationships with other prominent African American intellectuals such as W. E. B. Du Bois, Carter G. Woodson, and Charles S. Johnson. They also developed relationships with many important Jewish scholars such as Melville Herskovits, and white scholars such as Robert Park and others. Other important forces within this public sphere were relationships formed and maintained with Caribbean intellectuals such as C. L. R. James, Eric Williams, George Padmore, as well as with African political intellectuals such as Nnamdi Azikiwe.

Howard intellectuals functioned in a number of fields as experts in the study of race and race relations. They undertook activities such as travel, lectures at conferences, participation on committees and bodies such as the American Council of Learned Societies' Negro Studies Committee, activity as experts for domestic civil rights and other black organizations, and influence on and participation in global and Pan-African networks such as the Pan-African Congresses, the black Britain intellectual collective, the American Society for the Study of African Culture, and the American Negro Leadership Conference on Africa. Of course, these intellectuals also regularly undertook speaking engagements on a variety of issues in churches and other institutions within the black community.

Chapter Five depicts Howard during its golden years as a prototypical black studies institute. The chapter examines the Howard intellectuals' contributions, in terms of scholarship and activism, to the development of African, Negro/black, and Africana studies in the United States. The chapter also explores ways that the policy research nucleus at Howard helped to pioneer Africana/black policy studies. I make a brief examination of Howard University's contribution to the development and evolution of black institutes and think tanks in America. Among the institutes influenced by, modeled after, and inspired by the efforts, scholarship, and representation of the Howard intellectual community we can find the American Negro Academy, Kelly Miller's National Negro Library and Institute, the Africa-America Institute, the Institute of the Black World, the William Monroe Trotter Institute, the Institute for Research in African American Studies, and the Joint Center for Political and Economic Studies. Howard was also important for the critical role played by its school of religion (headed by Benjamin Mays and Howard Thurman) in the development of a theology of race relations—as well as for the impact that Charles H. Thompson's *Journal of Negro Education* and the efforts of the law school (headed by Charles H. Houston and William Hastie) had on the dismantling of racial segregation in America.

In conclusion, I consider the impact of Howard intellectuals on the next generation of black intellectuals, including those whom the media have dubbed the "new public black intellectuals." I examine both the legacy of the Howard community of scholars and the lessons and unfulfilled legacies passed on to the current and future generations of black academic intellectuals. I attempt to provide a brief retrospective examination of the role, activities, and overall contribution of the Howard intellectual community to black intellectual life—past, present, and future. I illustrate some of the links between scholars such as black cultural critics Sterling Brown and Henry Louis Gates Jr., in order to show both continuity and change, similarities and differences between black male intellectuals and their present-day counterparts. I end with a comparative assessment of the black public intellectual, during the era of these Howard scholars and the current state of black intellectualism. Despite the popularly held belief that Howard public intellectuals failed to make any significant impact beyond its golden years (a period whose beginning and ending dates are under significant debate by scholars), I advance the position that the impact and legacy of this stellar community of scholar activists goes well beyond the narrow confines of a decade or two. In many ways, the Howard University public intellectual legacy is an ongoing and enduring one. If in doubt, just mention the names considered in this book and discover the overwhelming responses you receive. Even if academic scholarship has relegated this community to relative obscurity, those most impacted—namely, students and successive generations of black intellectuals—remember these critical thinkers very poignantly and fondly.

CHAPTER ONE

Prelude to Community

Foundations of the Howard University Intellectual Community, 1890–1926

T HE YEARS FROM 1890 TO 1929 saw the emergence of Howard University as the "Capstone of Negro Education," although as author Walter Dyson notes, Howard held that designation only from 1904 onward. Jonathan Holloway suggests it is more than likely that Howard was the Capstone in name only, and it was not until the administration of Mordecai Johnson that Howard gained its true prominence as an intellectual haven for black Americans.[1] I argue that the stellar Howard University intellectual community that blossomed in the 1930s had its foundation in this initial thirty-year period. Foundational figures such as Alexander Crummell, Kelly Miller, and Carter G. Woodson made a considerable impact on the intellectual environment. Many of the events surrounding the removal of the last white president, J. Stanley Durkee, were spawned during calculated strikes at Howard by the student body, in addition to strident protests by the faculty and alumni.

Howard's rise to intellectual prominence happened at the same time as the rise of the Harlem Renaissance and the emergence of the New Negro mentality in black middle-class and intellectual circles. Among the major leading lights of the movement, philosopher and social critic Alain Locke was a professor at Howard.[2] He contributed mightily to the intellectual foundation of the university, and he acquired considerable visibility as a public intellectual and for being one of the main leaders of the New Negro movement. I argue that, concurrent with the active nature of the black middle class there, Washington, D.C., was also a special seat of the New Negro renaissance, which extended far beyond the boundaries of Harlem. The black middle class in D.C. included many foundational figures at Howard and helped to carve a rare and important cultural and intellectual haven for black Americans. The culture and nightlife of D.C.'s famous areas such as U Street attracted many noted entertainers and intellectuals. The nation's capital was the perfect backdrop for a university such as Howard to become elevated to a celebrated intellectual status, partly because of its proximity to the seat of government and partly for the presence of countless philanthropic foundations, think tanks, policy organizations, and for the existence of a large, active, and prosperous black population. All these conditions served as the proper impetus for the events that brought Mordecai W. Johnson to the presidency of Howard in 1926. These characteristics also created an environment that was conducive to Johnson's plan to make Howard a thriving center of intellectualism and activism.

The 1920s witnessed the rise of the New Negro movement. The great migrations north by southern blacks created a prime opportunity for someone like Johnson and his activist intellectual ambassadors to harness and mobilize networks for social change, not only in the city but nationally and internationally. During the period from 1890 to 1929, the nation's capital experienced the same level of Jim Crow segregation as was simultaneously spreading across the American South. Neither black Washington nor Howard University was immune to the innumerable constraints imposed by segregation both customary and encoded in law. Although located geographically between the American North and the South, Washington, D.C., nevertheless was a very southern and segregated city. Much of the history of race relations in the nation's capital attests to this fact. It was in the city, not far from the doorsteps of Howard, that the U.S. Supreme Court in 1896 handed down the infamous *Plessy v. Ferguson* decision that legalized segregation not only in D.C. but throughout the nation. This decision would alter and dramatically affect race relations and everyday life in D.C. from 1896 to the time in 1954 when many of Howard's legal and social science scholars would collaborate to finally bring an end to Jim Crow.

Throughout their tenure at Howard, the university's scholars and activists felt the sting of racism and segregation, both in academia and outside its hallowed halls. It was easy for Howard professors to see a natural connection between life at the university (referred to as the academy) and life in the black community. Many professors lived in the heart of the black community. Their everyday lives centered around its institutions such as churches, schools, and other businesses. They were intimately familiar with the concerns of the community and its needs. Outside of campus activities and academic circles, professors were in constant interaction with other members of the black community. Because they experienced the effects of racism on their careers and their community, few Howard professors could fail to understand the consequences of segregation. Many became activists, directing their scholarly pursuits toward the achievement of racial equal-ity and social justice. Many who helped sound the death knell of segrega-tion—in fact, Howard scholars such as E. Franklin Frazier, Ralph Bunche, Rayford Logan, Charles Hamilton Houston, and Charles H. Thompson who constitute what historian Michael Winston calls the "policy research nucleus"—had either grown up in the black middle-class community of D.C. and the surrounding areas or were heavily impacted by Black Wash-ington's political and cultural milieu. Winston characterized this policy research nucleus as being "very active in criticizing public policy as well as the strategies adopted by various Negro groups." Thompson, to his credit, along with Logan "recognized the significance of policy research," which had been the sole preserve of whites until Thompson started the *Journal of Negro Education* in 1932. Illustrative of the significance of this journal to the development of African American policy history and studies is the January 1936 special issue that focused on relevant topics such as the New Deal, the race question, social planning, economic development, socialism, and communism.[3]

During this initial period in Washington, as well as in other major cities and all across the nation, a new attitude of self-esteem, self-evaluation, and cultural self-determination was growing among black Americans emerg-ing from the aftermath of slavery. In postslavery America, this cultural revival arose amid unprecedented attacks on black life and culture, dur-ing a period of violence (including lynchings) and other forms of social injustice so severe that Howard history professor Rayford Logan coined the term "the nadir" to describe the period from the end of Reconstruction in 1877 to the first decades of the twentieth century. The nadir, the lowest point in black life, was characterized by the significant loss of gains won by African Americans during the Reconstruction period and by unprec-edented anti-black violence, terrorism evidenced by the rebirth of the Ku Klux Klan and revived by the 1915 release of D. W. Griffith's film *Birth of a Nation*, legalized racial segregation coded into law with the 1896 *Plessy v. Ferguson* Supreme Court case instituting the doctrine of "separate but equal," race riots—in particular, in East St. Louis in 1917 and the Red Sum-mer of 1919 in numerous major cities including Chicago, and Tulsa in 1921—as well as unchecked, virulent expression of white supremacy.[4] The concomitant violence suffered by blacks in the rural areas of the American South as well as by blacks in other areas of the country served as a major impetus for the great black migrations to the North and Midwest. This period also saw the legal entrenchment of segregation as reflected in law by *Plessy* and by other state and local laws, as well as other cultural forms of inequality practiced in the form of custom.

* * *

Considerable debate has taken place in more recent years concerning the origin and actual center of the New Negro movement. Today, many who are familiar with it associate the movement exclusively with Harlem, and many call it the Harlem Renaissance. However, noted intellectual historian Wilson Moses, in a work analyzing black literary and intellectual life in the period before the 1920s, offers an alternative discussion of this time-honored notion. He calls for a reexamination of the New Negro movement and its roots, challenging the notion that Harlem was the center of the renaissance and the New Negro movement. In his view, Washington was in fact more of a center than Harlem, and he gives some reasons for its anonymity and exclusion.[5]

Citing the consistently negative portrayals of the black elite in academic and popular circles, Moses suggests that Washington's significant literary and intellectual life during the 1920s and 1930s has gone unnoticed and unappreciated. Contributing to this poor portrayal of Washington's black elite was "the over-reactive condemnation by artists and intellectuals of the follies and foibles of the black bourgeoisie." Commending Constance McLaughlin Green's social history of D.C., Moses argued, however, that it was too general, almost leading one "to believe that black Washingtonians simply did not participate in the life of the mind in America."[6]

To substantiate his claims that the coverage of black Washington's cultural and intellectual vibrancy has been historiographically insufficient, Moses makes mention of the minimal attention given to the contributions of Mary Church Terrell, NAACP cofounder and first president of the National Association of Colored Women's Clubs, and Alexander Crummell, founder of the American Negro Academy who served as Episcopal priest and rector of St. Luke's Episcopal Church in D.C., and as spiritual guru of Du Bois. These examples point to a vital role played by D.C. in fomenting the New Negro mind and spirit. Harking back to its roots in abolitionism and evangelical Protestant reform efforts, Chocolate City, as it is fondly known today, served as home for the likes of Howard professors E. Franklin Frazier and Alain Locke, two of the more notable figures of the New Negro movement. Also, D.C. was home to Carter G. Woodson, the father of black history, who in 1915 established his black history movement there, known then as the Association for the Study of Negro Life and History. Citing Harold Cruse (the influential historian who shook the foundations of black intellectualism with the publication of his 1976 tour de force *The Crisis of the Negro Intellectual,* which inspired generations of black intellectuals and thus paved the way for the modern black public intellectual), Moses highlights Cruse's consideration of what Woodson called the "Migration of the Talented Tenth." This discussion centered around the migration of black politicians, artisans, teachers, and others of the professional class to Presbyterian, Episcopal, and African Methodist Episcopal churches in the nation's capital, forming the base of black Washington's emerging intellectual leadership class.[7]

Some of black America's most prominent intellectuals, though they remain obscure to current generations, functioned as foundational figures and scholar activists of the intellectual community of Howard University and of black Washington. One of the most noted among these was Alexander Crummell, a popular Episcopalian clergyman, teacher, and missionary who challenged Booker T. Washington on the proper social and educational course of the race. Crummell and his contemporaries were very active in black Washington's intellectual circles and were known by many as the District's "New Negroes." They served as mentors to Du Bois and to other black scholars around the country, as well as to those in Washington, at Howard University.[8]

Crummell taught at Howard University for two years and then, in 1897, embarked on his life's crowning legacy and intellectual achievement, the establishment of the American Negro Academy (ANA), whose purpose was to encourage intellectual excellence in the race. The ANA was known by many as the first major sustained black think tank in the country. According to Alfred Moss, the ANA represented an elite cadre and community of predominantly black male intellectuals.[9] Although severe restrictions were placed on membership in the academy, it included some of Howard University's most established intellectuals, such as Alain Locke and Kelly Miller.[10] Apparently there was some connection between Howard and the ANA. Some ANA meetings were held on Howard's campus, for example, and the ANA could have furthered subsequent attempts by Miller, Logan, and Locke to start an institute for the study of the Negro at Howard.

Although historian Carter G. Woodson—known by many today as the father of black history and the second black American to receive a doctorate from Harvard—only taught at Howard for the year of 1918, his impact on its intellectual growth is evident.[11] On September 9, 1915, Woodson established the Association for the Study of Negro Life and History (ASNLH), with offices located in D.C., to promote his Negro history movement. This was an organization dedicated to the preservation of and continued research on the global black experience, and to counteracting racist scholarship and public portrayals concerning black people. Soon thereafter, Woodson established a number of related institutional apparatuses, such as the *Journal of Negro History* in 1916, the Associated Publishers (his own publishing house) in 1921, Negro History Week in 1926, and the *Negro History Bulletin* in 1937, all to further his mission to promote Negro history. The ASNLH's public mission was "to promote, research, preserve, interpret, and disseminate information about Black life, history, and culture to the global community."[12] Howard public intellectuals Sterling Brown, Alain Locke, E. Franklin Frazier, Rayford W. Logan, Charles Wesley, and others partnered in various capacities with Woodson in his life's mission to correct errors and mistruths concerning people of African descent.[13] Historian Pero Dagbovie also notes the significant contributions of a number of black women, namely, Mary McLeod Bethune (ASNLH president in 1936), Lucy Harth Smith, Lois Mailou Jones, and countless others, all who ably assisted Woodson in his efforts to establish the association and the black history movement.[14] As president of the association and editor of its principal publication, the *Journal of Negro History*, Woodson maintained close contact with many of Howard's "talented tenth" faculty, up to the time of his untimely death in 1950. Reverend Mordecai Johnson, prior to his assuming the presidency of Howard in 1926, maintained a frequent correspondence with Woodson.

Woodson involved some of Howard's faculty in the interworkings of the Association for the Study of Negro Life and History, such as fellow historians Charles Wesley and Rayford Logan. Because of Woodson's temperamental nature and tightfisted control of the ASNLH, however, he often came into conflict with Wesley and Logan and on occasion ostracized them in order to maximize his control. Woodson had a strong distrust of affiliating his organization with any university, particularly Howard University, even though the potential intellectual capital provided by its faculty would have offered the critical mass of scholars necessary to make Howard "officially the mecca" for the study of black people. Woodson's fear of institutional control was in fact well warranted. About two years after his arrival as Howard's first black president, Mordecai Johnson gained annual appropriations for the university from the federal government, but these appropriations came at an extremely high price.[15]

Many Howardites know that sometimes this price was an intrusive federal intervention attempt to control the thoughts and affairs of the university and its intellectuals. The tension involved is most evident in the challenges to academic freedom at Howard during the Red Scare in both 1942 and 1953 as Howard became the target of FBI investigation. Initiated by Wisconsin senator Joseph McCarthy, the House Un-American Activities Committee sought to root out and curtail the spread of communism in the United States. Black professors, intellectuals, and activists were known targets of McCarthy's Red baiting tactics. Some of them, such as Du Bois and Paul Robeson, and others, for example, were continually harassed. Added to this tension was the often complex and charismatic personality of Mordecai Johnson, who butted heads with many of the faculty at Howard, including Woodson. Understanding Woodson's temperament, it is unlikely he would have taken too kindly to the tremendous attempts at control by either the federal government or Johnson. Unfortunately, Woodson's health and peace of mind was always challenged as he struggled to gain significant financial support from the black middle class. Rejecting university affiliation, Woodson could not support the ASNLH on funds from the black community alone. He had to rely on an even more problematic relationship with white philanthropists, including Julius Rosenwald, the Carnegie Corporation, and the Phelps Stokes Fund. Woodson was of course not the only black scholar whose career and activism was hindered by the control and intrusive preconditions of white philanthropic groups—who agreed to fund research projects for black scholars only if they were not overtly offensive to whites and did not challenge the status quo. Many longer-tenured members of the Howard faculty (namely, Locke) were restricted by philanthropic mandates similar to the ones placed on Howard University itself by its board of trustees and by the federal government.[16]

One can only imagine what the addition of Woodson, the "father of black history," and W. E. B. Du Bois to the faculty would have meant for Howard University's intellectual community, and for Negro studies across the country. Du Bois was arguably the leading black male intellectual of the twentieth century. He applied to become a professor at the Capstone in the 1890s and later in the 1940s but was never actually employed there. Along with the emergence of the New Negro mentality, espoused by many Howard professors, there arose the responsibility of many scholars at the Capstone to grapple with two of Du Bois's main ideas.

The first idea was that of the color line, a social and cultural boundary that was understood to separate the races. The second was the philosophy of the "talented tenth," which admonished college-educated blacks to become race men and women to lead the race to social equality. Later, a few of Du Bois's contemporaries and the younger black scholars, including many of those who formed a part of the Howard community, found themselves on many sides of this debate. Their ideas spanned a wide gamut in perspective on the significance, meaning, and relevance of the talented tenth, concerning its connection to their professional and personal lives as well as its relationship to the larger community (especially the black masses) beyond the walls of the ebony tower. In essence, Du Bois's initial concept of the talented tenth was the responsibility to develop a cadre of black intellectuals who would lead the race in its drive for social equality and advancement.

The complicated relationship between Du Bois and Woodson would have added much flair and many sparks to an already heady brew of egos and intellectual genius. Other black scholars were contemporaries of Du Bois and in various ways functioned as part of the talented tenth, either directly or indirectly, but the two most prominent black male intellectuals of the twentieth century were Du Bois and Woodson, and the two had a complicated, oftentimes uneasy professional and personal relationship. Many of their disputes—especially the one involving control of an Africana encyclopedia project, designed to produce the first comprehensive encyclopedia of global black life—and other disputes among scholars within the Howard community involved heated competition for research projects and funds awarded by noted philanthropists representing foundations such as the Carnegie Corporation, the Rockefeller Foundation, the Phelps Stokes Fund, and others.

In addition to these points of difference, scholars also disagreed in terms of philosophy. For instance, other contemporaries such as Alain Locke were also critical of Du Bois, even as both he and they suffered the same constrictions imposed by life in the segregated academy and segregated America. For many scholars at Howard, Du Bois served as the standard or model to which they aspired, and although uneasy with his personality, many, whether they admitted it or not, had to come to terms with what it meant to be a member of the talented tenth and what it meant to operate as a scholar activist in the era of the color line. Indeed, many Howard scholars who debated with Du Bois—such as sociologist E. Franklin Frazier, economist Abram Harris, and political scientist Ralph Bunche—were also constrained and plagued by internal ambivalence and feelings of inferiority, coupled with desires to assert, awaken, or give birth to the New Negro within them.[17] Du Bois also wrestled with this condition, characterizing it as a state of double consciousness, or a seemingly perpetual situation where black Americans—and in this case black scholars—wrestle with the assertion of an identity that is both Negro or black and American. Du Bois described this double consciousness as the existence of two competing souls, at war one with the other.[18]

The color line was very evident in Howard's governance as the twentieth century began. Since its founding in 1867, the university had been led by a succession of white presidents, the majority of whom were Congregationalist ministers or other men of the cloth. Historian Raymond Wolters recounts that racial tension expressed by students and faculty at the Capstone did not begin during the 1920s. Wolters argues that "intermittent criticism of Howard's white presidents [had] persisted" long before but was originally tempered by the tremendous influence of the university's black deans, namely, those known as the Triumvirate. This group, in the early 1900s consisting of Kelly Miller, Lewis B. Moore, and George William

Cook, was said to have "established semiautonomous spheres of power within their colleges," which curtailed the power of the white presidents and placed tremendous influence in the hands of the deans.[19]

In 1903 President John Gordon, in an attempt to usurp the power of the Triumvirate, moved to establish one-year terms for deans at Howard. Although not completely racial in its intent, this move took on predominantly racial overtones and sparked increased protest among students and deans alike, mostly Cook and Moore. Soon afterward a black lawyer, Archibald H. Grimke, led a campaign calling for Gordon's resignation. Suspicions were expressed by Grimke and other black university officials concerning Gordon's ambivalence toward black students and faculty at Howard. They charged that he acquiesced to the color line, as evidenced by the fact that he broke with tradition and enrolled his children in white schools in Washington rather than at Howard. In 1906, amid continuing pressure, accusations concerning his inadequacy, and calls for a black president, Gordon finally resigned.[20]

Gordon's resignation spurred a race for the highest office at the Capstone. Because of a lack of consensus behind any one black candidate, Wilbur Thirkfield, a white Methodist and former president of Gammon Theological Seminary, was chosen as Howard's next president. Thirkfield had a reputation of being able to negotiate effectively with interracial relations and was believed to be, according to the board of trustees, the remedy to the presidential instability at the Capstone. This seemed apparent, as there was relative approval of Thirkfield's appointment within D.C.'s black community. The promise associated with Thirkfield was short-lived, however, as he resigned in 1912 to become a bishop in the Methodist Episcopal Church. So there was another mad scramble for succession by varying black factions at Howard. This time each member of the Triumvirate vied for the coveted office. Had any two withdrawn or some consensus been determined among the three, Howard might have had its first black president in 1912; the implications of this would have been immeasurable.[21]

Unfortunately, no consensus was reached among the Triumvirate, and the board of trustees selected another white Congregationalist pastor, Stephen M. Newsome, to head Howard. A compromise was reached, however, as Newsome agreed to defer in many ways to the desires of the black deans. Even with this concession, black Howardites had missed a golden opportunity. During the course of Newsome's administration from 1912 to 1918, the black deans wielded a great deal of power. Furthermore, the presence of approximately two-thirds black professors on the faculty and the ever-waning influence of whites evidenced that, in both subtle and overt ways, winds of change were abroad, and blacks were assuming greater levels of autonomy at Howard. At the Capstone, a rising racial consciousness among faculty and administration was gaining momentum that would eventually, in the 1920s, dovetail with the New Negro spirit.[22]

J. Stanley Durkee became Howard's eleventh president in 1918. Durkee was a Congregationalist pastor who had at the top of his agenda the moral and religious development of the students. He often admonished the faculty to play a central role in the moral development of students. With regard to students, he heavily enforced the rule of mandatory chapel attendance despite the opposition he faced from a number of students and faculty alike. Even though Durkee acquiesced and agreed to end the chapel requirement, he remained undaunted in his emphasis on character development at Howard.[23]

Despite criticism of his administration of Howard University, Durkee did make an effort to recruit more black faculty and was fairly successful. By the early 1920s, there was a stalemate over the question of Howard's presidency, with an impasse between the predominantly white-controlled board of trustees and the predominantly black alumni. Most of the trustees were content to continue the line of liberal white university presidents with theological backgrounds. By contrast, the alumni (infused in large part by the New Negro mentality) were resolved that it was long past time for Howard University, a predominantly black university in one of the world's most populous black cities, to have at its helm a black man who had some connection to the field of education. Current Howard professors such as educator Dwight Oliver Wendell Holmes and historian Charles Wesley had expressed interest in the position, but they were not acceptable to the university trustees.[24] Despite the resolve of the alumni and many on the Howard faculty such as Locke, their urgings were not enough to persuade the board to give in to their demands.

During Durkee's administration, Howard failed to participate in the New Negro renaissance. Despite the individual participation of Locke and other professors such as Frazier and Hansberry, the university administration failed to embrace the movement and hence missed a historic opportunity. Howard's failure to participate was not surprising, however, given that the predominantly white and religious-oriented board of trustees and administration shunned black studies. Two notable examples demonstrate this fact.

First, in 1901, despite the urging of then Dean Kelly Miller, the board of trustees voted down a proposal for the university to subsidize the scholarly works and publications of the American Negro Academy. It can be argued that the lack of university-based support coupled with the lack of interest by the private foundations precipitated the eventual demise of black studies think tanks such as the ANA. The board refused even as it was known that a few of the university's professors such as Locke, Woodson, and Miller were active members of that exclusive institute. The ANA incident was just one example of the lack of respect and support received by the black faculty at the Capstone from its administration and board of trustees. Furthermore, any attempts at reconciliation between the opposing sides were designed merely to temporarily appease unhappy professors rather than to make any real effort to reform a short-sighted policy.[25]

Another notable example of the board of trustees' disdain for black studies was the situation surrounding the movement for courses concentrating on the black experience. Both professors Carter G. Woodson and William Leo Hansberry tried in vain to convince Durkee and the board of trustees to support black studies courses.[26] Despite a course on American Negro history being organized by Woodson in 1920 and a course on African history organized by Hansberry, the administration, historian Raymond Wolters says, "found it difficult to recognize the academic legitimacy of black studies[,] and its commitment to the field was slim." Even with Hansberry's efforts, the course he established in African history was deemed expendable, and despite an outstanding teaching and research effort, the "prophet without honor" taught for years without tenure, retiring as an associate professor in 1959.

Carter Woodson, professor and dean of the College of Liberal Arts after working at Howard for one academic year, in 1919, angrily severed his ties with Howard after the administration refused to allow him to establish black history and black studies courses. Unfortunately this would prove a huge blow to Howard's intellectual community, although Woodson continued to maintain close contact with a number of Howard faculty. The snub scarred him and made him all the more distrustful of affiliating his black history and black studies movement with the university. Had Woodson stayed and had the university supported both the ANA and other efforts to institutionalize Negro studies, perhaps Howard would have become even more of a legitimate and prominent center for black studies and for black policy studies. Howard failed to gain an inestimable source of intellectual vitality and renown from Woodson and the ANA. Perhaps the affiliation of the ANA would have ensured that institution's survival, and the addition of Woodson might have extended his efforts, and his life, and curtailed his subsequent descent into isolation—especially with the presence of a viable university intellectual community that appreciated his work and his contribution to black studies.[27]

Thus board of trustees meetings evidenced a lack of support for early black history initiatives at Howard. Among the Triumvirate, Dean Kelly Miller stood out in his support of the New Negro movement and the institutionalization of black history. Miller was a member of the prestigious ANA, and he led an effort in 1901 to have Howard subsidize that academy's scholarly publications. The initiative was not successful. Along with the board's lack of support for Miller's proposal, they also shot down Locke's proposal for a course in interracial relations, and a request from Woodson (as dean in 1919) to develop a course in African American history.[28]

Alain Locke was a major proponent of making Howard University into one of the "radiant centers of Negro culture." His 1925 epic anthology, *The New Negro,* gave form to the modern beginnings of a black renaissance and arts movement. Locke, Miller, Benjamin Brawley, Logan, Frazier, and others desired to make Howard the center for the study of the Negro.[29] Among others, they were adamant about developing a center for the study of the Negro at Howard, which would in many ways have foreshadowed modern-day black studies research centers. These men proposed to establish such a center, but their views fell on deaf ears during the Durkee administration—and then faltered during the Johnson administration, also, due to the untimely deaths of Professors Miller and Brawley. In the late 1930s they supported an initiative started by Miller a decade earlier, to establish a National Negro Museum, Library and Institute at the Capstone. The National Negro Museum was a precursor for the Moorland-Spingarn Research Center, which serves today as one of the world's premier research repositories of Africana historical materials.

Among Howard's black deans of the New Negro era, spanning the 1920s and 1930s, Kelly Miller stands out above Lewis B. Moore and George William Cook in promoting the study of what was then known as Negro history. Rayford Logan's phrase "the revolt of the Negro intellectuals" foretells of the years 1903–1915, when many black scholars were caught up in Du Bois's strident critique of Booker T. Washington's accommodationist political philosophy and parallel emphasis on vocational education for the black masses. During these years, Howard University began collecting top-notch intellectual talent among its faculty members, providing a solid foundation upon which Mordecai Johnson, beginning in 1926, would then build. In addition to Alain Locke, who received the prestigious Rhodes Scholarship to Oxford in 1907, the Capstone's intelligentsia boasted the literary scholar Benjamin Brawley, administrator Dwight O. W. Holmes, and cell biologist Ernest Everett Just. Exposed to this early intellectual flowering at Howard between 1903 and 1918 were future deans Miller, Cook, and Moore, who were important members of the faculty. Historian Walter Dyson characterizes Cook as "the rich man of the campus," Miller as "the scholar," and Moore as "the diplomat."[30]

* * *

President Durkee did not have his finger on the pulse of the New Negro movement and the tremendous impact it would have on Howard students and faculty (most notably, Locke). He was last in a line of thirteen white university presidents who placed a major premium on religion, rather than on more humanistic disciplines such as black history. In fact, Durkee at first required mandatory chapel services for students and faculty, although this policy ended as soon as it was proposed. Durkee's reluctance to support the early attempts by Miller, Woodson, Hansberry, and others to institutionalize Negro history and Negro studies at Howard conjoined with a changing moral tide on campus and a more open embrace of the New Negro movement to signal that the clouds were gathering to end Durkee's term as president.[31]

During the 1920s Professors Frazier and Locke expressed discontent with the kind of education being offered to the students at Howard. They joined the likes of Hansberry in pushing for a significant adaptation in the university curriculum—one that would allow for the proper training of able black leadership. Unfortunately (as we have seen), the board was still not particularly receptive to any substantive introduction of black studies on campus. Wolters notes that the board offered some degree of official resignation toward black studies but then failed to substantiate this tolerance and summarily rejected numerous proposals for black studies courses. One barrier in this apparent stalemate was the racial composition of the board. Sixty-six percent of the board's members were white, which allows a conclusion that they exhibited a sort of white paternalism. This paternalism contributed to the lack of urgency toward the emerging discipline of black studies, even as its growth paralleled the growing renaissance in black Washington itself.[32]

The traditional religious-oriented education, both Locke and Frazier felt, was devoid of any teaching about black culture or about service to the community, the two main tenets of black studies. Locke and Frazier felt that too much emphasis was placed on the acquisition of a "prevalent materialistic individualism of middle-class American life." This attitude— combined with the university's lack of appreciation for the role of black studies in the lives of students—left even more faculty, students, alumni, and members of the D.C. black middle-class community up in arms over the administration of Howard and very desirous of an immediate change.[33]

In response to the generally dictatorial maneuverings of the Durkee administration (such as a proposed retirement plan for professors over sixty-five years of age), the Howard University Alumni Club of New York argued that the administration's official explanation for its actions represented "but a pretext of the President to discipline those who have dared to differ with him on any issue." In supporting such a claim and in illustrating the resiliency of Howard's black intellectuals, the superintendent of D.C.'s Negro schools, Roscoe Conkling Bruce, stated that "these professors were simply too manly and too intelligent for Durkee to dominate." Conkling Bruce asserted that Durkee's disregard for academic freedom was because of his inability to adequately comprehend the concept and thereby extend it to the disgruntled group of professors at the Capstone.[34]

Fed up with Durkee's misgivings and lack of regard for the concerns of the black faculty, Howard's alumni began organizing a campaign to oust the president and force his resignation. Their method was to amass significant public opinion in their favor. The alumni collected various documents including letters, sworn statements, resolutions, and personal narratives that were eventually published by G. David Houston under the pseudonym "Alumnus" in the *Baltimore Afro-American*. Houston published this flurry of criticism against Durkee in fifty different articles that ran in the *Afro-American* virtually every week from April 1925 to about July 1926.[35]

One prime example of the very critical letters printed in the *Afro-American* expressed the view of one alumnus that Durkee attacked the manhood of Howard's black professors by coercing their loyalty or punishing those he considered disloyal. One alumnus believed the president was punishing scholars at Howard, "humiliating them until he is satisfied that servility has displaced scholarship and manhood." This behavior by Durkee and his other unfavorable actions galvanized increased opposition against him. The same alumnus articulated that the president displayed a "widespread tendency to intimidate and crush real manhood displayed by Negroes." It was believed that these attacks went beyond purely academic actions and were in fact racial in intent and nature.[36]

One of the major areas of concern among faculty was salaries. The period immediately following World War I was a difficult time for the "traditionally hard pressed professoriate," as the general cost of living increased dramatically by 50 percent from 1915 to 1920. During this time, academic salaries across the board increased by only 5 percent. To properly support themselves, many science and technically oriented faculty took positions in business and industry, for example. Others chose to devote sabbatical leaves and summer vacations to working jobs that earned extra money as opposed to devoting time to scholarly research.[37]

In the mainstream academic community, the commercialization of scholarship also created widespread concern. Noted economist Thorstein Veblen expressed concern that what he deemed to be the ideal of scholarship, a community of scholars working stridently to reveal truth to the world, "was being perverted because only the well-to-do could afford the luxury of research." And if salary conditions were difficult for white scholars, the situation was doubly extreme for black scholars operating in segregated academia where salaries were lower than at white institutions. Calls came from the national press that universities should invest more in faculty, rather than giving top priority to physical plants and buildings.[38]

The dire economic position of Howard professors was not addressed by private philanthropy. In the 1920s the Rockefeller Foundation earmarked $50 million to aid the economic difficulties of professors by providing colleges with the ability to increase faculty salaries by about 25 percent. But Howard and its professors did not receive any of these funds. Although the need was there at the Capstone, conditions at other black colleges were far worse. Professors at Howard gained salaries comparable to the average of many private colleges, and perhaps this is a reason Howard was not awarded funds. From the perspective of the Howard professors, the numerical parity that the Rockefeller Foundation said must exist between their salaries and those of professors from many private colleges proved inconsequential. Howard professors struggled hard to support their families on inadequate salaries. Howard also received some federal support, and this might explain its lack of success in receiving private philanthropy, in this situation and others, because philanthropists such as the Rockefellers—because of limited funds of their own as well as the selectiveness and restrictions in their search process—were intent on awarding funds only to those schools deemed most in need of resources. In these circumstances, and with seemingly no relief in sight, Howard professors organized to press for their demands in the area of faculty salaries.[39]

In June 1921, with philosophy professor Locke as secretary of the Faculty Salaries Committee, Howard professors pressed their claim for higher compensation to the administration. After much back-and-forth maneuvering and with no apparent salary increase on the horizon, Locke mounted a counteroffensive entitled the "Correspondence of the Salaries Committee," which was then signed by fifty-three professors and published in the national press. This correspondence consisted of a prepared statement that explained in further detail the distressing condition of faculty salaries. It described meager salary raises as "aggravating pittances" and criticized the board of trustees for neglecting faculty salaries for buildings and equipment. Professors understood all too well that Congress looked down upon salary increases of any kind and demonstrated favoritism toward the subsidizing of buildings and equipment. Despite this understanding, professors continued to press for a more equitable pay scale.[40]

Not only were salaries low, but there were significant inequities among Howard professors that contributed to faculty discontent. Ultimately, these inequities were attributed to favoritism on the part of President Durkee. Locke believed that Durkee awarded higher pay raises to professors who were loyal to him and punished those who opposed him with only meager raises. Locke shared his dissatisfaction with Du Bois in private:

> In the salary campaign . . . we have stressed not merely the raising of salaries but the standardizing of grade by a definite salary schedule. The real reason for refusing this has been that it would take political patronage and favoritism out of the hands of the administrative officers—their best club in breaking faculty morale and prestige. All sorts of anomalies exist—many associate professors receiving more than full professors, and assistants more than associates, etc., not so much because of limited funds as because of favoritism and pay for political service and espionage. . . . Dr. Durkee has repeatedly insisted on "personal loyalty and cooperation, and favored, promoted, and made close counselors of men who would give it, and persecuted, embarrassed and demoted men who would not."[41]

Locke would come to a personal understanding of these circumstances in the spring of 1925, when mathematician Alonzo Brown, accounting instructor Orlando C. Thornton, and French professor Metz T. P. Lochard were fired temporarily, because they had grievances with President Durkee and his administration. Each was accused of having supported the student opposition to ROTC and opposed other university practices. It was believed that, if professors did not acquiesce to the will of the president, they would suffer the consequences. Harking back to Veblen's characterization of the commercialization of scholarship, Locke understood that inadequate salaries stymied effective and comprehensive research and scholarly productivity.[42]

Durkee's administration came at the same time as African Americans' heightened push for equality. The New Negroes of Washington, D.C., were especially determined to attain equality, and the faculty at Howard were most certainly of the same opinion. Their determination was underwritten by the belief that, since many black Americans (including numbers of Howard students) had fought courageously in World War I in order "to make the world safe for democracy," they should be able to immediately and fully enjoy the same spirit of democracy and equality in every institution in American society. Also, so close to the seat of government in the nation's capital, the belief was that there was no justifiable reason blacks must accept business as usual and return to the old ways of segregation and second-class status.[43]

Historians Jonathan Scott Holloway and Wilson Jeremiah Moses give two different accounts of black Washington, which in many ways help explain the growing opposition to the Durkee administration. This opposition paralleled the rise of the New Negro movement (in the District as well as around the country), although the movement itself can be dated back to the 1880s and 1890s. Holloway does a good job of offering a visual map of the District. He argues that, while "Black Washington may have been generally confined to a certain geographic space within the District," this does not signify that members of the community were united in their thinking, especially those privileged members of the black elite, whom Howard sociologist professor Frazier later called the black bourgeoisie.[44] Members of the black elite, including the intellectual elite and the black masses, were said to have "shared the same spaces—the former in large row houses, the latter in the alleyways." Holloway asserted that in such an amalgam of sorts, "aristocrats, politicians, store owners, professionals, domestic workers, students, and professors made their homes in the neighborhoods around Howard," such as U Street, Shaw, and Georgia Avenue. Although Holloway concentrates his study on the era of the New Deal, his contention that the history of black Washington and Howard University are both complex and interwoven applies also to the period prior to the celebrated rise of the New Negro movement. Connecting this larger cultural movement with the intellectual culture beginning to amass at Howard, Holloway adds that, just "as New York City's political, literary, and artistic worlds molded the famous 'New York Intellectuals,' Washington's social, cultural, and political rhythms duly affected the Howard intelligentsia."[45]

Writing on black literary and intellectual life before the "Renaissance," Wilson Moses offers a more in-depth portrayal of the black middle-class and intellectual elite in black Washington and their relationship to the New Negro movement. Critiquing a definition of the movement put forward by literary scholar Robert Hayden in his 1968 reprint of *The New Negro,* Moses characterizes any popular notion that associates the movement with "iconoclasm" or "bohemianism" or that "equates it with the Harlem Renaissance of the 1920s" as being "the antihistorical, but largely unchallenged, prevailing view of the New Negro Movement." Offering a genealogy of the term "New Negro" that predates Locke's use of the term, Moses goes on to question whether Harlem was the only place the New Negro renaissance occurred, and even if Harlem was really the centerpiece. "Perhaps fortunately," Moses affirms, "no term has yet been invented to describe the literary and intellectual life among black Americans that was centered in Washington, D.C., during the 1890s and [that] had its roots in the traditions of abolitionist political rhetoric and evangelical Protestant reform." According to Moses, prior accounts of black Washington (including Constance Green's *The Secret City*), although very important to an accurate understanding of this community, fail to provide any insight into the intellectual life of its scholars, leaders, and activists. "One would almost be led to believe that Black Washingtonians simply did not participate in the life of the mind in America."[46]

In his account of black Washington, Moses provides contextual insight into the sociocultural environment that Howard University's impressive intellectual community provided. Based on his interpretations, one walks away with the view that this community was squarely grounded in the social milieu of black Washington's cultural elite. "The existence of an elite group of serious and educated Black Americans in turn-of-the-century Washington," he argues, "made possible the existence of an E. Franklin Frazier and an Alain Locke, two of the most important figures of the Harlem Renaissance"—and also professors at Howard University, "who ironically lived in Washington." I disagree that it was ironic that Frazier, Locke, and other Howard professors were in Washington. Even in this early period of the 1880s, and onward, Howard was still emerging as the Capstone of Negro education, and it already had some of the most able black minds in the country. Coupled with the intellectual and literary environment provided by the M Street School (black Washington's best-known high school and a pipeline to Howard) and its professors, who were also members of the black intellectual elite in D.C. (namely, Mary Church Terrell, Francis Grimke, and Carter G. Woodson), black Washington boasted a very well-regarded cadre of thinkers. With other religious and intellectual figures such as Alexander Crummell and institutions such as the ANA, the Bethel Literary Society, and later the ASNLH, black Washington was not in need of a renaissance, since its cultural and intellectual movement had been going strong for years prior to Harlem. The genius emanating from Washington was more independent and more autonomous than in the Harlem movement. Continuing his claim for the legitimacy of black Washington as a major center of the New Negro renaissance, Moses adds that "there was a cultural movement in Washington, and much of the Harlem Renaissance did, in fact, take place there." As further evidence of black Washington's central role in the New Negro movement, Moses argues, "a Washington Renaissance had predated the one in Harlem by at least twenty years."[47]

In many ways, it was with the support of such a community in black Washington (always involved either directly or indirectly in the affairs of Howard) that protests by the black deans, faculty, and alumni began to intensify, calling into question the authority of President Durkee. Many of these protests reflected the New Negro attitude shunning paternalism and calling for the free expression of black self-determination. Trustee Francis J. Grimke, for instance, argued in a February 1916 letter that "any white man who aspires to be president of Howard University or any colored institution must be absolutely square on what is popularly known as 'the Negro Question.'" Grimke adds that "A white man who isn't openly and above-board straight on the race question is entirely out of place at a colored institution." The men and women of black Washington, including deans, faculty, and alumni of Howard, all sympathized one way or another with Grimke's statement, echoing and identifying with it. After the groundwork was laid by these and other groups, the rising tide of racial consciousness finally engulfed the student body, which initiated a strident protest in 1925. It was this protest that finally broke the back of the Durkee administration. The 1925 strike acted as a "catalytic agent that dramatically underscored the chaotic situation of affairs on campus" and provided further evidence of the need for Durkee's resignation.[48]

The student strike at Howard was inspired by strident student opposition nationwide to compulsory ROTC. Before the spring of 1925, opposition to ROTC was not extreme, mainly because the ROTC department suffered a shortage of personnel, and student absences and refusal to attend classes and drill were largely ignored. However, Howard faculty soon responded to requests from the ROTC department to institute some form of discipline for students who did not comply with its requirements. The final agreement was that when a student accumulated ten unexcused absences in either physical education or ROTC (or both), he would be called before the dean and given a warning. If a student accumulated twenty absences, it was recommended that he be dropped from the college. On May 5, 1925, five students who had amassed twenty absences were suspended, although the faculty voted the following day to reinstate them. Despite the reinstatement, however, there was still much student resentment against the new policies.[49]

This continued dissatisfaction caused student opposition to the policies to intensify. Days following the reinstatement, the Howard University campus was flooded with posters declaiming, "Don't Be an Uncle Tom," or posing the question, "What Is This Going to Be—an Army or a University?" Protest activities such as picket lines, the circulation of petitions, and regular meetings became commonplace on campus. The majority of the students supported a strike, and Howard professor Kelly Miller praised the students for their "solidarity," characterizing them as "future leaders of the Negro race" who demonstrated "that the race must hang together or hang separately." In addition to reporting the petitions, meetings, and picket lines, the local press told of "human barricades formed at the entrances of classroom buildings," as strikers kept "lukewarm" students from attending class. In his assessment of the situation Miller noted that "these Howard students waged an orderly campaign," whereby "they did not create excitement, damage property or injure persons." Miller added that, in his mind, "never" was there "any real need of the police, though the blue coats paid the campus a visit, only to return for the lack of business."[50]

Even though the students conducted themselves in an orderly manner, most of the faculty resented receiving ultimatums and felt it would be irresponsible to compromise with students in their defiance of faculty authority and university policy. But the faculty was far from unanimous on the issue. Some professors pressed for the faculty as a body "to stand firm and issue" nothing less than "an ultimatum." Others clamored for the faculty as a body "to be human and grant the students' demands." The debate continued for four days and concluded at a "marathon meeting" on May 12, 1925, when the decision was made to issue to the students an ultimatum stating that those who continued "to obstruct other students from attending classes" would "be suspended." Furthermore, students who were absent from class for fourteen days would be "flunked." However, on a more conciliatory note, the committee relented and reported to the students that they were "willing to consider any complaint or grievance after [the students] return to normal relations with the University." Faculty suggested by such actions that, if students "would only return and recognize the authority of the faculty, their demands would be granted."[51]

Student responses to this proposed resolution evidenced disdain for the faculty refusal to negotiate with them during the strike, and many students disregarded the numerous warnings of looming suspensions. Naturally, the reaction on the part of students intensified the situation at Howard and captured the increased attention of the local and national media. Howard professors such as Kelly Miller even believed that "it is a safe bet that this strike will be carried to the floors of Congress," at a time "when the appropriations are discussed."[52]

The strike garnered significant congressional criticism from Alabama Democratic congressmen Henry B. Stegall and Miles C. Algood. Algood attributed the situation to the fact that "This whole university is simply a Republican vote-catching machine." Other forms of criticism of the students' actions came from the black press such as the *Dallas Express*, which felt that the students' actions played into the hands of the enemies of the race. With considerations of congressional appropriations in jeopardy and continued ridicule in the national press, the local alumni association set up a reconciliation committee. This committee conducted nonstop negotiations and convinced the students of the merits of the faculty's position, and vice versa. On May 14, 1925, the students agreed to return to class, and the faculty reinstated the five students whose initial suspensions had initiated the strike. Amnesty was granted to all students who had participated in the boycotts of class, and the faculty further agreed not to require attendance at ROTC until a special committee had concluded its study of the twenty-cut rule and thoroughly examined the military training and physical education programs at the university.[53]

The student strike may have been resolved, but its resolution did not lessen the general consensus that President Durkee had to go. Many more blacks began to believe that Durkee's removal was the only recourse left to ensure peace on the Hilltop. Unless there was definite resolution to the entire matter, many felt that there would be only continued and "ceaseless conflict between the president and the student body as well as hesitant and growing loyalty and devotion on the part of the members of the faculty," who only offered allegiance to stay on the good side of the president. English professor G. David Houston, who published collected documents, letters, sworn statements, resolutions, and personal writings in a column for the *Baltimore Afro-American* under the pseudonym "The Alumnus," assessed the Durkee years as being "consumed with bickerings and clashes." Many came to the conclusion that there was no alternative other than Durkee's removal. A writer in the *New York Age* characterized the "root" of the problem at Howard to be a "lack of teamwork between the president and the faculty," adding that "The Board of Trustees must recognize the fact that harmony and cooperation are necessary elements in maintaining a great university."[54]

Despite ever-increasing calls for Durkee's removal, Howard's board of trustees remained resolute in continuing its support of the president. In a statement printed in the *Chicago Defender,* board members expressed "confidence in the devotion and efficiency of President Durkee." The board president, Charles R. Brown, conveyed to the public that the trustees were in control of the situation and had the final say on the matter's resolution, that "the trustees of Howard University and not a group of disaffected people are in control of the university." Durkee's reaction to this staunch affirmation of his character and administration conveyed the assurance that the matter would be adequately handled even as he still remained as the head of the Capstone.[55]

In reaction to the inflexible position taken by the board of trustees, a scathing editorial in the *Washington Daily American* characterized the board's position as extreme disregard for the opinions and concerns of the alumni and other involved parties whose position differed from the board's. The author accused the board of arguing that blacks were incapable of directing their own affairs and needed to be led. The editorial mocked the trustees and sarcastically expressed what were believed to be their real intentions:

> We trustees, the majority of whom are white and not alumni of the university, are your lords and masters. What we say is law, no matter

what you colored people and alumni think. As a matter of fact, we do not even care to hear your complaints against the administration, for anyone who dares to disagree with our policy of running your school belongs to a disaffected and disloyal group. We have spoken.[56]

This sentiment characterized a continued and growing sentiment on the part of Howard's black alumni, but the protest did not change the board's position concerning Durkee. To support their position, the trustees pointed to successes attributed to the Durkee administration, such as a Class A accreditation status and an increase in the university's annual appropriation from Congress. In their view, these successes justified continued support for the president and also gave credence to Durkee's claims that criticism came from only a few isolated faculty members and alumni.[57]

The alumni ultimately staged a protest directing their attention toward congressional intervention and a reshaping of the board of trustees. In addition to asking Congress to suspend university appropriations during an investigation of charges leveled against the administration, alumni called for a reform of the process of selecting trustees. Alumni were able to garner significant support for a bill sponsored by Rep. Royal M. Weller that would amend the charter of the university, to create a new board of trustees of about eighteen members, with one-third chosen by alumni, one-third chosen by the U.S. commissioner of education, and one-third chosen by these two groups. Although this effort failed, it did succeed in thwarting a bill by Rep. Louis C. Cramton to authorize annual appropriations for Howard.[58]

The battle between the alumni and the trustees and administration had the potential to damage Howard's financial well-being as it gave southern congressional opponents of Howard ammunition to derail the federal appropriations. On May 8, 1926, representatives such as Rep. B. G. Lowery of Mississippi and Rep. Butler B. Hare of South Carolina used the division at Howard to pursue their own agenda, damage the credibility of the trustees, and further their own argument against appropriations. Understanding the enormous effect of these charges and the vulnerable position in which they placed the university, trustees finally conceded slightly and agreed to hear the "extensive and persistent . . . criticism of, and charges against, the present administration of Howard University."[59]

According to historian and Howard professor Rayford Logan, there were many charges brought against Durkee during this particular hearing. These included his educational policies, his ignoring of protocol with respect to the hiring and firing of faculty without consultation with deans or department heads, the loss to Howard of a number of notable faculty because of their personal disagreements with the president, his disregard for the alumni in his appointment of a hand-picked alumni secretary to oversee their activities, and his "arbitrary and dictatorial policy" of overall administration. Durkee was accused also of interfering with the academic freedom of faculty and even with physically assaulting professors. He was charged with misusing appropriations designed to increase faculty salaries and redirecting these funds to employ new teachers who would be loyal to him. He was reprimanded for exhibiting favoritism and being "vindictive" in granting or not granting recommendations for promotions, salary increases, and other matters involving the faculty's interests. The final grievance concerned Durkee's acceptance of the presidency of the overtly racist and discriminatory Curry School of Expression in Boston, whose continued policy of open exclusion of and discrimination against blacks provided the last straw for both faculty and alumni already offended by the president's insensitivity to racial pride and self-determination.[60]

Indignation about Durkee was apparent in the pages of the black press. Articles were featured by some of Howard's professors, such as cell biologist Ernest Just and the recently fired Alain Locke, who gave testimony at the hearing. Their testimony was not included in the hearing record, but their sentiments were acknowledged, nevertheless, by reports in black newspapers such as the *Baltimore Afro-American*.[61]

The board of trustees exonerated Durkee, but the writing was on the wall, and he was aware of the mounting pressures from hostile testimony and the alumni's threats against Howard's congressional appropriation. Durkee realized his time as president was at its end, and he held sympathies with the sentiments of one black trustee who commented, "If a colored man is ambitious enough to be in hell, let him be elected to the presidency of Howard University." In March 1926, with the end in sight, Durkee accepted the pastorate of the prestigious Plymouth Congregational Church of Brooklyn. In his letter of resignation, he lamented the situation:

> I did give everything I possessed of time and talent and consecration and prayer to Howard University. . . . I did the things that had to be done, which no one else would do. I knew great opposition would develop, I knew that those who could not see would fight. I did hope that I might be spared to put Howard University into the class of one of the greatest American universities. Our colored people would not permit that, so I turned away to a greater task, which is the task here at old Plymouth Church.[62]

Immediately following Durkee's resignation, the shout went out for the next president of Howard to be a black educator. Du Bois recommended that Howard "elect a colored man as president[,] and this not because there are no white men fitted for the job but because no one of the white men best fitted will feel like stepping into Dr. Durkee's shoes."[63] Not long afterward, the board of trustees, on March 25, 1926, unanimously voted that the next president of Howard should be a person of color.

The first name offered was that of trustee Jesse Moorland, but his candidacy encountered two major obstacles. First, although he was familiar with many of the faculty, alumni, and students, Moorland had "been one of Durkee's most influential supporters." This fact alone would have proved problematic, even given Moorland's race, and placed him "in a very bad position to bring peace to the divided Howard community." Second, critics such as "Alumnus" (G. David Houston) argued that Moorland, at the age of sixty-eight, did not possess a college degree, and it was argued that, "when the president's training has been a joke, the faculty can hardly do otherwise than to hold their self-styled leader in disgust." Despite these claims, Moorland did in fact possess relevant educational experience for the post of president. Michael Winston asserts that Moorland attended the Northwestern Normal University in Ada, Ohio, as well as Howard University's theological department, where he graduated salutatorian in 1891. It is more than likely that Rayford Logan agreed with Winston on this, since they coedited the biographical dictionary of important Negro leaders, in which Moorland was featured. Many trustees were certainly aware that these two objections were insurmountable, especially with the mistrust pervading the campus. There were alumni staunchly opposed to Moorland because of what some termed his questionable credentials. "It is no secret," wrote Houston, "that the alumni are bitterly opposed to the proposition to make Dr. Moorland president." Houston added that the alumni "were opposed to any candidate with such vulnerable qualifications. They want a live wire, and not a person already certified as having reached the age of diminishing productivity."[64]

At a meeting with the board of trustees, the alumni stressed their desire to hire as Howard's new president either a graduate or a professor of the university. Not to do so would lay the university open to the criticism that Howard had "failed dismally to produce an educator competent enough to be its president." Most alumni, it was argued, were strongly in favor of the board appointing a Howard man. Most faculty pledged their willingness to support any professor chosen by the board of trustees. Among the notable candidates mentioned from among Howardites and who were supported by the alumni were Dean Kelly Miller, Dwight O. W. Holmes, and historian Charles Wesley.[65]

The board of trustees eventually shied away from hiring internally, however, apparently because most candidates mentioned—although capable men—had been too involved with the "factionalism of the Durkee years and would be at a disadvantage in restoring peace to the campus." Initially, the board offered the presidency to a bishop in the African Methodist Episcopal Church, John A. Gregg, who was a capable leader and a former president of Wilberforce University. At the announcement of Gregg's appointment, the *New York Age* rejoiced that it was a "momentous decision," which represented "a significant advance in the policy governing Howard University." All seemed to be settled—except for the fact that Gregg could not in good conscience accept the appointment because of his commitments as bishop. He declined the offer, and the search continued for the first black president of the Capstone.[66]

The board then offered the position to thirty-six-year-old Baptist pastor Mordecai Johnson, who certainly appeared to have the necessary credentials, having been educated at Morehouse, the University of Chicago, and Harvard. Despite the growing sentiment among alumni that the next president should be chosen from within, most soon accepted Johnson's appointment. The situation at Howard was attracting the attention of notable black intellectuals and the black press. Writing an opinion in the pages of the *Crisis*, the NAACP's principal communication organ, Du Bois admonished those at Howard to bypass "clannish feeling." Editors of the socialist journal the *Messenger* placed the situation in its proper context and expressed the importance of this moment in Howard's history. "The white world will watch this experiment with great interest: our friends, hoping that nothing will go awry; our enemies, ever waiting and expectant that the slave psychology will reassert itself and precipitate a state of hopeless confusion because of distrust in Negro leadership."[67]

Many black intellectuals and leaders could identify all too well with this sentiment. They understood the magnitude of the situation at Howard and its implications for black intellectual life, black education, civil rights, and other matters of the race. Howard was in many ways— as Dean Miller depicted it in Locke's *The New Negro*—the national Negro university. It was imperative that the Capstone, its alumni, faculty, and trustees, all come together and gain some sense of internal control. The best way for this to occur was to select a highly regarded black man for the job and have as many influential figures as possible pledge their support to the new administration.

While pleased to accept, Johnson did not think his honeymoon would last long. Not long after being selected, he was already preparing himself for criticism of his policies as soon as the period of good feelings passed. Especially in the early years he did what he could to avoid offending anyone and to gain the support and trust of the faculty, alumni, and students. So Johnson did not come into the fray with blinders on. He understood the situation all too well as he was very familiar with the history and climate at Howard.[68]

Indeed Johnson was no stranger to Howard. Durkee had often invited him to speak at chapel. In 1923 the university had conferred upon him the honorary doctor of divinity degree. He and Durkee had shared many conversations about Howard when Johnson was on campus during critical periods of Durkee's administration. During these times, Durkee conveyed to Johnson his feeling that, despite his best efforts, he was greatly misunderstood at Howard. Before Johnson attained his doctorate from Harvard's divinity school, Durkee had offered him a position as professor in Howard's school of religion and as a preacher for Baptist students. In addition to Durkee's insistence that Johnson take the position, trustee Jesse Moorland also talked with Johnson and admonished him: "You must heed the call. . . . God wants you here."[69] Johnson eventually turned down this first offer of a position at Howard, as he had many other offers from other universities (in large part because of his commitment to pastoring the First Baptist Church in Charleston, West Virginia). Johnson did have other reasons for not accepting the post. As he confided to Moorland, "I have written him that the offer is very attractive to me with two exceptions . . . that I should not care to accept the official status of Baptist professor and pastor of the Baptist students and . . . that I should find it necessary to request that he make a decided advance in salary."[70]

Before he came to Howard, Johnson's reputation was well-known within the black community. An important Young Men's Christian Association (YMCA) activist, Sherwood Eddy, first brought Johnson to the attention of the national black leaders. Eddy had met Johnson when the latter was serving as secretary of the YMCA, and knowing of his keen interest in the problems of the world, Eddy invited Johnson to participate in a seminar he was conducting in Europe. Johnson accepted the opportunity without reservation and had his expenses underwritten by the First Baptist Church of Charleston.[71]

Howard officials were also well aware of Johnson's reputation. Richard McKinney, a scholar and a contemporary of Johnson, notes that he was known for possessing a "sharp intellect," for being an "eloquent communicator," and for having "moral integrity." McKinney also reports that Eddy attempted (but to no avail) to discourage Johnson from taking the Howard post and to continue his lecturing with the seminar in Russia, China, and other areas and then return to America to conduct massive campaigns of social evangelism. Johnson could not concede to Eddy, however, despite his respect for the work he was doing. For Johnson, the Howard post represented more than just a position; it was to him what the seminars were for Eddy, a large part of "his major purpose in life."[72]

McKinney argues that the presidency of Howard represented "a calling, a challenge, and a duty" for Johnson. He understood from the outset that "any Black American who assumed the position was bound to experience tremendous difficulty and suffering, primarily because of the deep divisions in the Howard constituency." He strongly believed and articulated that "Any colored man in the United States had a bounden duty to the Negro people and to the cause of higher education to accept this position at Howard and to bear whatever suffering he was called upon to bear to clear up the internal difficulty which threatened the life of the institution." Howard's presidency would allow Johnson the position of a very publicly visible black religious leader and intellectual. It would allow him to be what McKinney called a "moral and spiritual engineer." He had not sought after the position but, rather, was chosen for it, and Johnson began to believe even more strongly that it represented his life's calling. "Because of the overall situation," McKinney states, "he was convinced that this was the arena in which he was destined to carry forward his mission," which he conceived as waging "the struggle on behalf of disfranchised and dispossessed members of the African American community."[73]

This view fit in well with Johnson's strong Christian beliefs as a pastor. His view of the Howard presidency was that it was no accident but, rather, a calling that he was chosen to assume after much personal deliberation and initial denial. As pastor of the First Baptist Church, Johnson in many ways had gained significant experience in the effort to mold the hearts, minds, and spirits of a diverse congregation—obviously incurring along the way much pain and suffering as well as joy, which he most likely attributed to being a servant of Christ, the same experience and view he could now bring to the situation at Howard.[74]

Where the New Negro movement was concerned, Johnson was one of many black preachers from the 1890s onward who espoused the philosophy of the social gospel, a religious movement in America that connected the truths of the scriptures to social change and activism. As others among his contemporaries, Johnson magnified the message of the social gospel to apply to a global scale. There were prominent black preachers such as Adam Clayton Powell Sr. who advocated that the church should function as a place to connect religious and spiritual service with social service to the community. In essence, as author Jon Michael Spencer suggests, Johnson and other black preachers believed that the New Negro movement "had become institutionalized in the black church in the form of social gospel ministry."[75]

As Johnson contemplated the storm he was about to enter at Howard, the challenge was to figure out how to be most effective in connecting these varying strands of the social gospel, Christianity, and divergent groups without furthering the dissension already present—and, more important for him, without meeting the same fate as Durkee had before him. One major obstacle before him was to determine how he was going to present himself as the first black president of Howard University, and thereby meld his two selves: that of a black leader and religious intellectual who adhered strictly to the philosophy of the Christian religion and the emerging emphasis on the social gospel, and that of administrator and president of Howard University, respecting and allowing academic freedom, even religious diversity. This challenge would prove enormous for Johnson. Only his belief that this post was his calling would sustain him throughout what lay ahead for him.[76]

Finally, in April 1926, following a lecture series Johnson had conducted at Howard, secretary Emmett J. Scott wrote Johnson about becoming Durkee's successor. Although Johnson was in agreement with many at Howard that the time had come for a black American to head the university, he no doubt felt torn because of the friendship and respect he held for Durkee. He was hesitant to offend Durkee, since it was during Durkee's administration that he had received his honorary doctorate. He also believed that the candidate should be chosen from among those already on the faculty. Johnson probably knew all too well that he would eventually be perceived as an outsider, just as Durkee had been, and that his race might well not prove adequate in garnering enough support to lead the university. Johnson stated that he did not want to compete with either of the two Howardites who had been considered for the position, Dwight O. W. Holmes and Charles Wesley. Perhaps he could see the writing on the wall and could foresee potential problems and conflicts down the road if he took the position.

Johnson found himself in a major dilemma, because although he understood the politics at Howard, he had a deep and genuine desire to assist in the improvement of higher education for African American youth. He could envision the role a school of the caliber of Howard could play in driving that goal and in promoting social change both in the United States and abroad. He wrestled with this dilemma for a while (and would later find out that his initial trepidation was warranted), but as of April 1926, he felt comfortable taking more time to decide. So in the meantime, he turned down the offer.

On June 6, 1926, Gregg was elected president of Howard but soon thereafter turned down the post because of lingering commitments in his duties as bishop of the African Methodist Episcopal Church. Even though Gregg had informed the committee that he was not available for consideration, the committee had nominated him anyway, against his wishes. This might have contributed to his refusal, in fact. Another reason was that, prior to being considered for the Howard post, Gregg had already twice served as president of institutions of higher education, and he was not excited to assume another position, particularly with an institution facing turmoil and uncertainty.

Once again the committee (led by Durkee's former secretary Emmett Scott) and the board of trustees turned to Johnson. The nominating committee met with him in New York on June 23, 1926, and discussed issues related to the presidency, such as his experience with overseeing financial matters and the likelihood that he would be offered the post if Bishop Gregg declined the offer (as it appeared might happen). Johnson at the June 23 meeting allowed his name to be considered. Once Gregg did decline, it was seven days later, on June 30, that Mordecai Johnson was elected the first black president in the history of Howard University.[77]

Within the first year, Johnson set about ensuring stability on campus and healing the rifts between the previously warring factions. Indeed, Johnson took advantage of the atmosphere of initial cordiality and cooperation and "laid the foundation for an enormously successful, although not always placid, thirty-four years as president of Howard University." He demonstrated a real commitment toward and respect for the faculty, as shown in a number of examples. First of all, in 1927, Alain Locke was reappointed professor of philosophy, which signaled a reconciliation of sorts for some of the faculty disputes that had occurred during Durkee's tenure. Faculty and department chairs were given a significant budget, as well as discretionary power in the appointment of faculty. Among the most important of Johnson's achievements in the early years came in 1928, when his leadership guided the passage of the Cramton Bill, which ensured the legality and actual appropriation of congressional financial support for the university. Despite all the turmoil and controversy, it seemed, Howard had emerged on solid ground, with a president primed to lead the Capstone to the level of national Negro university as designated by Kelly Miller.[78]

CHAPTER TWO

Messiah and Leader

Mordecai Johnson and the Making of the Howard University Intellectual Community, 1926–1960

I N MANY WAYS, Mordecai Johnson's reputation for sound character, good judgment, and strong belief in social justice preceded him, and it was this that made him seem attractive and well suited to become the first African American president in Howard's history. Johnson had a great vision for what Howard could become. From the start, he envisioned it possessing a caliber of faculty and facilities that would be second to none other American university, black or white. Johnson's contemporary Richard McKinney concluded that "Johnson viewed the presidency of Howard as a calling, a challenge, and a duty." Any African American who assumed the position was expected to "experience tremendous difficulty and suffering," mainly because of the deep divisions at Howard. Some faculty portrayed Johnson as one who underappreciated the same faculty he spent time recruiting to Howard. It is unclear where the line is drawn between Johnson's outright negligence of faculty interests and his consideration of appropriation politics, which restricted the school's annual funding. Nevertheless, the position of president offered Johnson the opportunity to be a "moral and spiritual engineer." He came to view the position as part of his life's mission, which was to help facilitate "the struggle on behalf of the disfranchised and dispossessed members of the African American community." Johnson had not sought the position, rather he had been called and had chosen to accept the challenge, and this was what to him made all the difference. In accordance with his mission and vision to make a significant contribution to the higher education of African Americans, Johnson set out to make Howard University a model for the entire country. With its placement in the nation's capital,

Johnson had the perfect backdrop against which to develop this mission. He intended to make Howard a training ground for future leaders of the race. He was determined to train them for service to their communities, to the nation, and to the world. He believed that a thorough liberal education could properly train and develop individuals to impact social problems in the United States and around the world.[1]

In his inauguration speech as president of Howard University on June 10, 1927, Johnson announced his intentions to develop a first-rate intellectual community. He recognized the growing crop of intellectuals at Howard and in many ways pledged his commitment to continue this tradition and further enhance it. By the fact that he already had some familiarity with Howard, in the first section of his inauguration speech titled "Sixty Years Struggle and Achievement," Johnson highlights the importance and achievements of Howard's intellectual community, expressing that he valued this part of Howard's tradition. Johnson understood that in order to develop Howard's graduates into global citizens and meet the needs of communities around the world, he had to build upon this outstanding faculty. He brought attention to the value of a strong intellectual tradition at Howard:

> There has been a decided increase in the number of Negro scholars gathered on the several faculties, it being the purpose of the original white founders of the university not merely to train Negro men and women for practical life, but to train educational leaders who participate with them on a basis of uncondescending equality in the whole enterprise of Negro education. Here during the years has gathered the largest body of intelligent and capable Negro scholars to be found connected with any enterprise of its kind in the civilized world. Not only have these scholars been able to teach their subjects, but also some of them have ventured into the field of creative contributions in the fields of botany, zoology, sociology, and history.[2]

In this address, Johnson unveiled his vision for Howard University. He traced its development and provided an update on its current state. Rather than being critical of the university's prior evolution and administration, Johnson chose to emphasize the strengths of Howard, while acknowledging the need to improve on its weaknesses. He gave specific attention to every aspect of the university and the various "publics" that made up the university community. He depicted the Capstone as "the first mature university organization" for blacks "in the modern civilized world" and characterized its growth from humble beginnings as "one of the great romances of modern American education."[3]

The president also evinced a strong support of black studies and its connections with the surrounding black communities of the nation's capital. He spelled out how Howard could contribute to solving social problems in the United States and around the world. Johnson noted that the disciplines of sociology, economics, biology, anthropology, history, social philosophy, and religion were among those areas that could "provide the intellectual resources by which African Americans and the nation as a whole could be advanced." Johnson's affinity for the social gospel made Howard a fertile ground in which to develop a theory and theology of race relations (see Chapter Five). He cited African American churches as the most vital institutions in the black community and charged Howard's school of religion with the task of aiding in the preparation of an educated ministry. For this task, specifically, in 1933 and 1934 respectively, Johnson hired colleagues and friends Howard W. Thurman and Benjamin E. Mays.[4]

Although, as far as we know, Johnson did not publish an official autobiography, he did make a significant account detailing his early experiences as president.[5] In this account, he stressed that his election as president of the Capstone "was in the form of a draft made upon me by the Board of Trustees and not as a result of any effort on my part to secure the position of president." During a five-year period beforehand he had come to Howard to deliver religious addresses and in that time had held extensive conversations with the president, J. Stanley Durkee. He mentioned how Durkee had courted him to become a member of Howard's faculty in the school of religion. Johnson acknowledged that during numerous conversations with Durkee he "became aware" that Durkee "was the subject of many distressing experiences in his relationship to members of the student body, faculty and the Negro community."[6] So Johnson knew from the beginning that he was stepping into a tumultuous situation as Howard's president. "I knew," Johnson recollected, that he was entering a situation, "dangerously confused and distressing. . . . it was inevitable that I would be called upon to suffer—to what extent, I did not know."

In his statement, Johnson outlined three major policy decisions that he envisioned making in the early stages of his administration. He stated that he made up his "mind" based on his handling of the congregation at First Baptist Church in West Virginia. He "would make no effort to determine in advance, who were the members of the two major competing sections of the faculty of the University." Undoubtedly, some faculty would be dissatisfied that the president chose not to take their side from the beginning—demonstrating what they saw as loyalty and Johnson saw as favoritism. Second, Johnson decided that he would not "allow" himself "to be guided invidiously toward any member of the faculty as a result of critical words brought against that member because of the situation existing before my time." Instead, Johnson determined that he "would deal with every member of the faculty on the assumption that he was a man of ability and character deserving my confidence and not to lose my confidence as a result of inefficiency or injurious conduct arising under my administration."

In Johnson's last policy move, he foreshadowed his method of dealing with the faculty in the Howard University intellectual community. His disclosure here is particularly interesting. Johnson notes his position on university politics, evidencing that certainly he was his own man. Johnson admits, "I decided in the third place that if I was going to overcome the cleavage as a result of the competition long prevailing there I would have to have no political party of my own, but make appointments on the basis of the ability of the candidate and would make no decision by reason of his own or opposing affiliation with the competing parties."

Many African Americans see Johnson as a complicated, multidimensional personality. In many ways he is renowned as a masterful preacher and orator. Other assessments of him contain harsh criticisms of his complex personality and autocratic managerial style. Other views of him revolve around his outstanding courage and profound convictions in the face of staunch opposition. Still, despite the various views of Johnson, he remains one of the forgotten historical figures, lost to the memories of many Americans, in general, and of African Americans in particular.

As a pastor Johnson maintained a strong interest in the philosophy of social gospel. The term *social gospel* refers to a movement within the Christian religion that addressed or attempted to address the major social problems of the era from the mid- or late 1880s to the early 1900s. For many black theologians of the nineteenth and twentieth centuries, the major issue that headed their social agenda was that of improving race relations, both domestically and globally. There has been significant criticism of the manner and effectiveness with which the social gospel movement addressed significant race issues such as segregation. Because of his interest in social applications of Christianity, or what was commonly known as American Social Christianity, Johnson felt a tremendous interest in both domestic and world problems, especially as they affected race relations, black Americans, and people of color. It would be this abiding interest in the social gospel that Johnson brought to bear upon his presidency. In turn, he would connect this with his belief in the higher education of African Americans—to fashion and undergird his administration philosophy at Howard.[7]

Upon his election Johnson enjoyed the support of much of the Howard community and the overall black community in the nation's capital and around the country. One of his contemporaries, Richard McKinney, said that "the Howard faculty took the appointment in stride," and the students "were quite proud." Various members of the black middle class in D.C. and nationwide celebrated that what was considered the nation's emerging elite university for blacks finally had a black man at its helm. As mentioned earlier, Johnson was no stranger to Howard. In 1923, the university had awarded him the honorary doctor of divinity degree. For five consecutive years prior to that honor, Johnson visited the Capstone as the annual speaker at the university's day of prayer and gave a series of lectures during that same week. At these lectures Johnson had impressed students and faculty so much that he always spoke to overflowing crowds. The national press also hailed Johnson's appointment as a significant milestone in the history of African Americans.[8]

In fact, in many ways, Johnson seemed to be in a rare position of enjoying the support of many on both sides of the previous protests. Added to this complicated equation was the temperamental nature of the federal government and of Congress, and the awarding of annual appropriations to Howard, which before Johnson's arrival had to be lobbied for annually. Johnson was aware of the university's tenuous position and attempted to maintain a balance without sacrificing his personal integrity and character. Initially, he turned down the offer to be president despite his solid belief that the time had indeed come for Howard to finally have a black president. In fact, at the time, Johnson requested that his name be taken from any future consideration.[9]

Despite general approval within the African American community, there were a number of Howard faculty members who were unhappy with the choice of Johnson as president, and these individuals would continue to express their displeasure throughout much of his administration. Johnson was well aware of the situation and showed the foresight to recognize the need "to elevate the faculty to a position of respect and control in University affairs" and to offer them significant concessions. Durkee had been unable to do this, but one of Johnson's strengths would be investing in empowering and upgrading Howard's faculty. Durkee encountered problems with the faculty because he had depended solely on his administrative officers to conduct university business, and often without the consent of the faculty. In order to capitalize on Durkee's mistake, Johnson sought to give the faculty more authority. He initially began implementing this plan by adopting agendas that had been brought before faculty members for consideration and discussion. He also began organizing the faculty into committees, whose members were appointed by their peers. Finally, he made a commitment to the faculty and raised their salaries to a level comparable with those of administrative officers. For example, Howard historian Walter Dyson cited that, during Johnson's administration, one professor received a salary of $5,000 annually, which was approximately $225 more than his dean, and a number of other teachers received salaries of $4,000 annually.[10]

In order for Johnson to implement such large changes for Howard's faculty, he had to deal with the difficult challenge of the budget. This action on his part, as Dyson noted, "was necessary to upset many vested interests." In essence, Johnson created a budget of expenses and admonished each department to operate within that budget. Prior to his arrival, in some cases the income from the tuition of students enrolled in certain academic departments went to increase the salaries of teachers in some of the professional schools. At the same time, professors in the academic departments were told repeatedly that there were no funds available to raise their salaries, despite the glaring fact that funds from their students were consistently being transferred elsewhere and not used to improve their lot. By 1931, opposition had arisen to Johnson's stringent supervision of income and expenses at Howard, and he faced a very bitter and harsh attack. Signaling the delicate nature of the situation, at a campus meeting on April 13, 1931, students rallied in support of Johnson. They endorsed him not because he was the first black president of Howard but "because he represents Negro leadership at stake."[11]

Dyson has suggested that this attack upon Johnson compelled him to alter the way he dealt with the faculty. Whereas before he had been more open to their suggestions, now Johnson determined that in order to secure faculty leadership in the university he had to develop a more autocratic method. Faculty leadership and development continued to be among his major goals at Howard, but he abandoned the democratic method of relating to the faculty and reinstituted "the right of the president" to select and appoint committees. In the process he made fewer propositions and offered fewer items for discussion to the faculty. Johnson probably could foresee another firestorm similar to that faced by Durkee and wanted to avoid it at all costs. From his experience as pastor of First Baptist Church he had learned how to deal with a variety of people and personalities in overseeing the administration of the church's affairs, including its budget. Although leadership in church and leadership in university administration are very different, Johnson must have found some approaches applicable in both. First and foremost, he realized that no matter what he did he could not please everyone, and that trying to do so would erode the goals of his administration and force him to expend unnecessary amounts of energy. Second, he realized the only way for him to lead Howard University, hoping to merge its competing factions into one, would be to employ an iron fist to lead. This method of administration earned Johnson the title of "The Messiah."[12]

* * *

As president of Howard, however, Johnson had to be more than just an administrator and an educator. He had a number of interrelated roles. To be sure, he was a significant public figure, a member of the nation's and the world's top and most influential black religious intellectuals. Blacks were still predominantly locked out of political offices and positions of public distinction because of racial segregation and prejudice in America, so the position of president of a historically black institution was equivalent to being the president of a significant portion of black America. Johnson's role as an intellectual and a visibly public one perhaps made some on the faculty feel devalued or even threatened. Johnson's opinionated personality and his background as a black religious intellectual meant he was not content to be relegated to purely administrative duties. As Logan has noted, Johnson became president at a critical time in the history of Howard—and in the history of the United States and the world. His presidency coincided with the onset of the Great Depression, Franklin Roosevelt's New Deal, and the rise of strong dictators around the world such as Italy's Benito Mussolini and Germany's Adolf Hitler. Considering this state of affairs and Howard's turbulent recent history, Johnson had to be a strong leader so that Howard would have a chance at survival in the midst of a rapidly changing world.[13]

When Johnson assumed the presidency, Howard was still maturing as an institution, although it had a growing reputation as a leading center for African American higher education. In total there were eight schools and colleges: the College of Liberal Arts, the College of Education, the College of Applied Science, the School of Music, the School of Law, the School of Medicine, the School of Pharmacy, the School of Religion, and the Dental School. At the time, none of the schools actually held accreditation. There were 200 faculty members and 2,268 students, with 1,701 of those students in the colleges. The university had an annual operating budget of $700,000 and its physical plant was estimated at a value of less than $2 million. Seeing the glaring inadequacies concerning the budget, accreditation issues for some of the schools and colleges, an undervalued physical plant, a small faculty, and its law student enrollment, Johnson set out on a mission to upgrade each of these areas. In his inauguration speech, Johnson explained how to implement his vision. In essence, he wanted to improve both the faculty and the facilities of Howard so that it could "compete favorably with any liberal arts university in America."[14]

In order to understand the politics surrounding Howard's annual appropriations, it is critical to examine the yearly appropriation data, offer some comparison of supplemental funding, indicate the specific usage of the yearly allotments, and trace the manner in which the annual appropriations either strengthened or weakened the intellectual life of the Capstone. Table 1 on page 48 provides a yearly listing of annual appropriations, dating from 1926 to 1966. The table also notes the years 1970, 1975, and 1980, thus covering the period of this study.

On December 13, 1928, Howard University received proposed annual appropriations by an act of Congress that amended Section 8 of the Act of Incorporation of Howard University. The bill read:

> Annual appropriations are hereby authorized to aid in the construction, development, and maintenance of the University, no part of which shall be used for religious instruction. The University shall at all times be open to inspection by the Bureau of Education and shall be inspected by the said Bureau at least once each year. An annual report making a full exhibit of the affairs of the University shall be presented to Congress each year in the report of the Bureau of Education.[15]

In receiving these appropriations, Johnson benefited from earlier work done by Durkee. He was able to gain appropriations only, perhaps, because of divine guidance, and the support and efforts of two House congressmen, Louis C. Cramton (who now has an auditorium at Howard named after him) and the New York Republican Alden Reed. Both congressmen submitted bills in support of Howard University, Cramton in 1924 and Reed the day after Johnson's election as Howard's president in 1926. Reed's bill resembled Cramton's earlier bill, which referred to Howard as "a national school to meet a national need." Both congressmen argued that the federal government must rectify the inequitable distribution of federal funds to colored institutions in seventeen states that had segregated schools. "It is this discrimination," Cramton stated, "that creates a national need for a great national university." The House approved the bill in favor of annual appropriations with a vote of 226 to 94 (112 abstaining), of which 162 Republicans and 64 Democrats voted for the bill. By contrast, 93 Democrats and Minnesota's Republican William L. Carss voted against the bill. The bill, issued by the Department of the Interior, included an annual appropriation of $600,000 for Howard. In the bill Johnson won the ability to use the funds to increase both the physical plant and the salaries of Howard professors, which probably also assisted him in future recruitment efforts. Johnson articulated to Congress that "our need[s] for additional personnel are so great that we are obliged to set before you the hope that substantial help in this direction may not be precluded." Although Johnson's request was not rewarded to the degree he might have wished, after 1928, federal appropriations were used in part to increase faculty salaries.[16]

The congressional bill allocating annual appropriations passed on December 13, 1928, "guaranteeing that Howard would receive annual

Table 1: Howard University Funding History: 1926–1967

FISCAL YEAR	APPROPRIATION	FISCAL YEAR	APPROPRIATION
1926	218,000	1946	2,591,950
1927	368,000	1947	4,744,444
1928	580,000	1948	4,721,750
1929	600,006	1949	8,254,425
1930	1,249,000	1950	4,262,000
1931	1,760,000	1951	3,767,000
1932	675,000	1952	4,031,499
1933	1,249,000	1953	2,555,000
1934	605,896	1954	8,678,000
1935	665,241	1955	5,082,000
1936	675,000	1956	3,901,200
1937	700,000	1957	4,212,000
1938	723,000	1958	4,636,300
1939	745,000	1959	5,498,000
1940	754,000	1960	7,148,000
1941	786,253	1961	12,010,000
1942	777,500	1962	13,109,000
1943	1,037,493	1963	15,507,000
1944	1,048,000	1964	11,470,000
1945	1,280,575	1965	13,902,000
		1966	13,344,000
		Total:	$173,815,316

Sources: Rayford Logan, *Howard University: The First Hundred Years, 1867–1967* (Washington, D.C.: Howard University Press, 1968), Appendix B, I, 589-91; Charles E. Williams, comp., *The Howard University Charter: Upon the Centenary of Howard University* (Washington, D.C., 1967), 29–33.

Howard University Funding: 1970, 1975, 1980

FISCAL YEAR	APPROPRIATION
1970	59,964,000
1975	81,700,000
1980	121,893,000
Total:	263,557,000

Source: Biennial Evaluation Report—FY 93–94, Howard University, http://www.ed.gov/pubs/Biennial/533.html.

Table 2: Yearly Usage of Federal Annual Appropriations by Howard University, 1925–1965

YEAR	AMOUNT	PURPOSE
1925	$370,000	Medical Building
1927	150,000	Women's Dormitory
1928	340,000	Chemistry Building and Women's Dormitory
1929	280,000	Chemistry Building and Women's Dormitory
1930	739,000	Douglass Hall and Women's Dormitory
1931	885,000	Douglass Hall and Women's Dormitory
1933	460,000	Power Plant
1936	1,120,812	Founder's Library
1943	229,500	Power Plant
1945	181,575	Dentistry Building
1946	1,377,920	Engineering and Architecture Building, Women's Dormitories
1947	2,242,080	Men's Dormitory, Law Building, Administration Building, Fine Arts Auditorium
1948	2,571,750	Engineering and Architecture, Dentistry, Fine Arts Building, Women's Dormitories
1949	2,408,460	Medical, Law, Biology Buildings, Men's Dormitories
1950	1,762,000	Medical, Law, Biology, Administration and Engineering Buildings, Women and Men's Dormitories
1951	1,292,000	Pharmacy and Engineering Buildings
1952	1,091,779	Medical, Dentistry, Biology, and Engineering Buildings
1953	20,000	Vacuum Pump Steam System
1954	5,958,000	Medical, Administration, Law, and Biology Buildings, Power Plant
1955	2,130,600	Law and Administration Buildings, Men's Dormitories, and underground telephone conduit
1956	386,200	Dentistry Building and Men's Dormitory
1957	412,000	Home Economics and Dentistry Buildings
1958	286,000	Physical Education Building and Men's Dormitory
1959	881,000	Power Plant and Fine Arts Building
1960	1,658,000	Power Plant, Classroom and Home Economics Building
1961	556,000	Hospital, Warehouse, Men's Dormitory, and Fine Arts Building
1962	86,000	N/A
1963	6,245,000	Planning and Architectural and Engineering Services, Site Acquisition
Total:	$40,850,676	

Source: Taken from Appendix B, II in Rayford W. Logan, *Howard University: The First Hundred Years, 1867–1967* (Washington, D.C.: Howard University, 1968), 592-93.

appropriations for its operations," but it also placed a restriction on using the funds for "religious instruction." Johnson had written to Julius Rosenwald to secure his support for the Cramton Bill, and in kind, Rosenwald met with the secretary of the interior, Roy O. West, urging his support of the bill. Following the bill's passage, West arranged for a conference with relevant governmental agencies and philanthropic organizations whose interests impacted the future of Howard. The goals of this conference were to reexamine the entire university program, to determine the exact amount of income needed to run Howard on a first-class basis, and to decide how much funding the government would provide for this effort. According to McKinney, "The commitments growing out of this conference established the bases on which Johnson could appeal to Congress and private philanthropies for needed capital and operating expenses. Both the federal government and private philanthropies began to [respond] to these resolutions." Cramton continued to support Howard's fund-raising efforts even after he stewarded the annual appropriations bill through Congress. He remained actively involved for the duration of his congressional tenure.[17]

While receiving annual appropriations, Howard also received external grants. In 1926, for example, the school received a grant from the General Education Board (GEB), with the condition that $250,000 must go toward a $500,000 medical school endowment fund. The university also received $153,431.07 from assorted anonymous colored people, $25,000 from Julius Rosenwald, and $63,843 from other donors. "Private philanthropy had continued to show a decided interest in the development of a first-class university organization at Howard University," Logan noted.[18]

Among the largest private grants received by Howard during the 1929–1930 academic year were one of "$250,000 from the estate of Conrad Hubert of New York, an additional appropriation of $211,970 from the GEB, and the availability of $70,656 from the Julius Rosenwald Fund," which, along "with smaller gifts, represented announced appropriations of approximately $535,000 from private gifts for 1929–1930, to be used, for the most part, in the year 1930–1931." President Johnson wrote that these private gifts and federal appropriations were "a hopeful sign of the possibility of establishing here in Washington an educational service of far-reaching significance to the colored people of the United States."[19]

The impact of federal appropriations—in strengthening or hindering the intellectual life of the community—was especially pronounced in the areas of salaries, teaching loads, and the scholarly development of the faculty. In 1929–1930, benefits in the professional schools saw an increase of $65,000 in federal appropriations, which gave Howard the chance "to take a first and substantial step toward the improvement of instruction at its very foundation, by bringing in an increased number of full-time teachers and assistants for an enrollment held to a point slightly below that of last year." In his *Annual Report to the Secretary of the Interior for 1929–1930*, President Johnson stated "that the Law School had been enabled to complete the requirements of the American Association of Law Schools." President Johnson's Annual Report for the year 1930–1931 indicated, for the previous ten years, what was termed an unreasonable burden on all teachers especially "with classes of unreasonable size and with teaching loads beyond all standards." By 1930–1931 these loads had been significantly reduced. "For the first time [the teachers] have had an opportunity to attend significant educational meetings and to entertain the wholesome fermentation of ideas derived there from, as well as to enter into discussions with their colleagues to discover what added significance may be gained from cooperation in research projects, a matter far more important for the creation of the proper cooperation among the departments of the university than any administrative reorganization, operating from above, can possibly effect."[20]

Furthermore, the 1930–1931 academic year witnessed sixty-three members added to the university faculty and teaching assistant groups; sixteen joined the liberal arts faculty, now numbering eighty-eight (sixteen professors, twenty-three assistant professors, twenty-six instructors, and seven assistants). President Johnson stated that the future of the university's graduate division was "on solid grounds, . . . a major purpose of the administration." Graduate work at this time was relegated to master's degree work. The general library acquired 2,937 volumes in the year 1930–1931, which brought the total number of volumes to 53,061. Johnson's 1931–1932 annual report illustrated that federal appropriations for salaries rose from $350,000 to $450,000. That same year, however, the university suffered losses in both federal aid and private donations. Teacher's salaries were reduced, which added to the burden experienced as a result of teacher personnel reductions. Restrictions on funding for the school of religion hampered President Johnson's vision of making it a first-rate school of religion—even with him bringing in Rev. Howard Thurman in 1933, whom he characterized as "an extraordinary personality."[21]

Federal appropriations had a mixed impact on the scholarly development of the Howard intellectual community. Johnson, despite his decided strong-arm control of the institution, worked to balance both academic freedom and adherence to mandates set forward by the federal government in its allocation stipulations. Johnson had inherited a difficult political, economic, and social climate at Howard, often indicating in correspondence his understanding of the keen challenge before him. Howard archivist and historian Clifford Muse noted a complicated relationship between Johnson and the federal government. Emphasizing the relationship during the Herbert Hoover and Franklin Delano Roosevelt years (1928–1945), Muse highlighted the manner in which Howard "benefitted from federal legislation" and examined "whether racial, political or economic factors, or a combination thereof, determined the scope and dynamics of the institutional relationship between Howard and the federal government, and by extension the degree to which the federal government supported or impeded the development of black private higher education at Howard."[22]

Muse indicated that Howard University's relationship with the federal government was navigated through the executive and the legislative branches. Complicating the tenuous relationship were "a myriad of forces arising from the internal politics of Howard and from power blocs external to the university." Howard's ten-year plan, laying out its future institutional development, spearheaded its strong appropriation support during the Hoover and Roosevelt administrations. In response, the federal government committed to support Howard's educational, financial, and physical development.[23]

Muse pointed to the powerful influence of philanthropic foundations who ensured the sustainable development of Howard. In addition to playing a crucial funding role, foundation representatives such as Julius Rosenwald, Edwin Embree, and Clark Foreman (all from the Rosenwald Fund), Abraham Flexner (GEB), Anson Phelps Stokes, and Thomas Jesse Jones (both from the Phelps Stokes Fund) also played strong advocacy roles on behalf of the university. Other foundations that supported Howard include the Rockefeller Foundation, the William C. Whitney Foundation, the Guggenheim Foundation, the Social Science Research Council, and the American Institute of Chemists. The major three figures remained Edwin Embree, Anson Phelps Stokes, and Thomas Jesse Jones.[24]

Black organizations also kept tabs on Howard politics, through the black press, for example. Howard's federal support was usually strengthened when the institution's politics reflected a "smooth, efficiently-run, non-controversial educational institution." By contrast, political controversies such as the squabble between Johnson and Ernest Everett Just over the latter's research funding caused Howard to receive more outside scrutiny than during calmer times.[25] Furthermore, "bouts of internal dissension, chaotic conditions and controversial policy decisions or activities weakened its effectiveness to advance its cause and to solicit the necessary support and assistance for growth and development." Even though Johnson was disliked by many Howard faculty, Muse reasoned, these internal personality conflicts had little bearing on the manner or amount of federal appropriations received by the university.[26]

A definite "Howard lobby" assisted Howard in maintaining its annual appropriation and private supplemental status. In addition to the afore-mentioned foundations, the National Association for the Advancement of Colored People (NAACP), the National Council of Negro Women, mem-bers of the Black Cabinet (namely, Mary McLeod Bethune), and the black press all played vital roles in promoting Howard's cause before Congress and the American people. In particular, the black press played a compli-cated role as it related to Howard's public presentation.

> The black press played the dual role of supporting and criticizing Howard's administration. In its positive role as a Howard "lobbyist," the black press reported on the diverse social and educational activities and programs at the university. The black press assisted Howard in its recruiting programs, and also informed black America about the many accomplishments of the university. These news stories reinforced How-ard's collegiate image as the Capstone of black higher education, and served as public declarations to the Roosevelt administration, which consistently wooed black voters, of the importance of Howard to the national black community. Howard used the black press to explain and defend university policies, actions and events. Its standing among major black newspapers fluctuated as different "political" issues con-cerning the university developed. Some newspapers, like the *Norfolk-Journal and Guide* and *Pittsburgh Courier,* were generally pro-Howard.[27]

Such a lobby also benefited greatly from the staunch support of the first lady, Eleanor Roosevelt. Her public support of Howard (more than that of President Roosevelt) ensured that Howard remained an important federal and legislative priority. Having the ear of the president, Mrs. Roosevelt publicly and privately advocated on behalf of the university. She made regular visits and addressed faculty, staff, and students, while taking note of the institution's successes and continuing needs. In contacting cabinet officials, she served as the major policy broker between Howard and the federal government during the Roosevelt administration.[28]

In guiding annual Howard appropriations through Congress on an ongoing basis, President Johnson faced a firestorm of obstacles that required careful negotiation. He had to overcome the "pioneer" label, as well as many "traditional methods, policies, positions, and attitudes for-merly existing at the university." Johnson's personality also factored into this delicate negotiation of appropriation politics, especially as it related to on-campus perspectives regarding the matter. Johnson's positive qualities included "integrity, earnestness, courage, and [his] unselfish dedication" to transforming Howard into "a credible and efficient educational institu-tion." This positive portrayal earned Johnson numerous academic, corporate, federal, and lay public supporters. He also earned a reputation as being the "right man for the right time" and "one of the most outstanding University Presidents in the United States."[29]

On the other hand, Johnson's charisma and outspokenness, when taken as negative qualities, garnered him much derision and many detractors. He was often characterized as lacking in "finesse," in "tact and discretion," a portrayal emanating from various verbal battles he incited with faculty and administrative staff. Johnson exhibited "impatience with views sharply at variance." To his credit, his strong demeanor also served to buffer faculty from external attacks. For example, at times he supported his faculty with considerable courage, as when he defended school of law vice dean Charles Hamilton Houston and fellow law professor Leon Ransom from accusations of Communist affiliation.[30] Even with these and numerous other challenges, both internal and external, Howard continued to make economic progress toward sustainability. Factors leading to decrease of funding, over the years, were attributable to the 1930s Depression; the retirement in 1931 of one of Howard's prime supporters in Congress, Representative Louis C. Cramton; and a period of "diminished influence" of the Howard lobbying apparatus.[31]

After securing ten- and twenty-year plans for appropriations for Howard, Johnson set out to build the intellectual community. One of the first methods he used toward this goal of a more vibrant intellectual community at Howard was to secure accreditation for each school in the university. Among his first preoccupations was the school of law. Other attempts by the school's deans to achieve accreditation had been dashed as it became known that serious and extensive reorganization was required in order for the school to meet the standards of the American Bar Association. The school of law placed great emphasis on its night school, in effect promoting large enrollments rather than admitting only those students who were academically well prepared and therefore most likely to work at a high level and pass the bar. The combination of the heavy work schedules of most of the students and the night school setting did not allow for extended collegiality and fraternity among the students, or between students and professors, and did not allow students adequate time to conduct library research. All these attributes would be part and parcel of a daytime law school, but until Johnson's arrival a day law school had been considered impractical.[32]

Before acting, Johnson sought the counsel of Associate Justice Louis D. Brandeis of the U.S. Supreme Court, who advised him to focus his efforts on attracting a small cadre of able students and "to train them in how to identify a good case involving civil and constitutional rights," and to prepare them to develop those cases until they were able to argue them before the Supreme Court. After receiving sound advice from Brandeis, Johnson tapped a young Washington lawyer, Charles Hamilton Houston, to reorganize Howard's school of law. Houston had been teaching part-time at the law school since 1924 and, in the meantime, also worked as a practicing attorney in a joint law firm with his father. He was a Phi Beta Kappa graduate and valedictorian of Amherst College and held the bachelor of laws degree from Harvard Law School. He also had a passionate vision and zeal for developing a first-class law school. Johnson recognized this and believed that appointing Houston as vice dean of the law school would promote an even stronger intellectual community, committed to active social change.[33]

Despite objections, the board of trustees in 1929 came to a decision to finally transform the focus from a night program to a strong daytime law school. Another piece of the puzzle came about in 1929 as the dean of the law school, Fenton Booth, was appointed Chief Justice of the U.S. Court of Appeals. With this appointment, the board of trustees named Houston vice dean of the law school. Along with this appointment came the legal and administrative counsel of Harvard law school's dean, Roscoe Pound (giving Houston both legitimacy and credibility), and two of his former Harvard professors, well-known legal experts Felix Frankfurter and Joseph H. Beale who, as frequent lecturers in law school classes at Howard, also supported Houston.[34]

Historian Genna Rae McNeil notes that Houston was a demanding teacher who expected and received the most from his students. He demanded excellence and did not tolerate mediocrity in any form. As a lawyer Houston was known for his belief that a lawyer existed "either to be a social engineer or a parasite on society." Houston's commitment to excellence was apparent in the way he expelled any student who did not attain the law school's academic requirements.[35]

Houston headed the law school administration according to the concept of social engineering. He believed that black lawyers should have a thorough command and understanding of the U.S. Constitution and should demonstrate a clear ability to use this knowledge to drive social change for the underprivileged and maligned—and especially to promote African American rights. Houston's emphasis on social engineering was intended to instill in his students the capability to "guide . . . antagonistic and group forces into channels where they will not clash," and to ensure that "the course of change is . . . orderly with a minimum human loss."[36]

Howard boasted an impressive array of recruits to its law school in the early 1930s. In addition to appointing Charles Hamilton Houston, between 1926 and 1935 Johnson also employed Leon A. Ransom, James M. Nabrit, and William Hastie. Ransom was a distinguished graduate of the Ohio State Law School while Nabrit was a graduate of Morehouse College and Northwestern University's law school. Nabrit is significant also because he was the first scholar at Howard to introduce a course on civil rights law. The 1930–1931 academic year proved a significant one for Howard's law school, for in that year it boasted a full-time faculty, had a fully functioning and successful day school, and finally achieved the much sought after accreditation from the Association of American Law Schools and the American Bar Association. Even with the resignation of Charles Houston in 1935 to assume the position of chief counsel for the NAACP, Howard's law school continued its steady growth with the appointment of William Hastie as dean. Hastie was a Harvard-educated lawyer, a notable character who possessed great leadership ability. Also, the law school attracted a number of notable students such as Spottswood Robinson III, Oliver W. Hill, Robert W. Carter, and Thurgood Marshall. Under both Houston and Hastie, many of the graduates of Howard's school of law became important civil rights lawyers, who were prominent in the dismantling of racial segregation in America.[37] Historian Michael Winston argues that the Howard law school team of professors Charles Houston, William Hastie, James M. Nabrit, Leon Ransom, and George Haynes, along with students Thurgood Marshall, Spottswood Robinson III, and Robert L. Carter, "pursued an unremitting attack on the legal foundations of segregation." It was the Howard law school's efforts, along with the social science research of Howard historians Rayford Logan, John Hope Franklin, and Charles Wesley and social psychologists Kenneth and Mamie Clark that (despite Houston's life being claimed in 1950 from a heart attack) culminated in the landmark 1954 *Brown v. Board of Education* decision that struck down *Plessy v. Ferguson*, thus legally ending racial segregation in the United States. Counting from the 1930s to the 1950s, Winston refers to this august body of figures as providing "the best example of policy research at this time." He considers their legal research as having "probably had a greater impact on American life than the research activities of any other Negro scholars."[38]

In fact, Howard's law school became one of the most important training centers for black lawyers in the twentieth century. Inspired by Houston's philosophy of social engineering, these professors were responsible for training many of the nation's most capable black lawyers at a time when the shortage of lawyers in black communities across the country was severe, in the face of constant and escalating challenges to black equality because of legalized and institutionalized racial segregation. Many lawyers around the country were either trained or influenced in some way by members of Howard's law school faculty or students. With the emphasis on social engineering, the law school contributed mightily to the growing intellectual community Johnson was building at the Capstone. The cadre of legal scholars at Howard functioned as the "catalyst for some of the most significant decisions affecting the civil rights of the Black community."[39]

Johnson's second major step in elevating the status of Howard's intellectual community was to revive the school of religion. As a theologian, he considered the school of religion a major priority. However, by 1928, Johnson was facing an uphill battle in his attempt to provide support for the school because of the stipulation in the appropriations bill that prohibited any federal funds being allocated for religious purposes. By 1934, the school still did not have full accreditation status and it was struggling.

In 1933 Johnson brought in theologian Howard W. Thurman as dean of the chapel and, in 1934, Benjamin E. Mays as dean of the school of religion. Together, Mays and Thurman transformed the school of religion into a respected and pioneering leader in the development of a theology of race relations, thereby attacking racial discrimination in the church and in society. After Mays stepped down in 1940, Johnson recruited theologian William Stuart Nelson, who continued the tradition of black religious intellectuals at Howard.[40] During their respective tenures at Howard, Thurman, Mays, and Nelson, as well as Johnson, traveled around the country and the world spreading the message of the social gospel while challenging racism, imperialism, and discrimination worldwide.

Howard W. Thurman had been a Baptist preacher and pastor in Oberlin, Ohio, a black religious intellectual who came to Howard at the insistence of Johnson. Thurman and Johnson had maintained a close friendship while Thurman was pastoring in Ohio, before his appointment in 1933. Thurman became enthralled with Johnson's vision to create a stimulating scholarly community at Howard, to make it into a vibrant intellectual center. In his autobiography Thurman noted, "I was caught up in Mordecai Johnson's vision to create the first real community of Black scholars."[41]

Over the years President Johnson, Dean Mays, and Dean Thurman came to be very close. Each had a tremendous influence on the other two, and all three had great respect for one another. They shared a number of commonalities that connected their lives and callings. All three were graduates of Morehouse College, former Baptist pastors, and articulate debaters, as well as practitioners of nonviolence and the social gospel philosophy. Mainly because of his leadership as dean of the school of religion, Mays earned the opportunity to become the president of Morehouse College in 1940. The Howard years were equally gratifying for Thurman in that they proved critical to his evolution as an intellectual and theologian. Despite the turmoil that often visited the university campus or its political entanglement, these three black men retained the bonds that brought them together and remained on common ground, forming a formidable triumvirate of their own.[42]

Each of them was a significant and active black religious and public intellectual throughout his tenure at Howard. Each served on the school of religion faculty as educator. They functioned as teachers, preachers, social activists, prominent scholars, and public intellectuals. Thurman evidenced his social activism and intellectual abilities in community with other members of the faculty such as Alain Locke, E. Franklin Frazier, and others. His biographers Catherine Tumber and Walter Fluker argue that Thurman's contribution to social activism is evidenced by the fact that he was "a public intellectual, who influenced some of the most important social movements of the mid–twentieth century."[43]

Upon becoming the university's first black president, Johnson had set out on a mission to establish a committed and impressive community of scholars at Howard. This vision became ever more a reality as many noted scholars gravitated to Howard mainly because of his aggressive recruitment. The origins of this community also lay in the very nature of racial segregation in America, which offered few alternatives for black scholars such as Mays. In a very real sense, a scholar's appointment to Howard meant that a Negro scholar had arrived. It often signaled the pinnacle of his or her career. For some such as Mays, it also represented a jumping off point as well.[44] In recollecting his decision to come to Howard in 1934, Mays articulated:

> I was eager to go to Howard for several reasons. I felt the challenge to make the School of Religion outstanding, to lift it, if possible, from its stepchild role to a place of respectability in the institution. Moreover, I had great admiration for Mordecai Johnson. . . . I had more than a casual interest in Mordecai Johnson's success at Howard. I am basically a "race" man. I believe in the black man's ability, and my heart leaps with joy when a Negro performs well in any field. For me, it was imperative that the first "Negro" President of Howard University be an unqualified and triumphant success. I was eager to help him build a great University by making the School of Religion a first-rate institution.[45]

From this statement, one can discern that Mays understood all too well the difficult position Johnson was in. Since its founding in 1867, Howard had been headed by a succession of white men. Mays commented that various questions were raised by "doubting Thomases" concerning Johnson's competency to succeed in his duties as president. To his credit, Mays argued that there were a number of precedents where black men had demonstrated the capability to be successful presidents of institutions of higher learning.

As examples he cited Booker T. Washington and Robert Russa Moton's leadership at Tuskegee Institute as well as the leadership of John Hope at Morehouse College. A larger question Mays prompted was whether Johnson could gain annual and substantially greater appropriations from Congress, overcoming the opposition of a number of southern congressmen. Even after Johnson's successful lobbying for consistent appropriations, Mays observed that the university president had a number of other barriers to contend with, such as congressional interference with affairs at Howard that would soon cloud his administration.

Understanding the challenges faced by Johnson in general and the school of religion in particular, Mays established six goals that he wanted to accomplish while dean of the school of religion. These were an increase in the school's enrollment, an improvement in faculty, the rehabilitation of the physical plant, the enlargement and improvement of the holdings of the school's library, the establishment of an endowment, and the attainment of accreditation by the American Association of Theological Schools. Mays believed that, in his six years at Howard, five of his six goals were met. These five were the larger enrollment, a more scholarly faculty, accreditation, the growth of the library, and the improvement of the physical plant. The goal that was not achieved was the establishment of an endowment. He added that only four of those goals were fully realized because the challenge to improve the physical plant continued from prior to his arrival until years after he left. In addition to being active in improving the school of religion, both Mays and Thurman traveled extensively abroad—to India, Europe, and other countries—to work as public intellectuals and promote the school of religion.

In addition to pressures from racism, segregation, and the standards of mainstream society, Mays articulated what he considered an even greater obstacle facing Johnson's administration: that of the "systematic undermining of self-confidence" by other black intellectuals at Howard. According to Mays, a small group of professors at the Capstone were adamant in their dislike of, and opposition to, Johnson, many believing that he administered the university in too dictatorial a fashion. Johnson has often been characterized as a champion of academic freedom for Howard intellectuals, but other faculty believed that this applied to everyone except in his relationship with the faculty.

Never fully grasping the reasons for the intense animosity against Johnson, Mays went so far as to suggest that Johnson himself may not have been fully able to comprehend the depth of opposition he experienced from some members of the faculty. Mays admitted that he, himself, was caught somewhat between divided loyalties since he and his wife, Sadie, were close friends with many of the dissenters. It seems that, because of a keen sensitivity to the precarious position of black men in academics, Mays found ways to remain above the fray and managed to maintain good relations with both Johnson and his detractors in the university community.

Johnson's appreciation of the value of the intellectual talent already present at Howard when he arrived as president was matched by his desire to build an even more impressive community of scholars committed to outstanding scholarship and service to the black community. He appreciated the contributions of scholars such as Alain Locke and Charles Wesley and, at the same time, envisioned a more extensive community of scholars and an even more important role for them. Already part of the faculty when Johnson arrived were noted cell biologist Ernest Everett Just, philosopher and Rhodes scholar Alain Locke, and English scholar Benjamin Brawley. Within a few years of his appointment, Johnson attracted more top-flight scholars. Under his direction, the Howard University intellectual community grew in both quantity and substance.

The social and natural sciences witnessed significant infusions of talent. Educator Charles H. Thompson was recruited to head the college of education, and in 1932 he founded a very important publication, the *Journal of Negro Education*.[46] This was to become the major voice for Howard's legal scholars and other black scholars around the country, in their opposition to segregation in higher education and in the larger society. Physician and professor of medicine Henry A. Callis, chemist Percy Julian and hematology specialist Charles Drew, who pioneered research in the development and usage of blood plasma, sought to train more black doctors and scientists to help tackle the health challenges facing black Americans at the time.[47] Johnson brought political scientist Ralph Bunche on board to head the political science department. Bunche went on to serve in the United Nations, and in 1950 he became the first black American to win the Nobel Peace Prize. E. Franklin Frazier, sociologist and author of works on the black middle class, the black church, and other black institutions, graduated as an undergraduate from Howard and returned to serve as the chair of the sociology department. Frazier was influential on the committee that established African studies at Howard in 1958. Also, economist Abram Harris, while at Howard, contributed mightily to an understanding of the effects of capitalism on the black community—as did historian Eric Williams, who expanded the examination of the effects of capitalism as it related to the global institution of slavery. Williams, while at Howard, aided in increasing the enrollment of Caribbean students and, following his tenure, became prime minister of Trinidad and Tobago.[48]

History and literary studies flourished under Johnson's presidency.

Historian Rayford Logan, recruited by Johnson in 1938, headed the history department and also served on the U.S. national commission of the United Nations Educational, Scientific, and Cultural Organization (UNESCO). Historian John Hope Franklin—author in 1947 of the classic textbook on African American history, *From Slavery to Freedom*—also served on the U.S. Civil Rights Commission in the 1960s. Historian William Leo Hansberry increased the enrollment of students from various countries on the African continent and also pioneered African history and African studies. Poet and literary critic Sterling Brown greatly enriched the community at Howard through his scholarship and active personality.[49] Along with Locke, Brown promoted the New Negro movement in Washington and around the country. He also served as director of the Federal Writers' Project in the 1930s. Other notable members of this community included historian Merze Tate and literary scholar Arthur P. Davis, the classicist Frank Snowden who authored a key Afrocentric study entitled *Blacks in Antiquity*, the historian Chancellor Williams who along with Hansberry pioneered early African history at Howard, and many others.[50] By the early 1930s Howard had amassed some of the most notable social science and humanities scholars black America had to offer and boasted one of most impressive intellectual communities of black scholars of its time.[51]

Despite his success in recruiting notable scholars, however, there were numbers of critics and detractors both at Howard and around the country. Many were critical of Johnson's outspokenness. Even some supporters, such as his friend and colleague Morehouse president John Hope, showed concern over Johnson's public utterances, which Hope felt might be taken out of context and used to attack Johnson's character and goals. Some of Johnson's public statements caused people to be critical, especially his expressed criticism of capitalism and his support of socialism. In numerous speeches Johnson proclaimed his belief in American systems, but he did not steer away from directly criticizing their shortcomings. As McKinney argued in his biography, Johnson was not interested in avoiding controversy. His personality was of a type that was driven to press on even in the face of staunch opposition and adversity. Other critics emphasized the fact that Johnson had limited experience as an administrator before becoming president of Howard. This same faction had been critical also of Durkee's lack of qualifications, and of previous white presidents of Howard. Johnson's experience in higher education prior to Howard was limited to two years of teaching and one year as dean at his alma mater, Morehouse College. Critics believed that Johnson's lack of experience in higher education would hinder Howard's progress. Many of the critics among the faculty and the administration probably felt that, without experience dealing with and understanding faculty culture, Johnson would do a poor job of understanding their needs and requests.[52]

Johnson steadily went about building an even stronger intellectual community than had existed at Howard prior to his assuming the presidency. A good example of the viability and influence of Johnson's community of scholars on one individual was the person of Benjamin E. Mays. "While at Howard," Miles Mark Fisher argues, "Mays was a member of the greatest community of African-American scholars of that day and possibly of all time." Fisher adds that, for Mays, in particular, this intellectual community "sharpened his mind through the exchange of ideas and stimulating discussions."[53]

Many longtime Howard faculty held on to the belief that Johnson's autocratic style damaged the reputation of the university, isolating and ostracizing a number of talented faculty, who either left the university in disgust or remained, but in a state of intentional protest toward the man many labeled "The Messiah." Professor of history John Hope Franklin recalls his own ambivalent view of Johnson's presidency. Initially, Franklin viewed Howard as the pinnacle of his own career as a black scholar in segregated America—in much the same way as did his close friend and fellow Howard historian Rayford Logan. Franklin noted, "I never had any real plans to leave Howard." In fact, he wrote, "in the middle 1950s, I didn't think I could leave Howard." Soon the renowned historian came to form a very harsh view of the Capstone, however, believing that Johnson's administration functioned in ways that diametrically opposed his own views of higher education. It appeared to his friend Logan that the needs of the faculty and student body were far removed from the understanding and concern of the president and the university board of trustees. In Logan's estimation, Johnson's administration seemed to privilege "self-preservation" over and above "efficiency, effectiveness, and accountability." Franklin bristled with hostility in an environment spoiled by a lack of administrative accountability, and by managerial incompetence—especially, among other matters, in regards to his requests for basic information, referrals, and an office telephone line. In the final analysis, this barrage of administrative problems soured Franklin's otherwise positive experience with students and colleagues and left him feeling disenchanted with Howard. In 1956, as Brooklyn College was looking for a department chair, Franklin jumped at the opportunity to escape the institution he had once held in high esteem.[54]

Franklin continued his criticism of the Johnson administration even many years after he left Howard, which suggests to many that he harbored a feeling of resentment. Fellow historian Yohuru Williams writes that the source of Franklin's bitterness toward Howard stems from his philosophical disagreement with the manner in which the university was run while he was there. Franklin had his own perspective on how a university should function. He summed up his nine years of experience there as reflective of a "series of frustrations."[55]

The first part of Johnson's tenure was marred by controversy and conflict with other influential members of the Howard intellectual community as well, not only faculty but also alumni and trustees. Among others, Johnson warred with Abram Harris, Rayford Logan, Alain Locke, E. Franklin Frazier, Kelly Miller, Ralph Bunche, Harold Lewis, and Percy Julian. Many of these scholars felt it unconscionable for the board of trustees to elect a Baptist preacher who had very little prior administrative experience in higher education. They considered Johnson both unfit and unqualified to lead a great university such as Howard into the remainder of the twentieth century. Critics claimed that Johnson was unyielding in his stances, that he possessed a messianic complex, that he was a dictator. Adding insult to injury for the faculty were the mandatory chapel services, held in Andrew Rankin Chapel, when Johnson's commanding voice would boom out pronouncements and declare theological views affirming the idea of predestination and chosenness. To be fair to Johnson, he was not alone among his college president contemporaries during the twentieth century in being labeled an administrative autocrat. Fisk's Charles S. Johnson faced similar scrutiny from certain wings of the faculty. However, it was true that Johnson viewed his role as president of Howard as being in line with the will of God.[56]

In the centennial history of the university, Logan recounts that particularly noted disputes occurred between Johnson and sociologist E. Franklin Frazier and economist Abram Harris. Logan characterized Johnson during his "Messianic Moments" as ridiculing Frazier and Harris, by trying to tell them what kind of sociology and economics to teach and write.[57] The hostility between Harris and Johnson arose over the fact that Johnson made no effort to retain Harris when he was offered a position to teach at the University of Chicago. Even though the Chicago position was of less stature than his post at Howard, Harris left because he felt he was not valued enough. He made it known that he would have stayed had he been made to feel that he was an important member of the faculty. In fact, over the course of their tenure at Howard, Harris and close friends Frazier and Bunche would often meet to share their mutual dislike for Johnson's administrative style and personality. Each of them complained about Johnson's unfair dealings with faculty and chided him for being more of a preacher and less of an academic. Essentially, for the faculty critical of him, the latter criticism made it seem virtually impossible for him to understand their perspective as scholars.[58]

The slight to Harris is interesting in light of a similar tiff between Johnson and Logan in 1947. Kenneth Janken notes that upon the establishment of a new salary scale to reward faculty who had taught at predominantly white universities and colleges, Logan had been left out. Of course, this was because Logan had not been able to teach at a white institution, but the new salary scale also created a new level of professor, the *super-duper* professor. This position paid annually six thousand dollars, which, considering the low salaries made by many black professors at Howard and across the country, was a great amount for the black faculty. Professors appointed to this level were E. Franklin Frazier, Alain Locke, and Sterling Brown. Upon demanding an explanation for his omission, Logan was informed that the position was available only to those who had previously taught at white institutions. In his struggle for acceptance in the academy, this incident was particularly hard for Logan to swallow. For example, Frazier in fact had only ever been offered a position by New York University. Johnson elevated him to the "super-duper" level in order to match that offer. One wonders why Johnson chose to match some offers by schools that courted his faculty members in some instances and yet, in other situations (as with Abram Harris), showed complete indifference. The fact that Johnson matched NYU's offer in order to keep Frazier demonstrates that, despite his apparent differences with some faculty members, he was cognizant of the importance of retaining quality faculty.[59]

Alain Locke and Johnson had a very difficult relationship. Many believed that the two in fact hated each other. Professors such as Logan, a temperamental figure in his own right, viewed Johnson as an autocrat and a dictator. Just and Frazier thought Johnson too overtly religious in his administration of Howard. Faculty who held this view of Johnson felt that he tried to force his moral prescriptions upon them. Frazier and a number of other social science faculty members, including Ralph Bunche and Harold Lewis, met on Saturdays at Bunche's home to compare notes and criticisms of Johnson and his administration. Some members of the faculty felt Johnson was out of touch with true scholarship, and that his treatment of some faculty members demonstrated this disconnect. They criticized him for possessing a messianic complex, for being insensitive to faculty needs, and for being an untouchable insofar as criticism went. Johnson's harshest critics felt they could not bring their criticisms to the board of trustees because they felt they would not be seriously acknowledged. Johnson was also criticized for alienating and pushing away some of the most talented faculty, including such scholars as linguist Lorenzo Turner and educator Dwight O. W. Holmes.[60]

* * *

Relationships between Johnson and members of the Howard faculty were obviously as complex and diverse as the many-faceted personalities of each member of the university's intellectual community. Even with those faculty members who were critical of Johnson, there are evident instances of mutual respect and collegiality, however. This demonstrates a complicated relationship between Johnson and the faculty that has not yet been thoroughly examined. It stands to reason that, with Johnson's great vision to amass a stellar intellectual community, he would also possess at least some understanding and empathy with the role of black scholars in the age of segregation. This point is further supported as one examines how vigorously Johnson supported and protected members of his intellectual community during the McCarthy Red Scare, and especially those whom many regarded as Johnson's bitter critics such as Locke and Frazier.

To be sure, scholars and preachers have egos, and with so much intellectual diversity at work at Howard, tempers and ego battles were bound to flare at times. Even the closest of colleagues had heated disagreements in the pursuit of common goals. Even though their areas of expertise and emphasis were different, however, they all shared a similar passion for the equality of African Americans, who lived constantly shaded by the curtain of segregation. Methods and egos would get caught in extensive political webs, as the system itself created animosities between many scholars of national importance (even noted black intellectuals Du Bois and Woodson). The segregation system was designed to create certain binaries that made it difficult for many leaders to function, but it is in spite of all the barriers and disagreeable moments that we need to look at the legacy of the relationship between Johnson and his community of scholars. The nature of segregation was so crippling on black intellectual life that it forced or contributed to many of the conflicts that ensued at Howard.

The wars at Howard should not obscure, however, the many instances where Johnson and faculty members demonstrated some form of professionalism, mutual respect, and collegiality. For instance, in 1929, Professor Locke wrote Johnson detailing the happenings at a Haitian luncheon. The tone of Locke's letter is one of respect, and there is no hint of animosity or hatred. Locke disclosed to Johnson that Du Bois "really exceeded himself and spoke constructively for once." He added a commentary that the addition of Charles Johnson to the Haitian commission was a good move, "a happy escape from what might have happened," and further added, "Let us pray for a similar deliverance for Haiti." This last statement goes against the view that Locke was completely antireligious, not able to find any common moral ground with Johnson, for it shows concern for the plight of black people the world over. Despite their particular idiosyncrasies and moods, the one matter that united Johnson with the scholars at

Howard was the plight of black people globally and the fight to achieve full equality for them.[61]

Other examples demonstrate that professionalism and respect—as well as interpersonal clashes—did characterize the relationship between Johnson and professors at Howard. In a 1935 letter, Johnson praised Locke and recognized him for his vision in heading up a "Minority Problems Conference." Johnson took the opportunity to "congratulate and to thank" Locke for his "arduous and valuable work" on the conference. "The number of distinguished speakers, the general character of the program and the growing interest manifested all indicate that the conference was a decided success." Johnson disclosed that he hoped the conference would occur again the following year, and he shared with Locke that he had already provided for it in the university budget, having already cleared it with the board of trustees.[62]

Johnson did also have very strong supporters, who felt that his style of administration at Howard was necessary. Without these strong supporters (Mays, Thurman, and others) Johnson would not have lasted as Howard's president for the thirty-four years he served. In 1960, the year of Johnson's retirement, Mays published an assessment of his friend's administration in the *Pittsburgh Courier*. Mays articulated: "I have great admiration for Mordecai Johnson. I worked with him as one of his deans for six years. The test of a man's leadership is determined by the respect and admiration you have for him after observing him up close."[63]

Mays wrote the article as a "salute to Johnson" and his service to Howard and the higher education of African Americans. In his article Mays outlined six major contributions that Johnson made while serving as Howard's president. By this time, Mays had a greater understanding and appreciation of Johnson's role, because Mays himself had been president of Morehouse College for twenty years. First, Mays credited Johnson with securing "millions of dollars" for Howard without involving the university unduly in partisan politics. Mays argued that "no strings were ever attached to the appropriation" and that no member of either house of Congress, no U.S. president, member of the cabinet, or any other government official "ever dictated the educational policy of Howard University." Mays stated that the board of trustees did all the hiring and firing "without political pressure." In this latter statement, Mays challenges the view that Johnson himself was solely responsible for the hiring and firing of many of the talented faculty at Howard, even some of those he initially courted.

Mays went on to assert that Howard was "academically free." On the question of academic freedom, Mays says, "The professors are free to teach the truth as they see it and at no time have they been afraid to follow the dictates of their conscience in the classroom. Academic freedom is one of the great signs of a great university. The fact that the university is academically free is due in a large part to the leadership of Mordecai Johnson." Mays continued by saying that "inseparable from academic freedom" was "faculty of able men and women devoted to the cause of education." Here, he pointed to the fact that, to his knowledge, each school of the university held accreditation status. He pointed to the great improvements made to the university's physical plant during Johnson's administration. He characterized Johnson as "a man of great integrity," possessing "insight, will power," and remaining "a man of conviction." He further added, interestingly, "There has been no scandal at Howard under his administration." Mays continued his salute to Johnson with the assertion, "He has given the university and the nation a courageous leadership. Few university Presidents would have had the character and the ability to speak the prophetic word in criticism of the social and political ills of our times as he." Mays ended by stating that the leadership demonstrated by Johnson was "difficult to follow," but he expressed full confidence in Johnson's successor, James M. Nabrit.[64]

In his numerous encounters with the president, Mays disclosed that not once did he experience the tyrant some others saw in Johnson. This assessment could be partly attributable to the educational and religious connections between the two mutual friends and clergymen. Instead, his assessment of Johnson depicted the president as "a man of honor and integrity." Mays was careful to add that Johnson, as all other human beings, possessed an imperfect nature.

The apparent animosity other faculty felt toward Johnson at times could have been spawned by viewing Johnson as a black version of the prior white presidents, particularly when he was either indifferent or inflexible to both individual and group faculty requests. Johnson was his own man, and this characteristic was perhaps more of a reason for animosity toward him. Another reason was perhaps the dilemma of the black religious leader as defined by theologian Willie James Jennings, who stated that these figures were torn between the dilemma of espousing black nationalism or race pride while simultaneously promoting American democracy. This dilemma, a crisis of the black religious intellectual, is very reminiscent of Du Bois's classic dilemma of double consciousness.[65]

Others echoed Mays's sentiments concerning Johnson. His childhood friend P. L. Prattis reminisced on his memories of Johnson and his administration:

> If my arithmetic is right, "Mordy" had the floor at Howard for nearly 34
> years. There were all sorts of schisms and inner conflicts, but "Mordy"

rode these well, ignored the yapping at his coat tails and went on to wheedle more out of Congress for Howard than had been wheedled in all the years with the so-called bacon. Howard has not reached its full stature yet, but one wonders where it would have been without Johnson at the helm. . . . To his credit, it must be said that he never bit his tongue—whether he liked to hear himself talk or not. Some folk may have trembled, but "Mordy" roared his convictions. He frightened the faint of heart, but he got what he went after. . . . Pick him apart if you will, but he was Howard's greatest president.[66]

Another strong supporter of Johnson was the trustee Jacob Billikopf. In a response to a questionnaire posed by the *Associated Negro Press* editor Claude Barnett, Billikopf mentioned the tremendous contributions Johnson made to Howard, noting his uncanny ability to garner substantial financial support from Congress, the Julius Rosenwald Fund, and the GEB. Billikopf said he could not "think of any individual, who could have obtained so whole heartedly the support" from these three entities, "all three of which have made it possible for Howard to make rapid growth and to lay a foundation for marvelous future development." Billikopf added that Johnson's personality was so impressive "he is trusted implicitly and his word carries enormous weight with them." The trustee attempted to establish his own credibility by asserting "intimate relationship with outstanding Negro leaders in the United States," especially members of the NAACP.[67]

In discussing the sentiments of members of the faculty, Billikopf credited Johnson with elevating the status of the faculty. "Purely of their own volition, distinguished members of the Howard faculty have, on various occasions, spoken to me in glowing terms of the high standards Dr. Johnson has created," indicating his "whole-souled devotion to their interests, material and otherwise." Billikopf disclosed that with Johnson's high ideals and "passion to make Howard University a seat of great learning and far-reaching influence, . . . it is only natural . . . that he should have found it imperative to make occasional changes, with the result that resentments and antagonisms were bound to be created." These changes, Billikopf added, were never made "without a thorough discussion on the part of the Trustees." Last of all, Billikopf stated that Johnson had made "innumerable friends for the university, among all sorts and conditions of men," mainly because of the belief that "folk throughout the country appreciate his splendid qualities of mind, heart and soul" and understand that Johnson's overriding passion was "to serve wholeheartedly and disinterestedly his people in every sphere of activity."[68]

* * *

In fact, Mays admonished Johnson to publish his recollections of his experiences as president of Howard in order to set the record straight. Mays continually urged Johnson to write his memoirs so as to tell his side of the story, something that Mays himself would do years later, before he died. Despite Mays's urgings, however, Johnson never did publish a full autobiography. What does exist, at least what is known to exist, is an auto-biographical statement that contains brief reflections on his life and career as pastor and president of Howard.[69]

Many of his supporters believed that during this period, the Johnson style of leadership at Howard, which used strong administrative tactics, was necessary. Johnson was not alone in his method of administration, as other presidents of black colleges and universities adopted a similar style. Johnson was placed in a difficult position, however, in trying to stabilize a tumultuous and chaotic situation. To be sure, Johnson knew he would have enemies. He set out to establish some sense of stability and order that would not otherwise have come to Howard following the turbulent Durkee years.[70]

As a preeminent black religious and public intellectual in his own right, Johnson was often misunderstood—as were many of those in his cohort. Although religion and the church played a special role in the lives of African Americans, especially during segregation, in black culture as in American society at large there existed a schism between church and state, and a divide between the secular and the sacred. Those who tried to meld the two—as did prominent black religious intellectuals such as Crummell, Johnson, and Mays—were faced with the unenviable result of being labeled either too religious, or too radical and outspoken for religious circles. This dilemma for the black religious intellectual was similar to that of the black intellectual who was not a preacher or theologian and who had no overt religious leanings. Both these cases were plagued with an evident anti-intellectualism in American society that found its way also into African American culture. Undoubtedly, a double consciousness existed. Many African Americans proclaimed education to be the key to black progress, but they were also skeptical of its excesses. The double consciousness was also evident in a division that developed between the secular and the sacred, though existing at the same time was a valuing of the interconnectedness of the two. In retrospect, Johnson managed to find a balance between the very difficult and different roles of black preacher, black religious intellectual, and black public intellectual, all while functioning as an effective and inspiring president of Howard University.

W. E. B. Du Bois speaking before an audience at the Andrew Rankin Chapel, Howard University. All photos reprinted by permission of the Moorland-Spingarn Research Center, Howard University Archives.

Mordecai Johnson.

Kelly Miller.

Dorothy Porter.

Charles H. Wesley.

Carter G. Woodson.

Rayford Logan.

John Hope Franklin.

William Leo Hansberry.

Merze Tate.

Benjamin E. Mays.

Howard Thurman.

Charles H. Thompson.

Sterling A. Brown.

Ernest Everett Just.

E. Franklin Frazier.

Alain Locke.

Ralph Bunche.

Eric Williams.

Mercer Cook.

Charles Hamilton Houston.

Thurgood Marshall.

James M. Nabrit Jr.

Lorraine A. Williams.

The "Big Six" of Howard University (left to right): James Nabrit, Charles Drew, Sterling A. Brown, E. Franklin Frazier, Rayford W. Logan, and Alain Locke.

CHAPTER THREE

Howard University Intellectuals and the Development of Community in Academia

P RIOR STUDIES OF HOWARD UNIVERSITY intellectuals have focused either on individuals or on small groups of three or so. These scholar activists are indeed interesting, when taken as individuals, but a collective examination, even if difficult, is useful in showing how Howard University became one of the preeminent intellectual communities of its time. Within this community of scholars there were all the attributes of a great institution of higher learning—including all the heated personal and professional politics characteristic of the ebony tower. At Howard, there was exciting intellectual exchange and inquiry. Creative ideas flourished, and the environment fostered intense professional and personal debates. The secular and the sacred collided, as differences in religious affiliation and personal identity militated against a homogeneous way of being or thinking. Uniformity in any of these aspects would not have improved Howard or made it the center of learning it became—the black Harvard of its day.

Like all great institutions, Howard ebbed and flowed as human beings came and went, but the legacy left by this intellectual community cannot be disputed. Certainly, there were other great intellectual communities during segregation such as those at Fisk and Atlanta universities, but none attained the prestige and presence that Howard developed and preserved during its golden years. Here the emphasis is on the community of scholars, which reached a level and a longevity that distinguish Howard from all others and justify the designations it has. Howard, in scholarly productivity and activism on a global scale, established itself as the pinnacle of intellectualism. Scholars at Howard were figures renowned throughout the world, whose interests, research, and scholarly work put them at the center of the major events and movements of the day—including antico-

lonialism, the Cold War, and the attacks on segregation. Their representation, work, and location in Washington, D.C., also brought them into
contact with many of the leading intellectual, civic, religious, and global
leaders of the day. While segregation in the academy contributed to the
formation of a magnificent intellectual community at Howard, it also created conditions that posed challenges. Ultimately, from the 1940s onward,
the softening and gradual demise of segregation exacerbated tensions
within the community and caused the brilliance of this close-knit network
to dim.

Segregation and the marginal position of black academics helped create
a strong sense of community. The African American intellectual community both benefited and suffered from racial segregation. The intellectual community at Howard University, as at most American universities
during the years between World Wars I and II, was composed of notable
women and men. Recent black intellectual history has sought to address
the specific challenges faced by black academic scholars and public intellectuals during the era of racial segregation and global colonialism. The
interactions and varied makeup of strikingly different personalities influenced the Howard intellectual community and culminated in a vibrant
tapestry of personal and professional narratives. Ultimately, the following
intimate portraits and mini-biographical sketches will serve to shed light
upon the lingering intellectual significance and challenges of arguably the
most noted intellectual community produced at a black American institution of higher learning.[1]

Heretofore, discussions of Howard intellectuals have been relegated to
biographies or studies focusing on two or three individuals. While help-
ful in assessing important aspects of individual personalities and contributions, this approach fails to explore the impact of community on
both individual and collective identity formation of scholar activists at
Howard. Some think it would be an impossible task to examine an entire
community of scholars. I argue, however, that this latter approach is vital
to a complete understanding of each member of the intellectual community, as well as to a proper understanding of the effects of segregation on
black intellectuals and their varied responses to it. Too often, as historians, we try to explain and compartmentalize the study of intellectuals as if
they were living and thinking through solitary lenses rather than actively
participating in the community of persons and ideas. There were multiple
levels of community that influenced the Howard group, simultaneously
personal, familial, and collegial, and even with the Howard community
as complex as it was, I argue that to examine an entire community is not
only possible but essential in order to see each member and the collective

as not merely the sum of individual scholars but rather as individuals who were all greatly shaped and influenced by one another. Indeed, it was in the crucible of community that both individual and collective identities of Howard scholars and other black scholars were shaped.

These intellectuals did not operate in a vacuum. Segregation played a fundamental role in forging the Howard intellectual community and shaping its contours. First, very few black intellectuals operated individually. Most had some kind of network, community, or a set of mini-communities, which they influenced and in which they were influenced. These networks were crucial because they served as forums in which black intellectuals such as Frazier, Mays, Charles Thompson, and others could discuss domestic and global issues in an affirming environment. The community also fostered discussion concerning their personal experiences as black men and women and their attempts to reconcile their sense of a double consciousness and of their marginality.

Whether one speaks of academia or society as a whole, segregation led to the creation of networks and organizations in which middle-class black men and women participated. These associations in turn created bonds that the Howard intellectuals brought with them and that facilitated community. The fact that all black people were adversely affected by segregation in obvious ways led to a shared interest in challenging it, both within the walls of the ebony and ivory towers and in the larger society. For many of these scholars, their experience of segregation in the academy proved just an extension of what they experienced beyond its walls. For black Americans living with segregation, the personal was professional and vice versa. Segregation and the constraints imposed on black life by its laws, values, and customs not only seemed to connect the university physically to the community but also further cemented a real psychological identification between their experiences as scholars and their experiences as black Americans subjected to a second-class status. Essentially, these dual identities and the double consciousness of Howard's scholars was always intertwined and interconnected.[2]

The reflections of many of Howard's intellectuals offer valuable insight into the legacy they left for the current group of black intellectuals. A rich intellectual tradition has been endowed by current black scholars because each member of the Howard group, each with his or her own personal strengths and weaknesses, has left a road map, as it were, of how to become and how to survive as an intellectual, a scholar, and an activist. Assessments offered by different members of Howard's intellectual community provide a contextual window providing light on the nature of this community as well as valuable perspectives on the personalities, complexities, and geniuses of some of its notable members.

* * *

One assessment was given by Mercer Cook, a former colleague of Ralph Bunche, who offered an insider's view of Bunche's impact on Howard.[3] "With his M.A. [the] young Bunche came to teach at Howard University in the fall of 1928, at a salary of $1500 per annum," Cook remembered. "Men liked him for his keen mind, his Western frankness, his amazing energy, and his engaging friendliness." Women, whom Cook characterized as "the gentler sex," viewed Bunche as "a romantic figure, with a youthful smile, handsome physique, and burning, deep-set eyes." He added, however, that "Bunche had little time or inclination for the social whirl; as acting head and sole member of the Department of Political Science, he had a job to do." In this capacity, Bunche had "papers to correct, lectures to pre- pare," and "students to interview." Much of his "surplus energy" went to participation in organizations such as the NAACP. Bunche's free time was also spent with William Hastie in founding the New Negro Alliance and spearheading its program "to obtain additional employment for colored Washingtonians." Amid this hectic schedule, Cook remembered that "to keep physically fit [Bunche] took up golf."

Cook went on to tell a story remembered by Hastie, then governor of the Virgin Islands. The story, concerning Bunche's interaction with a student, shows his personality, his manner as a teacher, and the way he had with his students. Cook recalled Hastie saying:

> During Bunche's early days as a teacher at Howard, he occasion- ally played golf with several of his students. One of the students was subsequently disappointed to receive a grade of "C" in one of Ralph's courses when he had anticipated at least a "B." An appeal to the instructor to change the grade was rejected pleasantly but firmly. The student then suggested a sporting proposition; namely, that student and instructor play eighteen holes of golf. If student won, the grade should be "B"; if the instructor prevailed, a "D" should be entered in the record. Bunche replied that he would accept the proposal with one minor modification, that the grade be "A" if the student won and "F" if the instructor won. The student decided to take his "C" and forget about it.

Abram Harris, former associate professor of economics at Howard and one of Bunche's closest colleagues, commented on his friend in an October 4, 1948, interview for the *Chicago Daily News*. Cook quoted Harris's recol- lection:

> Ralph never misses a football game if he can help it. . . . He told me once, "I could play billiards all day." He likes the game—any game. He likes to play the game. . . . He plays seriously, as one solving a problem. Yet he laughs heartily at his own mistakes or his bridge partner's. He

is not cantankerous. He really believes in fair play. . . . He can work ter-
rifically. I have known him to work 15 hours in a day while his leg was
strapped up for varicose veins and propped on a table. He won't crack
up, though. He knows how to relax. He never broods. He has a great
sense of fun. He's healthy emotionally.

Cook's account notes that Bunche, after two years in the classroom, was
named as President Johnson's assistant. "With his usual competence," Cook
recalled, "energy, and approachability, he rendered brilliant service in this
new post, yet found time to spend many of his evenings at the Library of
Congress working on his doctoral dissertation." Cook remembered Bunche
confiding to him, "You know, my ambition is to teach and to write; I'll be
satisfied with a full professorship—someone else can do the administrative
work." Following this, Bunche traveled to Europe and Africa and received
his Ph.D. from Harvard, winning a $250 prize for having written the best
doctoral dissertation in the field of political science. "This official recognition," Cook believed, "strengthened [Bunche's] determination to do more
writing, but [it] did not inflate his ego." Cook stated that Bunche "retained
a naturalness, a modesty, which made him even more likable."

Bunche published articles in black journals such as the *Crisis, Opportunity,* the *Journal of Negro History,* and the *Journal of Negro Education.* In 1936
he was commissioned to write his first book, *A World View of Race.* In the
book Bunche predicted:

> The world race war will never be fought, however. Unquestion-
> ably, wars involving White and dark peoples will be fought, so long as
> there are dark peoples to be conquered and held in subjection, just as
> there will be wars between groups of white peoples and wars between
> groups of dark peoples. There will be sporadic outbreaks when sub-
> ject peoples become restless under too harsh measures of imperialis-
> tic oppression. But the signs throughout the world are unmistakable.
> Despite the frantic efforts of many of those who control national and
> world policy to conjure up international race issues, the lies are form-
> ing in a totally different manner. Race issues appear but tend to merge
> into class issues. Throughout the world the issue between the working
> and owning classes is sharpening. The titanic conflicts of the future
> will be the product of the uncompromising struggles between those
> who have and those who have not. These conflicts now wage within
> all groups, racial and national.[4]

At the time the book came out, Bunche was planning a new volume, which
he knew would require more travel and research. To support this effort he
received "a sizable grant from the American Council of Learned Societies
and journeyed to Hawaii, East, West, and South Africa, and Japan." Cook

wrote that Bunche's "formidable array of documentation resulting from this trip was laid aside as he accepted the important assignment of assistant to Gunnar Myrdal in the preparation of the Carnegie Study. . . . Motoring through the South with his Swedish colleague," Bunche was "chased out of several towns but, with the perseverance that has always characterized him, he got the facts and helped Myrdal present them in what is unquestionably the most complete report on the race problem in the United States, *An American Dilemma*."[5] Cook recalled that he sat in on a conference in Atlanta "between Bunche, Myrdal, Benjamin Davis, Sr., and several other Negro politicians." Cook "marveled at Bunche's astute, pertinent questions, and the easy, disarming manner with which he handled the entire proceedings." Cook added that Bunche was "instrumental [in choosing] capable Negro scholars" such as Abram Harris, Sterling Brown, University of Chicago sociologist Allison Davis, and others. These scholars helped "to furnish Myrdal with trustworthy background material on various aspects of the vast project." Soon after, Bunche was recruited to serve in the Office of Strategic Services, and he was then called to the State Department.[6]

A number of noted intellectuals paid tribute to Alain Locke upon his death in 1954.[7] Among them were Locke's former Howard colleagues Ralph Bunche and William Stuart Nelson, as well as noted intellectual W. E. B. Du Bois. These tributes, made at Locke's funeral and published in the pages of *Phylon,* include intimate, personal, and professional recollections. Although physically unable to attend the last rites, Bunche remembered his friend and colleague in the following manner:

> It is with a sense of deep and personal loss that I contemplate the death of Alain Locke. As a colleague and friend I have known him, worked with him, sought and taken his sage advice and profoundly respected him for more than a quarter century. How much inspiration I have derived from his life and works I cannot possibly measure, but it has been great, for in my younger days, in the Twenties and Thirties, Alain Locke was a strong and unique beacon lighting an exciting new course for aspiring young Negroes. He is gone, but somehow I cannot fully believe it. One had the feeling that Alain Locke would be as permanent as he was ubiquitous and it would be good for the world could he have been so. I visited the hospital only a short time ago. I knew then that he was on his deathbed and so, I am sure, did he. But as we amiably talked and reminisced neither of us would accept the obvious nor can I still. And, indeed, he is and will be for long to come, with us. For Alain Locke's large influence and work survive though his frail little body and his very big heart are gone. Too few, perhaps, well understood or adequately appreciated Alain Locke. Those of us who did have lived

a richer life for it. Philosopher he was; thinker and writer; an intellectual; a man of conviction with courage of his convictions. The American society has lost a noted scholar and an outstanding citizen. Negro Americans have lost a great pioneer and a fervent protagonist. I have lost a good friend.[8]

Another of Locke's Howard colleagues, William Stuart Nelson, successor to Benjamin E. Mays as dean of the school of religion, offered his recollections of the noted Howard philosopher and intellectual. Nelson "on behalf of Howard University [expressed] a deep sense of community and personal loss" at Locke's death.[9] He characterized Locke as a "teacher, philosopher, and friend." Nelson added that the number of "years Dr. Locke spent at Howard University has its own significance, for he touched nearly ten generations of students" and had few equals in terms of service to the university. "But in this number of years," Nelson continued, "lies by no means Dr. Locke's primary significance to Howard University or the explanation of our profound indebtedness to him." According to Nelson, it "was the quality of [Locke's] presence that left its mark" on Howard, its administration, faculty, and alumni. Nelson addressed the rare depth of Locke's personality and his effectiveness as an intellectual and teacher:

> Here was a teacher who lived and taught through a period when University education succumbed increasingly and alarmingly to the factory method and the gladiatorial spirit, but here also was a teacher who, as one dedicated, walked a path where the guideposts were learning and thought—disentangled, unencumbered, unbeclouded thought. And yet he lived in no cloister, no ivory tower. He did not detach himself from concern with practical issues and the hurly burly. But he did not succumb to the event. He walked among the affairs of men with the eyes and the mind of an educated man, of one who bore the obligation and who possessed the ability to make choices. He was no unwilling victim of this movement or that. He was no faddist. If he was enthusiastic about an idea or a trend, it was deliberate choice and not by unwitting conformity. To use his own words, he was determined to be free from "blind partisanship." He understood the "puzzling paradoxes" which enshroud certain great human problems and the "long range perspective required to see and understand them." One need never think, however, that he was not a man of convictions, deep convictions, convictions which he not only held but expounded and invited others to share. The point is that in a university he stood for what a university should stand for preeminently—the fashioning of keen, discriminating minds and the providing of a learning and a capacity for learning upon which these minds can exercise themselves creatively.

Nelson added that the "singularity of purpose [Locke possessed] was matched by a remarkable breadth [and] an uncommon cosmopolitan quality." Locke "was fortunate from his youth in the opportunity to live in other lands and among different peoples." Nelson further characterized Locke's early exposure as "the genesis of his cultural pluralism[, his] rejection of the concept that any land or any people [held] a monopoly on the best in our cultural heritage or that any culture is without its virtues." Locke "learned to suspect absolutisms and dogmatisms" and "was wise enough not to fall victim to evil dogmas, but was also wise enough not to condemn those who did on grounds other than those related to the issues." For Locke, "Men were not good or bad because they lived East or West or were Black or white, but for reasons basically apart from geography or race." Nelson affirmed, "Dr. Locke possessed the breadth of knowledge, which all men—certainly educated men—are meant to have." Nelson believed Locke "seemed to know something about nearly everything—everything worth anything," adding that one could "scarcely think of a conversation among educated men to which he could not contribute something." Nelson argued that Locke "was familiar with the world in which he lived."

Du Bois, widely known as the preeminent black intellectual of the twentieth century, also paid a telling tribute to Locke. He described Locke "as a man who deliberately chose the intellectual life; not as a desirable relief from reality, but as a vocation compared with which all else was of little account."[10] Du Bois added that, "in the midst of money-making and gambling," it was amazing for a man such as Locke "at intervals to devote some time to thought itself or to the basis of human reason." Du Bois conceded, "But to give a life to thinking and its meaning, that is to most Americans quite inexplicable," adding that as a consequence "to many this lonely figure, who spoke quietly and smiled with little restraint, became often an object of pity if not evil gossip and ridicule." Du Bois ended his tribute with a stirring description of the wide sweep of Locke's great nature and persona:

> Yet in truth, Alain Locke stood singular in a stupid land as a rare soul who pursued for nearly half a century, steadily and unemotionally, the only end of man which justifies his living and differentiates him from the beast and bird; and that is the inquiry as to what the universe is and why; how it exists and how it may change. The paths pointed out by Socrates and Aristotle, Bacon and Descartes, Kant and Hegel, Marx and Darwin, were the ones Locke followed and which inevitably made him unknown and unknowable to a time steeped in the lore of Mickey Spillane. And yet in Locke's life lay a certain fine triumph. He knew life's greater things: pictures and poetry, music and drama, conversation which was not filth, laughter not clownish, and appetites which

never fell to cheap lust. His severe logic, his penetrating analysis, his wide reading gave him a world within, sparsely peopled to be sure, but finely furnished and unforgettable in breadth and depth. It was built for a man not fit for war, but nobly courageous and simply consistent, who could bear pain and disappointment and yet live and work. For his dark companions he had faith and fellowship; for their smaller problems advice and guidance. But for himself he had only truth.

Du Bois summed up Locke's meaning for him by saying, "his quest for truth and logic was no easy task." It "was often contradictory and disappointing." Du Bois felt that Locke's search for truth "either appealed in vain to understanding or found no understanding to which it could appeal." To search for truth, Du Bois believed (somewhat implicating himself), "was a thankless task to those who see life as money, notoriety, or dirt." He added, "yet its faithful pursuit is more than living" and "is more than death." Speaking for Locke by invocation, Du Bois declared that his contemporary, if he could have spoken at that very hour, would have proclaimed "that life is not length of days nor plethora of pleasure, but satisfaction of work attempted," and he added, "that [Locke] surely had."

In an interview with Charles H. Rowell at his home in Washington, D.C., before his death, Sterling Brown, noted by many as the "maker of community," reflected on many aspects of his career as a scholar activist, including his relationship with many of the scholars of the Howard intellectual community. With regard to a criticism thrown at Alain Locke by writer Zora Neale Hurston, Brown commented, "it is not true that he just read whatever other people wrote. Locke[, both] intellectually and intuitively, knew the importance of the spirituals, and when he wrote about them he was good." Brown went on to say:

> Now, just as Zora [Neale Hurston] couldn't get along with men, Locke couldn't get along with women, particularly a great big aggressive woman, like Zelma Duke. He caught Zelma Duke at something and she says, "Well Dr. Locke, everybody makes a mistake." She said, "You said in your book that Scott Joplin was a white man," and Locke turned to me and said, "Well, you know," he says, "you can't always tell what these creoles are. Isn't that so, Sterling?" And I said, "Dr. Locke, Scott Joplin was a Black man. Scott Joplin was as Black as the ace of spades." He tried to turn it off, but she had caught him, and he could get caught. He could be very inaccurate, but I do not agree with what Zora said about him.[11]

Admitting that Locke could be mistaken from time to time, no different from any other scholar black or white, Brown painted an intimate picture of Locke, very different from the portrait most people know today:

His contribution in establishing a respect for Negro folk culture is strong, is true, is genuine. It did not come, however, from an absorption or deep love. It came intellectually. The spirituals had a dignity and a beauty that he could respond to. He was still a bronze Beethoven. That was his upbringing. You see, Locke learned and Locke blossomed when he came to Howard. There were all these young men around there who were in there pitching: Ralph Bunche, E. Franklin Frazier, Abe Harris, Emmet Dorsey, and myself. Then later Rayford Logan. Locke had to get up and do something, and he did *The New Negro* in 1925. Then we started jumping back and Locke got back into it. Then he got a Carnegie grant and he did work on the Negro in art and the Negro in music. He had me do *Negro Poetry and Drama* and *The Negro in American Fiction.* He had Ralph [Bunche] do one called *The World View of Race;* he had Arnold Hill do something on economics; he had Ira Reid do something on adult education; and he had Eric Williams do something on the Caribbean. That series should be better known. You see, it was a series published at the end of the thirties, and it's not well known. A lot of stuff is taken from it without credit, and then a lot of stuff is being done that's already been done.[12]

Black women scholars also held a significant place within the intellectual community at Howard. Most notable among these are the political scientist Merze Tate (whose research and writings placed her in the history camp as well), the bibliophile Dorothy Porter Wesley, art professor Lois Mailou Jones, and historian Lorraine A. Williams. Historian Pero Dagbovie asserts that Lulu M. Johnson, Susie Owen Lee, Elsie Lewis, Helen G. Edmonds, and Margaret Rowley composed the "first distinguishable coterie of formally trained Black women historians." History predominates as the major discipline for African Americans at this time. In 1940, for example, Marion Thompson Wright (1902–1962) was the first black woman to earn a Ph.D. in history and the first black historian to receive a doctorate from Columbia University. Having written her dissertation on "The Education of Negroes in New Jersey," Wright returned to Howard specifically to train young black women in the significance of historical scholarship. Her publications appeared in the *Journal of Negro History*, the *Journal of Negro Education*, and the *Journal of Educational Sociology*.[13]

Dorothy Porter (1905–1995), known for her expertise as a librarian, scholar, and bibliophile of black culture, navigated Howard's intellectual community with great political skill, dignity, and savvy. Her single-handed development of much of the Moorland-Spingarn collection, the finest collection of black research materials in the world, is a testament to her dedication, intellectual brilliance, and keen ability to solidify important relationships with scholars at Howard, throughout the nation, and internationally. In a 1995 interview, she spoke candidly of how a conver-

sation with Eric Williams led her initially to gain employment at Howard University. While working upstairs at the Schomburg Library in New
York, she was propositioned with a job opportunity by Williams, trying
to woo her away from New York. Williams, who worked at the Schomburg during the summers, was able to persuade Porter to return to Howard and secure appointment as a librarian. In 1931, the first major task
Williams gave her was to build the black collection donated by Howard
trustee Jesse Moorland, in 1914. Needless to say, Porter, over the years,
proved immensely successful and she developed lifelong contacts and
resources for the collection.[14] Born in Warrenton, Virginia, she spent most
of her childhood in Montclair, New Jersey. She was married to James Porter, artist and renowned Howard art professor, and following Porter's
death in 1979, she married Dr. Charles Harris Wesley, Howard history
professor and dean. Her contribution lies in her incomparable manner
of fusing scholarly brilliance and administrative acumen. Thomas Battle
characterized Porter as "the embodiment of the scholar-librarian." She
ably assisted the research of fellow black intellectuals John Hope Franklin, Alain Locke, Sterling Brown, Richard Wright, John Henrik Clarke,
Langston Hughes, Alex Haley, and numerous others.[15]

Upon her retirement in 1973, she was heralded by colleagues for the
remarkable achievements she had accumulated over the course of her
professional career at Howard. In addition to being fondly regarded as
African America's national librarian, Porter Wesley also personally knew
fellow bibliophiles such as Arthur Schomburg, Jesse Moorland, and
Charles Blockson. As a scholar, she wrote a number of books, articles,
book reviews, and other works. Her most significant works include *The
Negro in the United States, Early Negro Writing, 1760–1837, North American Negro Poets,* and *Negro Protest Pamphlets.* She was cited as a Distinguished Alumnus at Howard and won prestigious fellowships from the
Ford Foundation, Harvard University's W.E.B. Du Bois Institute, and the
Julius Rosenwald fund. Lastly, Porter Wesley worked for the Ford Foundation as a consultant at the National Library in Lagos, Nigeria, and she
also attended the 1962 First International Congress of Africanists, held in
Accra, Ghana.[16]

Lois Mailou Jones, while at Howard, brilliantly balanced a professional
career as a talented artist and a professor of art. In 1928 Jones applied to
Howard for a position on the faculty, but she was informed that no positions were available at that time as James A. Porter (Dorothy Porter's first
husband) had recently been hired to teach art history. Pondering a suggested move south upon graduation from the Boston Museum School,
Jones recounts her first recollections of Howard University:

I recall going to a very lovely party at a friend's house and meeting William Leo Hansberry, who had come up to attend Harvard Summer School. I was greatly impressed by him and his intelligence, and he mentioned that he was a professor at Howard University. So I began to think that I should learn a bit more about the South and Howard University. In our conversation he suggested that I apply to teach at Howard. And so I did. I got a response that I would be considered for that next year, after graduating from the Designers School. . . . I received a second letter, however, from Dean Downing, who was Dean of the School of Engineering and Architecture, saying that they had decided finally to hire James A. Porter, who was just graduating, but that I would be the second person to be made a member of the faculty. Of course, I was a little disappointed, but I felt at least that the opportunity would come.[17]

Jones, instead, was hired by Charlotte Hawkins Brown to develop the art department at the Palmer Memorial Institute, one of the country's pioneering preparatory schools for blacks in Sedalia, North Carolina. During the summer of 1930, while she was at Palmer, James Vernon Herring, founder and chair of Howard's art department, spoke at Jones's invitation. So impressed by the work of her students, Herring offered Jones a position at Howard. That same year she joined the faculty and remained until her retirement in 1977. Together with James Porter and James Lesesne Wells, Jones created an innovative curriculum that became a model for other black colleges and universities.[18]

Jones also developed significant professional relationships as a member of the Howard intellectual community. In 1938, returning to Washington from a stint abroad, Jones met Howard philosopher Alain Locke. She informed him of her intentions to include one of her paintings depicting Parisian street scenes in Locke's forthcoming 1940 *The Negro in Art*. Locke, the cosmopolitan cultural critic and black consciousness advocate, advised her to explore her own African cultural heritage more seriously. Jones responded in kind by naming the 1940s period her "Locke period." Enhancing her intellectual and artistic talents, Jones took additional classes at Howard and graduated in 1945, magna cum laude, with an A.B. in art education.

By 1969, Jones went on to build further upon Locke's invaluable advice, receiving a grant from Howard to conduct research on contemporary art in Africa. Between April and July 1969, she traveled to eleven museums on the African continent, documenting biographies of African artists, administering interviews, and surveying museums. Simultaneously, her interest in all things African peaked as she conducted her research, fueled by, as Tritobia Hayes Benjamin says, "the African American's quest for cultural identity." Over the course of her career, Jones greatly impacted her

Howard students, instilling in them a great love of art. As a scholar she produced a "body of work characterized by technical virtuosity, consummate skill, versatility, elegance, vitality, structure, design, and clarion call."[19]

In Michael R. Winston's recollections of Howard's history department from 1913 to 1973, he includes a lucid history of the role of significant black women historians such as Elsie Lewis and Lorraine A. Williams. Winston argues that the years 1942–1962 culminated in a period of "slow, but steady increase in the research productivity of the faculty, [as well as] the addition of scholars, who were developing national reputations." Among those distinguished scholars were John Hope Franklin, Elsie Lewis, and Chancellor Williams. This activity occurred during the leadership tenure of Rayford Logan, who succeeded Charles Wesley as department chair in 1942. Lewis joined the Howard history faculty in 1956, as a specialist in the history of the Negro, the same year that John Hope Franklin left the Capstone to take up the position of chair at Brooklyn College. Lewis went on to serve as chair, ending her tenure in 1969.

Lorraine Williams was a gifted historian, who was as adept an administrator as she was a scholar. Williams's major works include a 1970–1974 series of historical publications, which she edited; *Afro-Americans and Africans: Historical and Political Linkages,* which came out in 1974; and *Africa and the Afro-American Experience: Eight Essays,* which she edited. This last volume featured eight prominent black historians, including William Leo Hansberry, John Blassingame, John Hope Franklin, Benjamin Quarles, and Rayford Logan.[20] Evidencing her own sense of political and administrative savvy, Williams was able to navigate the difficult political terrain of the Black Power era at Howard. She educated many Howard students who were seeking a relevant education that would enhance their cultural identity as a result of the Black Power movement's intense pull.

Receiving a Howard faculty research grant in August 1970, Williams set out for West Africa. In accord with her affinity for Pan-Africanism research and culture, Williams visited numerous African universities in an attempt to promote cultural exchanges and research projects. She conversed with history professors and visited historic sites, such as W. E. B. Du Bois's interment site as well as the memorial of Kwame Nkrumah.[21] During this trip, in Nigeria she collaborated with Dorothy Porter, who was there organizing the library collections at the University of Nigeria at Lagos.[22]

According to Deborah Newman Ham, Chancellor Williams would later serve as a strong ally of Lorraine Williams, as she attempted to transfer from the social science program to the history department. Ham recollects that every member of the department opposed Williams's transfer. Chancellor Williams, flexing his political muscle on behalf of his former colleagues, threatened other members with a potential down vote for their pursuit of full professor rank. Black male intellectuals, according to Winston, had to enter the ivory tower through the back door. For black women, within the ebony tower, their oppression was doubled, as they had to navigate the challenges associated with both race and gender. To be sure, concerns over disciplinary fit influenced the decision of many members of the history faculty. However, one must also consider the presence of probable sexism as a contributing factor as well. Added to this equation, a number of black male intellectuals at Howard made it a practice actively to recruit black women intellectuals to join the community, complicating the gendered politics at this "Black Harvard."[23]

Like Lorraine Williams, Merze Tate was a consummate scholar and public intellectual, whose work was widely respected within the Howard community and beyond. One of the first two female members of the history department, she was professor of history and a specialist in international affairs and U.S. diplomacy. The first African American woman to earn a Ph.D in government and international relations from Harvard, she joined the Howard history faculty in 1942. Her tenure lasted for thirty-five years, until 1977, and she produced some of the finest scholarship in foreign policy studies. Rosalyn Terborg-Penn underscores Tate's role as historian and public intellectual: "Tate saw the economic and social aspects of society as central to understanding history." In addition to her importance to the scholarly community at Howard, Tate was often called on as a foreign policy expert by both Congress and the United Nations. Her dissertation focused on U.S disarmament policies. Similarly, Tate's impact on students was as influential as the respect she commanded within the intellectual and policy community.[24]

To be sure the reception of black women intellectuals, on a campus dominated by black male faculty, reflected evidence of gender discrimination, patriarchy, and sexism. Not much scholarship has been dedicated to the study of black women intellectuals at Howard and not much has been written about their experiences, an omission that must be rectified. In oral interviews and other published accounts, commentary on the gendered aspect of the community is blunted (if it is present at all). For example, Dorothy Porter Wesley and Lois Mailou Jones were both highly active and influential members of the Howard community, yet interviews conducted expressed that these intellectuals faced challenges at Howard that were directly linked to gender discrimination. Dagbovie, in his pioneering work on nineteenth- and twentieth-century black women historians, argues that African American women faced tremendous obstacles in attaining higher education degrees. Dagbovie echoes a fact pointed out by William Banks that "Black women were widely and often systematically excluded from participating in mainstream U.S. and African American academic culture." Howard graduate and historian Paula Giddings asserts that, in spite of these obstacles, black women intellectuals at Howard and elsewhere pressed on and defied social, racial, and gendered conventions. Black women intellectuals such as Porter, Jones, Williams, and others were determined to fight these infringements by dedicating themselves to their work.[25]

A key point here revolves around the question of interpretation. Sexism, of course, existed at Howard. One manner in which Howard's black women scholars challenged gender insensitivity and oppression was through the clever negotiation of relationships with their black male colleagues. Dorothy Porter provides a good case in point. Porter developed a reputation for amassing a slew of contacts for the would-be Moorland-Spingarn Research Center, while also carefully and skillfully negotiating professional relationships with difficult personalities such as longtime president Mordecai Johnson. Porter recounts one occasion where she needed Johnson's approval in order to purchase the materials of the NAACP's second president and longtime board member Joel Spingarn for the evolving Moorland collection. Her office, located across the hall from Johnson's, provided a strategic opening to negotiate resources for the collection. Garnering Johnson's approval, Porter obtained the collection, despite administrative intransigence from the university treasurer.[26]

Obviously, another way in which these brilliant black women intellectuals challenged gender discrimination was in the recruitment and production of talented black women students, who then went on to pioneer in the areas of black women's history and women's studies, and particularly in black feminism and womanist thought. The best example here is Lorraine Williams, who personally recruited important black women historians such as Bernice Johnson Reagon, Elizabeth Clark-Lewis, Rosalyn Terborg-Penn, Sylvia Jacobs, and Debra Newman Ham. These women—matriculating through the heyday of the modern women's movement of the 1970s—were conditioned by a feminist and womanist consciousness, which influenced their scholarship in the intervening years after graduation. Also, with Congresswoman Shirley Chisholm's groundbreaking presidential campaign in 1972 (the first by an African American), undoubtedly, Lorraine Williams's cadre of black women historians would take up the mantle and challenge black male sexism in both scholarship and academic culture.[27]

* * *

Howard public intellectuals, within the community they formed in Washington, achieved very real accomplishments under difficult circum-

stances. Among the most notable were their pioneering efforts in scholarship and activism, which contributed to the then nascent fields of African,
African American, and Africana policy studies. The legacy of these public
intellectuals also included important public policy influences, the production of high-quality scholarship, a gender-neutral model of how public
intellectuals should function, and the building of bridges for white intellectuals to make strides at reconciling the tremendous dilemma of race in
America.

In 1970, Gregory Rigsby, acting director of the African studies and
research program at Howard, noted a few of the pioneering accomplishments of Howard in the areas of black men's studies and African American
studies. Rigsby wrote, "for more than half a century Howard University
has been a center for research and instruction [in] all phases of the Black
Man's existence in the United States, the Caribbean and Africa." The university and its scholars became pioneers in black studies by voting in 1968
"to establish a department of Afro-American Studies." Rigsby added that
this act was supplemented by the Ford Foundation's providing a grant to
allow a steering committee to oversee the department a year later. Howard
became a pioneer in African studies by founding one of the nation's first
departments in the 1950s. Howard was the first university in the United
States to offer a Ph.D. in African studies. The African Studies and Research
Program was developed to offer a master's degree in 1953. By 1969, this
had become part of the Arts and Sciences graduate school. In 1988, the
Board of Trustees changed the program into a department, offering the
B.A., M.A., and Ph.D.[28]

Members of the Howard intellectual community made significant contributions to a variety of areas in the social lives of African Americans as
well as in academic and policy cultures. Educator Charles H. Thompson,
in addition to founding the pathbreaking *Journal of Negro Education* in 1932,
also initiated important research in the areas of race relations, civil rights,
equal employment and access, and other relevant issues of the day. The last
article Thompson ever wrote served as a parting shot but also functioned
as a prophetic statement concerning a major problem that African Americans continue to encounter even today. Thompson's article "Race and
Equality of Educational Opportunity: Defining the Problem" appeared in
the summer 1968 issue of the *Journal of Negro Education*. In it he observed:

> The task of securing equality of educational opportunity for Negroes is
> an educational as well as a political problem. Not only does it involve
> the development of a reasonable consensus in support of the ideas,
> but poses a number of pressing questions relative to implementation.
> Despite the fact that practically every advance made in the attainment

of equality of opportunity for Negroes in general, as well as specifically in equality of educational opportunity, has come through legal
coercion, the problem is at the stage now where an almost equally difficult task is that of educational implementation. For even if every racial
barrier were entirely removed immediately and everyone agreed that
Negroes should have full equality of educational opportunity, such a
consensus would constitute only a partial solution of the problem.[29]

The *Journal of Negro Education* was part of Thompson's lasting legacy.
It still functions to address the overall challenge of education, and more
specific issues of educational access and equity. Richard Kluger noted
that, even though in 1932 Thompson had no funds to pay for printing and
postage costs for the *Journal,* he nevertheless created his publication for a
twofold purpose: to document thoroughly the condition of Negro schools,
and to examine the consequences and implications posed by segregation.
In many ways the *Journal* filled the void left by the *Crisis* magazine when
Du Bois was first fired. Kluger noted that although less polemical than the
Crisis, the *Journal* still maintained the function of informing, arousing, and
inspiring African Americans. To assist in this capacity, Howard University
and its president Mordecai Johnson provided office space, clerical assistance, and approximately one-third of Thompson's salary.[30]

Howard honored William Leo Hansberry, the noted Africanist and the
"Father of African Studies," in a tribute program on November 20, 1972,
on the event of his death. A number of Hansberry's former colleagues and
students paid tributes to the man and his legacy. Hansberry was a professor at Howard from September 1922 until his retirement in June 1959. In
a glowing statement, Lorraine Williams, chair of the history department,
described how Hansberry "traveled the thorny path of a pioneer."[31] From
the time he arrived on Howard's campus in 1922, "he inspired his students to study African history in order to revise the chauvinistic European
theory" that viewed Africa as a continent without a history. Making an
immediate impact on Howard's community of scholars as well as its students, the year following his arrival Hansberry wrote an article for the
Howard University Record entitled "Howard's Supreme Opportunity." He
admonished his colleagues to search for the real truth about the African
past and its people.

In this, Hansberry was a forerunner of Afrocentricity. He taught John
Henrik Clarke and was a colleague of Chancellor Williams. In many ways,
Hansberry paved the way for Molefi Asante and other Afrocentric theo-
rists. Lorraine Williams called Hansberry "the father of African Studies
at Howard University," although in the early to mid-1920s there was a

controversy involving Hansberry, Alain Locke, and Melville Herskovits concerning Hansberry's legitimacy as a qualified Africanist. Lorraine Williams noted that for much of his career, despite having the support of President Johnson, Hansberry was indeed "a prophet without honor in his own country." This label became all the more apparent as he was denied in his repeated attempts to secure a Ph.D. from Harvard University.

In many ways, like Du Bois, Hansberry's greatest tribute came from abroad. One of Hansberry's stellar students at Howard, Nnamdi Azikiwe, later became the first president of Nigeria, and he honored his mentor and friend on September 22, 1953, by establishing the Hansberry Institute of African Studies at Nsukka in Eastern Nigeria. On the day of Howard's tribute to Hansberry, the history department reissued the inaugural address that Hansberry had given to dedicate the Institute of African Studies in Nigeria. The department published his address as the sixth work in its second series of historical publications.

On October 10, 1964, one year after the Nigerian college was named after him, he was awarded the first Haile Selassie Award for African Research by the government and country of Ethiopia, as "their first prize for original work in African history, archaeology, and anthropology." The highest honors he was to receive came from African countries, where he tried to reestablish linkages with the African diaspora. It was fitting that Hansberry received the Selassie Award, as he had founded and pioneered the Ethiopian Research Council in the 1930s, which was very influential in protesting Italian imperialism in Ethiopia.[32]

English professor Arthur P. Davis wrote a telling profile of his colleague E. Franklin Frazier in the fall of 1962 in the pages of the *Journal of Negro Education*. This tribute came after Frazier's untimely death earlier that year, on May 17. In the editorial notes Davis was described as "a colleague and friend of long standing." Davis described Frazier as not a "proper" Negro. He argued that Frazier spent much of his life fighting "American racial injustice; the Negro's reluctance to measure up to national standards; and the shallowness, pretensions, and false ideals of the Black middle class." After teaching at Atlanta and Fisk universities, in 1934 Frazier returned to Howard. Davis noted that this year "was a propitious time for him to return to his alma mater" and that, by the 1930s, "Howard had brought together a group of brilliant young Negro intellectuals—a group that gave the University an academic and intellectual climate that no other Negro school had."[33]

Davis described Frazier and the young community of scholars at Howard during the 1930s as "nonconformists and gadflies." He observed that these scholars "needed the administration" but also proved influential in making Howard a center of *modern* education. Davis described Frazier as "an active and influential member of this group." Frazier "was never a blind follower of any one camp, and he criticized his colleagues as readily as he criticized deans and presidents." Davis quoted one of Frazier's consistent quips: "I am not polite when my colleagues do things that are foolish, I speak out." While praising Frazier, Davis also noted many of his shortcomings. "Impatient with all kinds of academic red tape, including reports and committee meetings," Davis added, "he felt that a professor, even though a department head, had only two real duties—to teach and to do research. He, therefore, ignored or refused to do many of the trivial things expected of a department chairman, but his department never lacked vision for the larger things."[34]

In 1950, Davis, in an address to a capacity Honor's Day audience at Virginia State College, spoke on the subject of "The Duties of a Colored Scholar." He identified "true scholars" as those "on whom rests the hope of our civilization." Davis argued that there was a great need for black scholars "who can discern real truth and worth in the midst of falseness and sham and hypocrisy." He added that these scholars would be "those, who could not only see clearly and objectively, but who will have moral courage to broadcast this truth no matter how unpopular it may be." In this regard Davis seemed to invoke the adage that the scholar—and here, specifically, the black scholar—functions to speak truth to power. He listed six duties that the black American scholar epitomized. First, black scholars had to "have a personal obligation never to cheapen or prostitute your dignity or talents because of the race situation." Second, Davis admonished black scholars with the duty to "render service to your people." His third characteristic dealt with the need for black intellectuals "to be thoroughly honest" with themselves. Finally, Davis challenged black scholars "to think big and act big [and] to be men of action [and] to be radical in your thinking and courageous in you[r] action."[35]

One manner in which segregation aided in the formation of community was through Howard faculty membership in black fraternities and sororities. Among the main principles espoused by the black Greek letter fraternities established on college campuses were brotherhood, scholarship, and service to humanity. Affiliation with black Greek letter fraternities became an important cultural and social marker for middle-class black men in early twentieth-century America, especially because these organizations came into being to create a sense of community amid the growing racial tensions throughout America at that time. The first fraternity to be established was Alpha Phi Alpha, on December 4, 1906, at Cornell University in Ithaca, New York. After this, chapters of the fraternity were established at historically black colleges and universities, the first of which was Alpha's second chapter, the Beta chapter, at Howard. In 1911 Kappa Alpha Psi was founded at Indiana University in Bloomington, and Omega Psi Phi founded its fraternity at Howard in 1911. In 1914 Phi Beta Sigma did the same at Howard.

Howard became a haven for black Greek letter fraternities and sororities, and for the social, intellectual, and service activities rendered by these organizations to black communities in D.C. and other areas. Since the founding of black Greek letter fraternities and sororities, many prominent scholars have joined their ranks, in many ways playing significant roles in the founding and furtherance of these groups. At Howard, physician and medical school faculty member Henry A. Callis served as one of the founding members of Alpha Phi Alpha. Later, Howard historians Rayford W. Logan, Charles Wesley, John Hope Franklin, and William Leo Hansberry, sociologist and mathematician Kelly Miller, sociologist E. Franklin Frazier, educator Charles H. Thompson, and law school dean Charles H. Houston were all very active in the fraternity over the course of their time at Howard.

Furthermore, other prominent black intellectuals around the country, who helped form an informal community of intellectuals and scholar activists, were members of these fraternities and sororities, and through these links strengthened the bonds with Howard's community of intellectuals. These scholars, members of Alpha Phi Alpha, include abolitionist Frederick Douglass, Atlanta sociologist and editor of the *Crisis* W. E. B. Du Bois, and Fisk University sociologist and president Charles S. Johnson. Even stellar students of many Howard faculty—including social psychologist Kenneth Clark and legal pioneer Thurgood Marshall—followed in the footsteps of their mentors at Howard. In examining correspondence between many scholars at Howard, one finds even some correspondence between "brothers," illustrating the critical importance of these links to their professional and personal identities. One of the most enduring relationships formed among scholars in the Howard community was between John Hope Franklin and Rayford Logan, for example. Both were historians exploring aspects of the African American experience, although Franklin identified himself primarily as a southern historian. Both scholars were active members of Alpha Phi Alpha Fraternity, Incorporated. Both men had been active in the organization since the founding of the Beta chapter at Howard, and letters they sent each other were signed "Fraternally."[36]

Also of note was the central role played by cell biologist Ernest Everett Just. He was one of the founders of the first black Greek letter fraternity to be founded on a predominantly black campus, Omega Psi Phi at Howard. Other Howard faculty who were Omega men included Abram Harris, Sterling Brown, James Nabrit, and Benjamin Mays, in addition to other noted scholars such as Carter G. Woodson. Alain Locke was a distinguished member of Phi Beta Sigma.

These affiliations and involvement with black male Greek fraternities is significant in one sense as it demonstrates the public activities these scholars engaged in simultaneously with their scholarship. Howard historian Charles H. Wesley, for instance, was the author of the first history book of Alpha Phi Alpha. More important, these scholars' public engagement demonstrates that the joint goals of holistic edification and empowerment of black men shared within each black Greek fraternity, regardless of individual distinctions, meant that affiliations in these organizations offered a closeness for black male intellectuals at Howard. It must be noted that even though members of the Howard community were in different fraternal organizations, this did not serve as a barrier to their forming other close relationships, regardless of affiliation or nonaffiliation. However, these fraternal ties did serve to connect members in various ways, as best evidenced in the relationship between Franklin and Logan.[37]

Black sororities also played a tremendous role in nurturing the foundations of the intellectual community at Howard. Alpha Kappa Alpha in 1908, Delta Sigma Theta in 1913, and Zeta Phi Beta in 1920 were founded on the Howard campus. During the early development of this intellectual community, each sorority created strong bonds of culture and community among black women students, faculty, and staff, all of which nurtured and sustained the overall intellectual community of professors and scholars. Lucy Diggs Slowe, the first African American woman dean of women at Howard University, for example, was also a founder of the Alpha Kappa Alpha Sorority. Slowe commanded a great deal of respect at Howard. She single-handedly developed a "female campus" there, modeling her powerful leadership presence among the young women students, faculty, and staff. Slowe, a self-determined race woman, was "an outspoken advocate for self-determination, respect, and advancement of college-trained African American women." Through her racial and educational philosophy, Slowe insisted strongly that African American women have access and representation in leadership positions. Following her appointment to Howard in 1922, Slowe presided over the National Association of College Women (NACW), a group modeled on the work of the D.C. College Alumnae Club. The NACW sought to enhance the life and success of African American women on black college campuses throughout the nation. In 1923, after establishing a committee of standards to examine black college academic program quality, members visited nine institutions listed as having an A or near A accreditation, including Howard, Fisk, and Atlanta universities. The report found that Howard had the most black women faculty members with Ph.Ds, eleven out of sixteen.[38]

* * *

Another avenue by which community was fashioned among scholars at Howard and beyond was through the development and maintenance of national networks. It was these national networks of black Ph.Ds and their connection to historically black colleges and universities that furthered personal interaction among black intellectuals, both before they arrived at Howard and after many moved on, either to other colleges and universities or to other sectors of work. Through these networks, intellectuals nurtured and shared projects that undergirded African American contributions and advanced the black agenda. These projects often led to the development of intellectual networks such as collaborations on scholarly projects, support for professional advancement, and cooperation in organizations and initiatives designed to challenge America's segregationist racial order. Certainly not static (like the community itself at Howard), these networks played important roles and continued to be replenished throughout the 1940s and 1950s and into the 1960s.

Alongside the diversity of figures at Howard, evident instances of continuity also existed. For example, the "Morehouse connection" was very evident among Howard's faculty. Of course, the pipeline from Howard to Morehouse was evident from the top down. President Mordecai Johnson was a former Morehouse graduate and a faculty member. In addition to Johnson, in 1933 and 1934, Howard Thurman and Benjamin Mays were brought on to the faculty of the school of religion, having definite ties to Morehouse, with the former having graduated from there and the latter having taught there. In 1936 James M. Nabrit, an honor graduate of Morehouse College who would later succeed Mordecai Johnson as president of Howard University, was brought to Howard as assistant professor in the school of law. English professor Benjamin Brawley also hailed from Morehouse, which only added to the strength of the connections among these scholars at the Capstone.[39]

Sterling A. Brown, characterized by some scholars as "the maker of community in academia," was central to the construction of community among Howard intellectuals and the surrounding black community of Washington, D.C. Brown's biographer Joyce A. A. Camper argues that "Sterling Brown made the connection [and] embraced both academe and those outside the university walls." Camper continues:

> In embracing the educated and the folk[,] he illustrated the interdisciplinary nature of the life of Black folk in America. He showed us that one doesn't exist without the other and that each has something necessary to the other's existence. For *Prof* there was no distinction between the street person and the educated person. Each had a voice and each voice was worth hearing, articulating, and remembering. By

embracing the community Sterling Brown stood as a bulwark against the splintering that has always plagued our people. He merged two parts to create one. In essence, he created community. And he did it despite the historical moment that dictated a different philosophical viewpoint. Professor Brown brought together entities that should never be separated.[40]

Although speaking in the important context of Brown's serving as a conduit for linking the university with the community, Camper here also speaks to the role Brown played in forging community among Howard's intellectuals. Brown maintained favorable and frequent correspondence with many of the noted members of this community of scholars. He viewed each scholar as being vital to the whole community. He was indeed the fulcrum of this community, and was grounded and well-rounded enough to maintain that role with amazing success.[41]

Further evidence of Brown's importance to this community and the high regard in which he was held was his relationship with the often fiery, brilliant Rayford Logan. Recalling his version of the events that led up to then President James Nabrit's selecting both Logan and Brown to write the centennial history of Howard, Logan noted:

> On January 19, 1962, President James M. Nabrit, Jr., appointed Sterling Brown and me to write a history of the University. The appointments seemed wise. Sterling and I were old friends. During my high school and college days, I had frequently visited the home of his parents and sisters. He had graduated from Dunbar (formerly M Street) High School in 1918, Williams (Phi Beta Kappa), A.B., 1922, and Harvard, 1931–1932, he and his wife, my wife and I sharing an apartment during the second semester of that year. In 1962, he was recognized as a distinguished poet, social critic, historian, and great teacher. I frequently referred to him as "the best mind on the campus."[42]

Brown was professor of English at the Capstone from 1929 to 1969. As he discovered, a number of Howard scholars formed very strong professional and personal relationships that sustained them during their tenure there. In the case of Brown, he went outside his departmental and disciplinary boundaries to forge strong ties with Ralph Bunche, E. Franklin Frazier, Abram Harris, and Charles H. Thompson, as well as with Logan.[43]

It was Brown's outgoing personality that enabled him to make friends with a wide array of scholars of different ideological perspectives at Howard and allowed him to avoid many of the "intellectual wars" that ensued within its hallowed walls. Among the subjects Brown discussed within his circle of friends and colleagues at Howard were the problems of tokenism, segregation in the nation's capital, programs and effectiveness of civil rights organizations, politics in Washington, D.C., the Scottsboro case and the issue of lynching, McCarthyism, and the promise of integration. "It was also in this circle" of intellectuals and scholar activists, Joanne Gabbin noted, "that Brown was able to cultivate a view of literature that issues from a deep understanding of the historical, economic, and political dimensions of American society." Indeed, Brown frequently acknowledged the influence that Bunche, Harris, Thompson, and Frazier had on his understanding of race relations. He viewed them as "social analysts rather than solvers of the race problem." Perhaps Brown had a knack for being sensitive. He appreciated the differences, in terms of personality and belief, among many scholars at Howard, and this allowed him to function as the fulcrum of Howard's intellectual community.[44]

Perhaps the tribute Sterling Brown paid to E. Franklin Frazier in memoriam is as much a telling demonstration of his ability to fashion community among black men from different backgrounds as it is a recognition of the complexity and less-known traits of a man whom many have characterized as prickly, temperamental, and high strung. First of all, in his memoriam, Brown shared that his "memories of E. Franklin Frazier go back a long way."[45] Brown recollected that, as a member of a group called "the Young Howards," he knew Frazier as "a campus leader" and "one of the campus big wheels, as one of the deep ones, the heavy ones, as one of the brains." Brown followed Frazier's career, as he attained a graduate degree from Clark University in Massachusetts and served as an American Scandinavian Foundation fellow at the University of Copenhagen in Denmark. Commenting on how other scholars became somewhat Europeanized by their experience, Brown remarked that Frazier, upon his return, "put on no airs, as so many, who took the European cure in those days did." He added that Frazier "was still easy to know[, that] he talked uncondescendingly, stimulatingly [and] was poised for the future." As for his scholarly writing style and abilities:

> He started writing early. I read many of his essays in *Opportunity* and *The Crisis*. The things he wrote about were things I wanted deeply to know. I remember the shock of recognition, the feeling of pride that came to me, then a young college teacher in Missouri, when the *Forum* magazine published his "The Pathology of Race Prejudice" in 1927. Here I felt, along with many others, was a clear, unequivocal revelation of an important truth about America. It was unsparing, it was sharp, it said what many had certainly suspected but had not been able to express so well. Here many of us saw that a man of learning, passion and courage had emerged.

Brown went on to make the connection between Frazier's thesis in "The Pathology of Race Prejudice" and current events of the 1960s in Mississippi, quoting its applicability to other areas of the American South and the entire country. Brown noted that Frazier's "career in teaching and scholarship was devoted to establishing and communicating [what he termed as] such objective facts" as the idea that "delusions of the white man under the Negro complex show the same imperviousness to objective facts concerning the Negro." From here, Brown traced Frazier's teaching career and paid special attention to the time Frazier spent working with fellow sociologist Charles S. Johnson of Fisk University. In a light moment during the memoriam, Brown recalled how their personal and professional paths had crossed. "When he came to Fisk, I was leaving for our paths were frequently crossing, he and his wife moved into the house that my wife and I were leaving. We made quite a ceremony of the transferral of the keys; we made a photograph of the scene but I need no photograph to bring it back; it is a vivid memory today, pleasant to recall."

As he continued his reminiscences, Brown spoke of their time as colleagues at Howard, mentioning that Frazier joined the faculty in 1934. In his tribute he stated "it is my assignment and privilege to speak of him as a colleague." Brown began by posing a question, asking, "What kind of man was this colleague, this friend and mentor whom we have lost?" In his statement, and from a careful reading of Brown's other memories, it is apparent that Brown and Frazier had a deep and multidimensional relationship that intertwined their lives and families, in both personal and professional ways.

Brown portrayed Frazier as paying keen attention to "scholarship, determination, and integrity." He declared that Frazier's honors were "too numerous" to mention, and that "experts in his field" of sociology had conveyed to Brown "how greatly in debt the social sciences are to [Frazier's] knowledge about race and culture contacts." Brown characterized Frazier as "one of the most important influences on our university thinking, on American thinking, on world thinking." He saw Frazier as "intellectually inquiring, insatiable in his search for knowledge, [and possessing] a capacity for hard and sustained work." Brown also noted the breadth of his colleague's work as he alluded to his "varied interest and ranging curiosities."

Describing Frazier as a teacher, Brown spoke of instances when he had witnessed his lecture style and classroom manner. Frazier "was in demand all over the land," he said, as "a peripatetic pedagogue." Brown described Frazier's classroom manner as "engaging, . . . unorthodox, challenging, at times prickly as a hedgehog." He described Frazier as wanting "no frills" and mentioned that "putting on airs was beneath his contempt

[, and] pedantic word-mongering was his bane." He highlighted that Frazier's "passion for truth alone shone out clear and bright." Sterling Brown lauded Frazier's confrontational manner, which, of course, had rubbed some the wrong way. Brown called it "a good thing for America to have this man—stimulating, energizing, sparking disagreements, demanding that cherished positions be reconnoitered again from another vantage point, with another perspective, with an arsenal of facts."

As this tribute demonstrates, Howard public intellectuals established important links between and among them, involving mentoring relationships with and influences on subsequent generations of black public intellectuals. Black literary scholar Houston A. Baker, longtime professor of African American studies at the University of Pennsylvania and currently professor at Duke University, offered great tribute to Brown, for example. He indicated Brown's impact as a mentor on him—and on a generation of those interested in becoming scholars of black literary studies. He described an encounter he and a friend had with Brown, telling of the tremendous connection and impact Brown had on him and other black public intellectuals of today.[46]

> On a cold gray fall day in Washington, D.C., my friend and I saw a tall, aged and slightly stooped man shivering at a bus stop. It was too cold for him to be in the open without gloves or a hat. His face was contorted with worry. And so we stopped our car and asked if we could give him a lift. "Yes, yes," he said. "I'd be most grateful." We were [sophomores] at Howard University doing a good deed on a winter's day. The man's wife had taken ill and been rushed to Emergency at Washington Hospital Center. He hoped it wouldn't be an imposition for us to take him there. Years later, at a tribute to Sterling Brown hosted by Larry Neal (who was then Commissioner of the Arts for the District of Columbia) Professor Brown approached me and my wife (the other party in the car on that winter day) and said: "I will never forget you all's kindness in taking me to see my wife that day. I was in trouble and that was wonderful of you."

In response Baker and his future wife "were dumbstruck." Baker continues the story, which made a huge impact on his life and career:

> We had no idea what genius we had been blessed to be close to on that winter day. Moreover, we were impressed by the scope of Professor Brown's memory and the generosity of his spirit in acknowledging such a minor kindness on our part. Many years later, Sterling Brown came back into our lives when we were his hosts during his sojourn to

Philadelphia. He had the generosity of spirit to tell our adolescent son that what made his parents special was not their "smarts" but their generosity in picking him up on a winter Washington day when he needed a lift. His granting priority to an enormously simple human act of kindness reminded me of Professor Brown['s] monumental folk character "Big Boy" Davis who thinks first to exclude "whuffolks" (white folks) from his imagined heavenly kingdom, only to remember, "But what is he to do / With that red brakeman who once let him ride / An empty going home?"

Brown was the son of a theologian and pastor at D.C.'s Lincoln Congregational Temple United Church of Christ. His father, Sterling N. Brown, had taught in Howard's school of religion, and he had spoken of his family's influence on his life and career. The "maker of community in academia" was heavily influenced, growing up, by his family's southern roots, and by the black vernacular, "whose forms, manners, functions, rhythms, and intonations Brown mastered." Sterling was "reared in the ways of hard, southern labor and rigorous Black aspiration for a better life." The influence of his father's education at Fisk University and Oberlin Theological Seminary, Baker offered, meant that Brown "was heir to intellectual ambitiousness, Black middle-class manners, and an inescapable long Black southern memory."

Baker noted that Brown had his first teaching position at Virginia Seminary in Lynchburg, Virginia. For Brown's three-year stint there, this position "proved equivalent to a magical, spirited, on the ground initiation into the ways of vernacular southern Blackness. Absorbing the speech patterns, lore, legends, myths, and manners of the country folk, who lived around the seminary, Brown discovered nearly the entire stock of his poetical repertoire." While at Virginia Seminary, Brown "discovered and embraced the Black southern vernacular as his enduring field of influence, themes, values, forms, and reference."

While acknowledging that Alain Locke was "the virtual father of the movement[, who] was tireless in his endorsement of folk forms and subjects for Black art," Baker was careful to add that "it remained for Brown to bring the vernacular to a precise voice, tone and form to draw readers and listeners seriously into a world of men and women, who keep on 'inching along' despite hardship [and] who relish their affinity with larger-than-life legends like John Henry and Old Jazzbo, who refuse to be brought permanently low by floods, hurricanes, starvation wages, or rampant White American violence against the Black body and soul."

Baker ended his tribute to Brown by stating that he was "a man of memory, who taught us how to pass on a kindness, how to remember beyond the material exigencies of life in the fast lane." He also lauded Brown for the extensive impact he had on countless generations of scholars, artists, activists, and "successors in Black art, intellectualism, and activism, such as himself, Ulysses Lee, Amiri Baraka, Stokely Carmichael, Michael Winston, Joanne Gabbin (who wrote the first biography of Brown), and others." Baker noted that Brown's towering scholarly contributions were his single-volume poetry anthology *Southern Road* and "his colossal achievement . . . the groundbreaking anthology *The Negro Caravan*," edited in collaboration with Ulysses Lee and Arthur P. Davis. Last of all, Baker was "personally grateful to Professor Brown for his consummate example as a poet, critic, scholar, and soul," which, he recalled, "spiritually instructs me to remember that a winter kindness must always be remembered and acknowledged, if we are to live a gracious Black life 'beyond the bone.'"

St. Clair Drake, in an interview for the *American Ethnologist* in 1988, offered his assessment of the impact and influence of the Howard group. Drake was a close friend and colleague of E. Franklin Frazier. He offered a general description of the importance of Howard intellectuals, and of the attention they gave to issues such as Marxism, scholarship, and social change. "Most who debated these issues were Black intellectuals concentrated at Howard; they could not teach at white universities. Howard was the most prestigious of the Black institutions. In the 1930s there were scholars such as E. Franklin Frazier, Alain Locke, Ralph Bunche and, eventually Bob Weaver and others like Kenneth Clark."[47]

When asked whether he had much contact with the Howard group during the 1930s, Drake responded, "No, only later." This later contact came through correspondence and relationships he developed with the likes of Frazier and others, who tried to woo him and get him to Howard to teach in the 1960s, at a time when Drake was teaching at the University of Ghana. Howard at that time was on a serious decline from the intellectual mountain summit of its golden years, 1926–1970. According to Drake, University of Chicago sociologist Allison Davis and Sterling Brown "were part of that generation."[48]

Allison Davis's first job was at Hampton, although "His peers were at Howard," as was the case with many other prominent black intellectuals of that era, including Charles Johnson and Horace Mann Bond.[49] Drake believed that part of Davis's "decision to retool himself came from contemplating what the Howard group of intellectuals were doing. If you want to use the criterion of relevance," Drake added, "the Howard group was continuously trying to grapple with the problems of class and the Black experience."

Drake, in many ways, was acknowledging what most contemporaries of the Howard group understood all too well—that the mark of excellence as a black scholar, activist, and public intellectual was set by the members of the Howard intellectual community. Everyone else was trying to meet that standard. Let it be added that the Howard group still stands as the standard-bearers of what it means to a black scholar, activist, and public intellectual, particularly because of the tremendous influence, either direct or indirect, that the Howard scholars had on the current generation of black public intellectuals.

Two other Howard scholars were heavily influenced by the community of personalities and ideas at Howard. These were theologians and black religious intellectuals Howard Thurman and Benjamin E. Mays. For Mays, being part of the Howard intellectual community was said to have "sharpened his mind through the exchange of ideas and stimulating discussions."[50]

Thurman was appointed chairman of the Committee on Religious Life and professor of Christian theology at Howard in 1932 and, according to Fluker and Tumber, "associated" with Harris, Johnson, Mays, Locke, and Frazier, in addition to other black intellectuals such as Du Bois. Between the time he became the first dean of Howard University's Andrew Rankin Chapel in 1932 and the time he left the university in 1944 to help establish the Church for the Fellowship of All Peoples in San Francisco, Thurman made a huge imprint on this scholarly community, and the community in return heavily influenced his political, intellectual, and spiritual beliefs. Thurman noted, "At Howard, I began to experiment with forms of worship other than usual religious services," adding that the sermon was not always "the centerpiece." Thurman continued, "Within the regular order of service, I provided stretches of time for meditation, a quiet time for prayers generated by silence[, and developed] a service that would permit greater opportunity for the play of creative imagination, a vesper service."

President Johnson, however, had to adhere to a strict separation between church and state on account of Howard's financial sponsorship by the federal government, and Thurman discovered that his experimentation was not welcome. Thurman believed the dependence on federal funding was responsible also for the subsequent "secondary position [given] to any emphasis on the place of religion in the academic community." Thurman's proclivity to experiment with various styles of religious liturgy, in light of the church-state separation issues, provoked a rift with Johnson, and this disagreement led Thurman to vacate his post as dean of chapel in 1944. Despite this regretted moment, Thurman held fond memories of his Howard experience. Even with the constraints placed on Howard by Congress, the school of religion still played an important role in helping to train and educate cadres of black ministers.

Thurman, in acknowledging how Howard and President Johnson influ-

enced him, recounted his decision to go to Howard in 1932 in his autobiography, *With Head and Heart:*

> I was no stranger to Howard University. President Mordecai Johnson
> had been a steady source of inspiration from my own high school days.
> Also, for several years I had visited the campus as Week of Prayer
> preacher and during that time I had made many friends. I was caught
> up in Mordecai Johnson's vision to create the first real community of
> Black scholars, to build an authentic university in America dedicated
> primarily to the education of Black youth.[51]

Another influential personality who played an important role in this
community of scholars at Howard was Kelly Miller, who served on the
mathematics faculty and as dean of the College of Arts and Sciences. The
venerable Miller—respected by many, no matter who disliked him or disagreed with him—was a strong intellectual presence. He proposed the
idea of a National Negro Library and Museum at Howard. He functioned
as a very visible public intellectual and debated the likes of V. F. Calverton,
the socialist scholar and magazine editor. He also wrote a long-running
daily column for the *Baltimore Afro-American.* Miller tried unsuccessfully to
connect all black organizations under one umbrella movement he termed
the *Negro Sanhedrin Movement.*

In delivering the eulogy for Miller, D. O. W. Holmes, then president of
Morgan State College and former dean of the graduate school at Howard,
characterized him as a "great college teacher," and "a rich source of knowledge," as he functioned as "a drill master" and served as "a great inspiration." Holmes proclaimed, "Kelly Miller was all three." Holmes identified
with others who admired Miller, intellectuals considered "his disciples"
who credited Miller with being "first of all the inspirer, who opened our
eyes and fired our ambitions."[52]

While acknowledging his ability as "at first a teacher of mathematics,"
Holmes explained why Miller was a one-of-a-kind race man:

> He was at first a teacher of mathematics and as such was very exact-
> ing. Those of us who were interested and followed him far enough
> realized that he could have been one of the greatest mathematicians of
> his day had [he] been willing to confine himself to the ivory tower of
> pure scholarship. But he saw early in his career that the greatest need
> at that time in Howard University and in all the colleges for Negroes
> was the awakening of the students to a realization of the problems of
> the race and an interest in their solution. To this end, there being no
> sociology in the curriculum, he skillfully mixed, in his classes, a study
> of race problems with mathematical problems in such a way that when

a course was completed all the students were keenly conscious of the American social situation.[53]

Again, it should be noted that in the Howard community of scholars, there existed a tremendous diversity in both belief and identification with religion, manhood or masculinity, politics, gender issues, segregation, and other differentials. Although in some cases this diversity led to heated debates and animated quarrels, the level of intellectual and cultural engagement that each member brought to Howard contributed to a vibrant atmosphere, where there was indeed a two-way transfer of influence. Each individual put his or her stamp on the others, and on the community itself, which allowed Howard as an institution and community to develop a life of its own. Simultaneously, the community as an institution left an indelible imprint on each member, regardless of their time or length of tenure there. The Howard milieu's tremendous influence on scholars is evident. Although the composition of the community changed over the period of this study, 1926–1970, each of the aforementioned scholars continued to interact with Howard intellectuals—through participation in conferences, involvement on civil and human rights groups, and through maintaining personal relationships or connections with religious or academic bodies.

It is important to note that the relationships among Howard scholars combined both the personal and the professional. This is evidenced by correspondence between scholars at the Capstone. For members of the Howard intellectual community, up against the backdrop of segregation, the personal was professional and vice versa. An unfortunate example of this situation is in the influence that the brain drain of black scholars had on Howard in general—and on E. Franklin Frazier in particular. Frazier biographer Anthony Platt argues that:

> Through his first decade at Howard, Frazier was sustained by his teaching and work on the curriculum, and his contact with a small circle of progressive colleagues, known as the "thinkers and drinkers," who met regularly to discuss informally the burning issues of the day. . . . In the 1940s Frazier became increasingly alienated from Howard as the brain drain took away important members of his circle—Bunche and W. O. Brown to the State Department, Harris to the University of Chicago, and Hylan Lewis to complete his doctoral studies. Just died in 1941 after a long battle with cancer sapped his strength and an even longer battle with Howard's administration completely broke his spirit. Disillusioned with the university, Frazier retreated more and more into his own research and writing, while looking for opportunities for research and travel outside Howard.[54]

Correspondingly, the varieties of manhood represented by Frazier and other Howard black male intellectuals signal that the issue of masculinity and the way in which segregation impacted and transformed this issue was of great importance, as these members understood their total identity as black men and intellectuals during a time when neither black men nor black intellectuals in general were accepted.[55] The issue of masculinity must be addressed because the experiences of black male intellectuals differed from those of black female intellectuals at Howard and around the country. Also, to properly understand the relationship of black male to black female intellectuals (either those who were colleagues or those who were significant others) one must begin to delve into the complex, multifaceted identity of black men intellectuals. So, it is impossible to discuss community among black men intellectuals at Howard without discussing—as part of their identity, everyday activities, and interactions, including activism, and other influences on their scholarship—the impact of masculinity on their psyche. As these black male scholars and others such as Du Bois rudely discovered, being an intellectual in the era of segregation did not discount the fact that these scholars were black, first and foremost, and that this identity held a degraded status, even to the point of rendering them invisible. What this created for black men scholars at Howard and elsewhere was a severe double consciousness applying to the academic context, whereby many, though interacting with each other, struggled with a mix of feelings of self-doubt, internal competition for resources, and other challenges.[56]

Jonathan Holloway argues that in the 1940s most scholars, black or white, paid a great professional price for promoting African American agency.[57] Perhaps one reason that some Howard scholars (notably Abram Harris) were ambivalent about their identity as black scholars was that, regardless of their personal feelings regarding race, they had to consider the consequences of representing oneself as a race man. Black scholars had to navigate very carefully through the political terrain of promoting racially progressive positions in their scholarship, because much of the predominantly white, conservative academic establishment would not welcome such positions, viewing such work as anathema to objective and true scholarship. Personal and professional sabotage was the consequence for openly advocating progressive or what was deemed "radical" thinking, as with the case of many of those Howard scholars who were attacked during the Red Scare.

President Johnson took a courageous stance during the Red Scare, which meant that Howard scholars continued to enjoy a certain measure of academic freedom despite harassment. Howard became a target for investigation in both 1942 and 1953. Johnson, to his credit, stood up for his faculty and publicly condemned the investigative probes. In another instance, in 1958, when he and the faculty invited the controversial Du Bois to speak, Johnson was determined not to buckle under congressional pressure, and he appeared on the podium with Logan, the venerable sage, who was introducing Du Bois.[58]

Although segregation fostered community, it did not promote uniformity of ideas or beliefs within the community of scholars at Howard or elsewhere. This was never the goal. Collegiality existed alongside debate, and even animosity did not diminish the importance of community. Indeed, debates showed a healthy degree of interaction as scholars were able to enter into heated argument, while demonstrating respect and even admiration for the other's perspective. This is particularly significant when we look at Mordecai Johnson's relationship to the scholarly community at Howard.

While conventional wisdom and accounts of Howard's faculty and contemporaries suggest that Johnson was indeed a tyrant whose relationships with faculty members were largely negative, correspondence and other sources concerning relationships between Johnson and these scholars suggest much greater complexity. It seems he respected and admired even those with whom he squabbled. In terms of criticism, a group of professors including Harris, Bunche, and Lewis often met on Saturday nights at Bunche's house to share their mutual criticisms of Johnson. These professors believed he should have a fuller appreciation for their worth and work. They thought Johnson administered Howard in a strict authoritarian manner, especially when handling his differences with faculty. However, faculty disputes remained tenuous and rarely amounted to any significant action beyond bitter public and private criticism of his tactics. This fact held sway, mainly because of the inability of any faculty members to garner enough support from the board of trustees to oust Johnson.[59]

Johnson's main critics included Locke, Frazier, Logan, and Harris, along with chemistry professor Percy Julian. In the 1940s, according to Logan, when Harris received an offer to teach at the University of Chicago, he jumped at the opportunity because he felt that Johnson made no real attempt to retain him. Later, it was documented that Harris might have stayed had he been made to feel welcomed. The real convincing point of this possibility is that Harris's position at Chicago was of lesser rank than the one he had enjoyed at Howard. For another example, although Logan believed Johnson and Locke actually hated each other, he also commented that, in introducing Locke to speak on behalf of the graduate school at a board of trustees dinner, Johnson commented on the love and appreciation that the Howard community, including himself, held for Locke. Despite harsh criticisms of his presidency, Johnson's tenure at Howard lasted as long as it did because he was—in instances such as this dinner—able to transcend his differences with faculty when necessary.[60]

Another example showing how President Johnson interacted with members of the faculty concerns the question as to whether Ralph Bunche was a Communist during his tenure at Howard. Walter B. Hill in an article in the *Journal of Blacks in Higher Education* argues that in 1952 Manning Johnson and Leonard Patterson, two African American former Communist Party members, brought charges against Bunche (at that time Howard political science chair) concerning his alleged membership in the party. Both Johnson and Patterson charged that Bunche's party affiliation "had been concealed so that he could operate covertly in Black communities." They also noted that the Communist Party felt Bunche's affiliation could bring respectability to its attempts to recruit African Americans. According to Johnson and Patterson, the CP believed that Bunche could "indoctrinate" students at Howard and that he could persuade them to become party loyalists.[61]

Although no conclusive proof was ever found to support these charges, Hill states that, between 1952 and 1954, "Bunche's career was dealt a crippling blow" as he was subjected to intense investigations from the Civil Service Commission and the Federal Bureau of Investigation. These events are ironic considering the amount of service Bunche gave to the State Department, his country, and the United Nations. But it signals that black scholars—despite their ascension to mainstream positions and unrelenting attempts to transcend the boundaries imposed by race—were still living in a segregated and colonized world.[62]

Ronald Walters, the political scientist and policy expert who taught in Howard's political science department for a number of years, described Bunche as "more of a radical" during his years at the Capstone than he was later, in his work as a diplomat with the United Nations, the global organization he helped create in 1945. Walters argues that, had Bunche stayed in academia instead of leaving it to work in the State Department and the United Nations, he would have been known primarily for his work in American civil rights. The case of Bunche is a prime example of the down side of the black brain drain, which began to grow steadily in the early 1940s. The brain drain began a slow migration of black scholars from the black academy into government service jobs and to serve on predominantly white university faculties. Eleanor Lee Yates contends that Bunche "hesitated to leave academia, but his knowledge was needed against the Nazi campaign in North Africa." It was a great loss to Howard University when Bunche left, although he did maintain both a professional and a personal correspondence with his former colleagues.[63]

Although the Howard community of scholars suffered many faculty changes during its golden years from the 1930s to the 1960s, it maintained a highly qualified and active crop of competent intellectuals. The Bunche scandal was not the only thing that happened with respect to the Howard community in 1952. Prior research has focused too much on isolated incidents, while giving inadequate attention to the totality of what occurred within this community of scholars. In September 1952, for example, sixteen new professors joined the community, others returned from leave, and still others obtained their doctorate degrees. Noted scholars W. Mercer Cook, Rayford Logan, and others returned to Howard from Fulbright fellowships. Among those granted faculty leave in 1952 were Franklin, Frazier, Vincent Browne, and Dean Charles Johnson, who was granted leave to complete a book. Finally, professors Harold O. Lewis and G. Franklin Edwards earned doctorate degrees. Carroll Miller completed his doctorate in education from the teachers' college, "bringing the number of Ed. D's on the faculty to an even half-dozen."[64]

While segregation helped to form and promote community among the intellectuals at Howard, it also served as a double-edged sword and elicited significant conflict and undeniable constraints. Segregation contributed to numerous conflicts at Howard. Among these was the presence of marginal finances at Howard, which created spats over "crumbs" in the area of salaries. Also, the marginalization of black academics and black men and women in general created a common rivalry for status and promotions at the Capstone. For some scholars this environment, which embodied the decline of segregation from national attention, further exacerbated personal and professional conflicts, but for others it opened the possibility of moving on to greener pastures and greater opportunities.

This scenario, whether it was the flight of scholars such as Harris and Bunche in the 1940s or that of the 1950s and 1960s, proved a further cause of discontent and jealousy among scholars at Howard. The decline of segregation led to a brain drain from black colleges, beginning in the 1940s and accelerating in the late 1960s and onward. By the 1960s, this brain drain left those still at Howard, such as Frazier, with a sense that perhaps either they remained at the Capstone to retire or they were committed to a dream that had come and gone.

To be sure, a number of prominent Howard scholars became disillusioned and disgusted with the university, and especially with the administration. Two faculty members, in particular, who were constantly at odds with the administration were Harris and Locke. In a 1947 letter to Locke, Harris disclosed his evident contempt for the university:

> When I was in Washington last [Christ]mas, we should have met and gone over one or two possible things to be done in connection with my plans to leave Howard University. Perhaps it is just as well because my disgust with the place is just about as great as yours and good riddance by no means expresses the Administration alone. I understand from a reliable source that the President in presenting my resignation stressed the fact that I was leaving for a higher salary. Neither he nor Price gave one moment of serious attention to the intentions I expressed last [Christ]mas. Lewis wrote several letters in the Spring asking me what I planned and I told him that unless I hear something from Howard about a substantial increase in salary and especially about the Administration's determination to build the social sciences, I would accept the offer of the University of Chicago. Lewis was never able to see Price who at the time, it appears, was writing his *annual report*. I am not certain whether he tried to see the President. It does not matter now.[65]

Harris felt bitterly slighted and offended by Johnson's actions regarding his leaving Howard. He wanted to stay—but not with the feeling that Johnson did not appreciate or even want him at the university. Harris already suffered, as many Howard faculty members did, feelings of inadequacy because of the marginalization of black scholars in the academy. But Johnson's slight, even if it was at the mecca of black institutions, proved too much for Harris to overlook. Harris confided in Locke because he knew Locke also felt hostile toward Johnson, and because both he and Locke had maintained good relationships with colleagues while at Howard. Perhaps, what stung Harris's pride the worst was how Johnson publicly humiliated him and portrayed him as a traitor and a seeker of fame and wealth at white universities. Harris flatly denied this portrayal and strongly believed it misrepresented his character. In light of these matters and other struggles with Johnson, Harris reached a final breaking point. He felt he had no other option but to leave. No longer hopeful that the situation would get better if he stayed, he moved to what he hoped would one day be greener pastures.[66]

In many instances, faculty members at Howard were drawn together by their opposition to President Johnson's administrative and personal maneuvers. However, by no means was opposition to Johnson the focal point of the whole intellectual community. Other instances, where members of the Howard community demonstrated both community and collegiality toward one another, transpired through collaborations on academic projects. For example, one of these great collaborations was among the scholars Sterling Brown, Abram Harris, E. Franklin Frazier, and Kelly Miller, whose influence on the New Negro movement is manifest in their contribution to Alain Locke's 1925 anthology *The New Negro*. Another instance of academic collegiality can be seen in the praise and support for the publication and work of Howard historian, Caribbean scholar, and future prime minister of Trinidad, Eric Williams. In a letter to Locke concerning Williams's seminal study *Capitalism and Slavery*, Harris mentioned that he "got a glimpse of Eric's Caribbean study." He praised it, saying it looked "like a good job." He offered further praise to Locke for his introduction, stating that it "is very timely in its remarks of the present situation."[67]

Other instances of community and collegiality can be found in the support Howard professors offered one another in regards to their receiving academic honors and awards. A number of Howard professors aided and encouraged each other in the attainment of prestigious academic honors, such as the Guggenheim Fellowship. Professors Sterling Brown and John Hope Franklin were among those who received this prestigious honor. Other Howard faculty were awarded various honors during their careers at Howard, such as Franklin and Hansberry, who were chosen by the State Department as Fulbright Fellows in 1954. In a letter to Logan dated May 12, 1953, Hansberry sought Logan's assistance in obtaining sabbatical leave in order to fulfill the terms and obligations of the Fulbright Fellowship. "Under the terms of the grant," Hansberry noted, "I shall spend the next academic year in research activities in Africa."[68]

The next day, Logan sent a letter of recommendation to the dean of the College of Liberal Arts, Dr. J. St. Clair Price, requesting "that Professor William Leo Hansberry be granted a Sabbatical leave of absence for the academic year 1953–1954 in order that he may accept a Fulbright grant for research in Africa." In praising Hansberry's accomplishments, and concerning the Fulbright, Logan noted, "The award is a deserved tribute to the quarter century and more of study and teaching that Professor Hansberry has devoted to a neglected field. The world of scholarship and his students will greatly benefit from this field investigation. I believe that the University should be proud of the fact that another member of its faculties, the third in the Department of History, has received the highest type of Fulbright award."[69]

Obviously, Logan's recommendation worked—along with Hansberry's record—for on August 5, 1954, Price sent a letter to Hansberry indicating that he had been granted sabbatical leave. This recognition for Hansberry was timely, for just five years later, he was sent a letter by the new dean, Frank Snowden, informing him of a new policy whereby professors at Howard had to retire by the age of sixty-five. Logan had supported Hansberry also many years before, when in 1946 he also recommended that the African studies expert be promoted to the rank of associate professor with a salary increase to $3,600 annually. Of Hansberry, Logan articulated his support for him and his "more than twenty-five years" in African history and studies: "some of the most noted scholars in the United States, notably Professor E. A. Hooton of Harvard University, recognized Professor Hansberry's work [as] one of the most significant in the field of American scholarship." Logan offered that Howard "owes it to itself to be among the first to give some public recognition to the high place that Professor Hansberry has attained among American scholars."[70]

Another instance of collegiality and mutual respect and aid can be seen when, in September 1949, Franklin asked Locke in confidence to be a reference for him and to advise him on applying for the Guggenheim. He mentioned that he was applying to "continue my work in the field of Southern intellectual history." Franklin told Locke he intended to use the fellowship to work on "Southern Travelers in the North," a work that eventually became one of Franklin's most important books on southern history.[71]

In 1950 Franklin then expressed his appreciation to Logan in a letter thanking him for his "congratulations and best wishes upon receiving the Guggenheim appointment. . . . I feel deeply of course that my appointment came, to a great extent, because of the generous expressions of confidence that persons like you made in my behalf. I am grateful to you for this and the many other expressions of faith in my scholarship and of encouragement. I hope that I shall live up to the expectations that you have."[72]

The deep personal and professional respect between Logan and Franklin was reciprocal and ongoing throughout their careers at Howard and beyond. In recommending Franklin to the rank of eminent professor in 1954, Logan spoke admiringly of his friend and colleague:

> Few, if any professors have brought so much honor and prestige to the University as has Professor Franklin. The accompanying statement reveals a list of accomplishments that is almost incredible. Even this list is incomplete. To it should be added his appointment to lecture during the summer of 1954 at Cambridge University, England [on] "Regional and Ethnic Influence in American History." We may confidently look forward to further productivity and higher honors.

Adding to his appraisal, Logan noted that Franklin was "a superb teacher" and was as "highly appreciated by other members of the Faculty as he is by members of the Department." Further, Logan continued, "I lean heavily upon him for sound advice in matters that require good judgement." In his estimation this appointment of Franklin would be highly regarded by historians in the United States and around the world.[73]

Another important relationship in the development of collegiality and community at Howard was the collaboration between Rayford Logan and Sterling Brown in researching and writing the university's centennial history. In a December 1961 letter to Logan, President Nabrit appointed a committee to be charged with the responsibility of writing an updated and detailed history of Howard University. It was to be "written and published in time to be one of the essential aspects of the University's centennial celebration in 1967." The responsibilities of the committee, as determined by Nabrit, would be first "to prepare guidelines regarding the history to be written." Second, the committee was charged with selecting a "person or persons in each school and college or other major areas to gather the data needed in the history, after consultation with the respective deans." Third, the committee was responsible for choosing the person or persons to actually write the history. Finally, the committee would function "as an editorial group with respect to the publication of the history." Nabrit selected Dr. Vincent Browne to serve as committee chair. Before ending the letter, Nabrit announced to Logan that he had appointed an executive committee, separate from the larger committee, to be "responsible for setting up a time table for the work involved in the writing of the history." In addition to Logan, this executive committee would consist of professors Sterling Brown, W. Montague Cobb, and Herbert Reid, Ms. Dorothy Porter, and Dr. Vincent Browne.[74]

On January 19, 1962, Nabrit "on the recommendation of the committee charged with the responsibility of having a history of Howard University written" extended to Logan, "in association with Professor Sterling Brown," the opportunity to work on this history. In his letter Nabrit relayed to Logan and Brown that, if they "find it possible to accept this important assignment," then they should arrange their semester schedule in order to "give one-half time to this work." Logan and Brown accepted.[75]

The only other history of Howard prior to this history had been Walter Dyson's *Howard University: Capstone of Negro Education*, published in 1940. Dyson's history provided a very general account of the evolution of Howard from its founding in 1867 up to 1940. It failed, however, to probe deeply into the complexities evident in relationships among members of this intellectual community, as well as into their relationships with President Johnson in the early years of his presidency.[76]

Up to 1962 it appeared that the writing of the centennial history of Howard University would be a celebrated and nonpolitical event. However, events occurring years later signaled that trouble had been on the horizon even then. In a twenty-one-page document, Rayford Logan recounted his experience of writing the centennial history of Howard. He responded in resounding fashion to the censoring of the history he was writing. Although it was indeed an honor for Logan, it was a bittersweet and difficult period of his career at Howard.[77]

Throughout much of the research and writing of the history, Sterling Brown struggled with sickness, which kept him from contributing as much as he and Logan had initially anticipated. Even more troubling were the political obstacles he and Logan encountered. According to Logan, "The heavy-handed attempt of Howard University authorities to censor my manuscript of the University's history [was awful]. . . . The writing and publication of the history under the title *Howard University: The First Hundred Years* (1969) constituted in many respects the most prolonged painful experience of my life."

Brown's absence from the book project contributed mightily to Logan's extreme difficulties in working with the university administration in order to complete the book. In July, commenting candidly that they were "old friends," Logan lamented that "*Howard University* would have been a better book if Sterling had been able to continue as co-author." On July 22, 1965, acting Howard president Stanton L. Wormley informed Brown that "it had become necessary for us to return you to your full-time position as Professor of English on September 1, 1965."

Despite all this turmoil and travail, Logan was able to complete the history of Howard with support from both colleagues and students. In addition to Charles H. Thompson, Vincent Browne, and George E. C. Haynes, most pivotal among this group were English professor Arthur P. Davis and a student, Michael Winston.[78] Logan, in the preface of the book, characterized Davis as "in effect the literary critic of the manuscript, which went to the publisher." Winston was noted as being instrumental in contributing "institutional research" and "the selection of photographs." He proved "invaluable . . . in the last stages of production, particularly with respect to the final format of the book." Additionally, Winston "made final arrangements for the publication" during Logan's absence in Europe in July and August of 1969.

With painful honesty, Logan admits that his research was "handicapped by the illness and death of my wife." Ruth Logan, his longtime confidante, had battled diabetes "for many years," and she had to have her leg amputated on Commencement Day 1964. Obviously harboring the pain and guilt he experienced during her final years, Logan pointed to Ruth's unselfishness while he worked on the Howard history. "When I called her from the University, she invariably answered: 'I'm fine Papa. Don't worry about me, I'm fine.'" Another time Ruth stated, "Papa, I am sorry that this [her amputation] had to happen to you." Besieged by guilt at his wife's challenging condition and weighed down by the enormity of the task involved in writing the university's history, Logan reeled as he recounted how he heard of his wife's passing. The afternoon of June 30, 1966, he received a phone call from Rupert Lloyd, a family friend, who informed him "that my wife was dead." Logan was devastated and went into obvious shock. He lamented his beloved wife, revealing that she was "Cheerful and courageous to the end, You worried more about me than about yourself."

Little time passed before Logan was dealt another serious blow. Three months later, still grieving his wife's passing, Logan received a letter from Howard University secretary G. Frederick Stanton, informing him that the university executive committee wanted to view the completed manuscript before it was sent to the publisher. Stanton added the hope of the committee that Logan would "understand that their interest relates to their office with respect to the legal and public relations of the University, and to the fact that their minutes are privileged."[79]

This act of grave insensitivity angered Logan for two reasons. First, he had written the history during a period of severe challenges, including the illness of Sterling Brown and the illness and death of his wife. Second, he had agreed with the committee, early in the project, to submit any chapters that might include statements indicating "any possible libel," particularly chapters focusing on Mordecai Johnson. Feeling infuriated and insulted, Logan paced the floor of his home "all day and part of the night" and finally resolved to write a letter of resignation from the entire project. In the course of a very thorough response, he retorted, "I refuse to be party to such outrageous censorship and therefore, I resign today, September 30, 1966, as HISTORIAN OF THE CENTENNIAL HISTORY OF HOWARD UNIVERSITY." He added that, when a new historian was appointed, he would turn over all the research materials in his possession.[80]

Logan turned the letter in to President Nabrit's secretary at around eleven o'clock on the morning of September 30, 1966. He did not receive a response until October 29, stating, in so many words, the university's "deep regret" in accepting "your resignation as Historian in accord with your wish." Acting president Stanton L. Wormley, articulating the university's tremendous investment in the project, requested that Logan turn over his materials to the Office of the Secretary "as soon as possible." Wormley concluded the letter by reiterating the university's sincere "regret" regarding "your resignation." In his letter of response, Logan listed the history of his working relationship with the university on the project, recalling particular stipulations, agreements, and conditions. "The action of the Executive Committee was offensive to me," Logan railed, "because it expressed a lack of confidence in my intellectual integrity, my scholarship, my judgment, and my loyalty to Howard University." He further declared that the committee's actions were not only "offensive" but "unrealistic" because of his charge that even the committee would not have the time to read the manuscript "in its entirety," adding his doubt whether under those conditions "there would have been a consensus as to what should be excluded in order to protect the 'public relations of the University.'"[81]

Logan blamed three factors for his inability to complete the history prior to his resignation. First, he pointed out "the failure of Professor Sterling A. Brown to carry out his assignment" as being "the major reason for my inability to complete the manuscript prior to my resignation." Adding a stinging addendum, Logan fumed, "During approximately three years, he did practically nothing to justify the substantial investment in his assignment." Added to this major issue for Logan was the amputation of his wife's leg in June 1964, whereby, despite the hardship, he "continued to work assiduously." Last, Logan mentions that, even though obviously emotionally heavy following her death, "he continued work on the manuscript and met several times with Dr. [Arthur] Davis." Logan signed off the letter to Wormley and the executive committee stating his feeling "distressed as you are that I deemed it necessary to submit my resignation."[82]

As Kenneth Janken notes, friend and fellow historian John Hope Franklin relayed to Logan his outrage at the evident censorship of Logan's manuscript, yet Franklin saw no conspiracy. He reasoned that it was standard practice for university trustees to approve official institutional histories. Franklin advised Logan to calm down and refocus on his other research. Unable to locate another scholar to take up the daunting task of completing the history, President Nabrit agreed to give in to "Logan's demand for an uncensored manuscript and reinstated him to the project."[83]

Logan put the finishing touches on the book in 1968, as the Black Power movement was gaining significant momentum. Logan, a product of the New Negro era, hated the label "Black," but at this moment it was bittersweet. He had gained a measure of respectability in being reinstated. However, the culture pointed to in the history reflected an uncertain future ahead for Howard University and the nation.

As successor to Mordecai Johnson, James M. Nabrit sought in many ways to maintain some sense of continuity in regards to the Howard intellectual community. In his 1963 address to commemorate the formal opening exercises of the university, President Nabrit described Howard University as an environment where the "common bonds" of community developed, and where current developments ensued.[84] Discussing the racial, religious, national, and cultural diversity apparent at the university, Nabrit opined, "This is, of course, exactly the way that the world is made up. It is because of these differences that there is so much value to be gotten from travel and study abroad. Each of us contributes to others and our lives are made richer by association."

Nabrit spoke of the method by which he envisioned "common bonds" being created at Howard. "Pulling together our diversities and making all people as one," Nabrit reflected, "are many common bonds. We spring from the same source. There runs in each of us the same fundamentals of human nature. All of us have capacities for good and evil. Our destinies are intertwined—for no man is an island unto himself."

This statement, referring to a larger aspect of the composition of the Howard community, is certainly applicable to the relationships being studied here. Very poignantly, Nabrit understood that, although many diversities of personality and ideology existed, what he termed the "common bonds" brought the community together. The fact that there was a link uniting the institutional mission of the higher education of blacks with the goals of each scholar's own racial advancement in a nonuniform fashion provided continuity within this community of scholars, despite the many personnel changes over the years. Evidence of the power in these common bonds is found in that, even with disagreements and departures from Howard, scholars developed close relationships with one another over the years and either continued to maintain contact after their tenure or continued to hold one another in esteem. Nabrit also recognized that each individual at Howard possessed both good and bad tendencies. He believed that through their common bonds both the institution and its scholars were mutually interdependent to the extent that they both sought to train and advance the race.

"Our common bond at Howard," Nabrit discerned, "is intellectual in nature—the pursuit of learning," but he added that this "common bond" was "deeper than" a purely intellectual endeavor:

> We seek knowledge not for its own sake, not to advance our own understanding, but also to make our world a richer and better one for all who live in it. The safety and welfare of none of us can be assured until we have provided for all. The concept of true university, is in the meaning of the Latin—"universitatas," is that it is an institution of higher learning, bringing together scholars from all areas of inquiry and joining them in a universe of knowledge. Thus, the university in its objective, the pursuit of learning, must be free from the biases of race, religion, nationality, politics, and all else which would obstruct its functions as a center of intellectual activity. Institutions of learning whether in the southern states of America or elsewhere which are

operated to serve narrow, parochial interests are therefore prevented from [realizing] the truly great purpose of education. There is a sovereignty of the mind which acknowledges no artificial barriers, and whose only limitation is that in human nature itself.

In his address, not only did Nabrit speak eloquently to the condition and challenge of any and every university in America at the time, but much of what he said applied directly to Howard itself. Nabrit had been at Howard as a faculty member in the school of law while Johnson was president. Many of his comments about the role of the university maintained continuity with those outlined and followed by Johnson in his 1926 inauguration speech.

Further documenting the success and legacy of this intellectual community, Mercer Cook spoke in glowing yet realistic terms of its substance and of the men who primarily composed it. As he remembered them at an Honor's Day speech at Howard on October 11, 1966, the professor of romance languages and former ambassador to Senegal spoke about the idea of community at the university. Cook lamented the passing of a number of "dedicated colleagues." Among the most noted black men he remembered were E. Franklin Frazier, William Leo Hansberry, and former head of the department of romance languages V. B. Spratlin. (It is a serious and curious omission that Cook failed to mention any of Howard's black women intellectuals.) In his address, Cook touched also upon the significance of critical work done by the Howard University law school in the 1930s:

> One of the best examples of the effective application of brain power to race relations started at Howard University Law School in the 1930s, while the late Charles Houston was Dean. Grouped around Houston were such outstanding NAACP Lawyers as William Hastie, Thurgood Marshall, James M. Nabrit, Frank Reeves, W. Robert Ming, and the late Leon Ransom. Their problem was to plan strategy for an attack on the legality of segregation in the schools. They began with the most impersonal of educational institutions: the law schools, and fought such cases as Murray [v]s. the University of Maryland and Gaines [vs.] the University of Missouri; then they moved on to the more touchy area of state Medical Schools before attacking the emotionally charged issue of the segregated public school. [The] whole doctrine of "separate but equal." In the larger context, the Supreme Court ruling of May 17, 1954, [no] matter how deliberate the speed with which it has been implemented, was a victory for the American people, but it was also a victory for brain power generated principally by Howard University's School of Law.[85]

Cook saw the value in and the evident contribution of this community of scholars, despite all the clamor and heated disputes. He viewed this community without uniformity as the most relevant point to remember, especially in light of the passing of many of its most prominent members.

Another perspective on this intellectual community comes from Professor Ralph Bunche who, although leaving early for a job in the State Department, had maintained contact with Howard's intellectual community and on many occasions continued to contribute to its continuance and development. Reminiscing on his days at Howard in a speech on April 8, 1953, at the installation of Howard's first Phi Beta Kappa chapter, Bunche spoke about his days as a professor there. "There is something thrilling about the title of 'professor,'" Bunche asserted, "a lot of dignity in it too, and even perhaps, an element of danger." This danger, Bunche believed, was that "no ego is constantly nourished as that of the college professor, before whose trough of knowledge students stand in never-ending queue." In a tone recalling his own personal odyssey at Howard, Bunche added:

> After all, there is something altogether unique about association with knowledge and the process of imparting it. There is, I think, nothing quite so rewarding; not to be sure, the material sense, but in the sense of self-satisfaction, the inner feeling which alone can signal true accomplishment. Knowledge gives, or should give, balance and perspective. For the challenge to the intellect is man's greatest challenge. What man, indeed, can fail to be humble in contemplation of the vast wisdom and the verities of the ages? I know, of course, that in academic as in other circles there are the bumptious ones, the brash know-it-alls who perceive themselves as the [center] of the universe, because they have acquired a little learning, which, in truth, may often be worse than none. But they are neither learned [n]or wise, for the learned man is he who is always acutely aware of how much there is that he can never know. Humility is the mark of those who have truly command with the goddess of learning.[86]

There were definite examples of the Howard group reaching out to the next generation of black scholars and public intellectuals. Historian Robert L. Harris Jr., a professor of history and Africana studies, wrote Rayford Logan in November 1978 asking him for advice about a book entitled *Afro-Americans and the United Nations: Petitions for Freedom and Justice*. Harris explained that he intended to examine the "U.N.'s place in Afro-American thought." Harris reminded Logan of the biographical sketch he had done on Daniel Murray for Logan and Winston's *Dictionary of the American Negro Biography*. Harris understood that Logan had enjoyed a long and distinguished career as a scholar and public intellectual and had done various stints of research and work with the United Nations. Even in the twilight of his career, Logan was still sought out as an expert in various areas of black studies. Logan was not alone in this, for his colleagues (including Brown and Frazier) were also often consulted by the next generation of black scholars and public intellectuals. Harris noted that he would be in Washington, D.C., "to participate on a National Endowment for the Humanities' evaluation panel" on December 18 and 19 of that year and inquired if he could arrange a time to speak with Logan. A note written below Harris's signature indicates that the two reached some sort of arrangement as, it seems, Logan wrote "will call after December 9."[87]

For all the diversity of thought and gender politics of black male and female intellectuals who constituted the intellectual community at Howard, there was unmistakably the presence of community. For them, community did not entail uniformity or a single way of being or knowing but was represented in a multiplicity of voices, personalities, and agendas. Although there was significant change and turnover of personnel over time, the influence of the Howard intellectuals still stands as testament to the presence and vitality of the concept of community in black intellectual life. Furthermore, their influence is noted in the legacy they bequeathed to generations of black intellectuals who have followed in their footsteps in search of community.

CHAPTER FOUR

Public Intellectuals and the
Black Public Sphere at Howard

T HE BLACK PUBLIC INTELLECTUAL is not a recent phenomenon. A public intellectual is in many ways both a scholar and an activist, but a black public intellectual is an altogether different creation. Black intellectuals by their very nature either are forced or choose to be both scholars and activists, and they embrace a synthesis of the two, so as to each become in many ways a scholar activist. This is the result of circumstance, with the most visible circumstance being an environment of segregation and continued discrimination. For some time mainstream white academia looked down upon those who mix the "intellectual" with the "political"—but black intellectuals, regardless of their brilliance or wit, have been relegated to a second-class status both as intellectuals and as human beings.

In the case of the Howard intellectuals, their lot as second-class citizens was inextricably bound to an unwarranted second-class status as intellectuals. In essence, for black public intellectuals at Howard University, the public was private, and vice versa. The discrimination they experienced at work was the same discrimination they experienced outside the ebony tower, when they were not teaching, lecturing, or writing books. Well before book deals and lecture tours became lucrative, black intellectuals engaged the black public on issues of race and world affairs. These intellectuals were a loose collection of individuals and organizations that were at the same time transnational and global in composition, perspective, and outreach. These men and women were cosmopolitan. They traveled the world, acutely aware of and deeply engaged in the important issues of the day such as segregation, integration, anticolonialism, and the like. For them, the realities of life under the veil of segregation were never far from their minds as they wrote, taught, and thought. For them, the development of theories was useful only if it could effectively bring about social change in America and around the world for people of African descent.

Members of the Howard University intellectual community were active and influential black public figures who operated within the context of a domestically segregated and globally colonized black public sphere. The black public sphere consisted of a larger network of black scholars in the United States, along with African and Caribbean scholars throughout the world, and mainstream white and Jewish scholars. Within this web of interconnected relationships were representatives of philanthropic groups such as the Phelps Stokes Fund and the Carnegie Corporation. The backdrop of this global black public sphere was a highly segregated and colonized world, where many black scholar activists were not welcomed in mainstream academic circles.

Most would argue that the phenomenon of the black public intellectual is of recent origin. By definition, a public intellectual is an educated individual who engages the people on public issues and whose thought and work influence, define, and transform those issues. Harvard University government professor Martin Kilson offered "an operational definition of Public Intellectuals and their function."[1]

Kilson argues that public intellectuals "historically and presently" operate "to fashion moral, ethical, and policy criteria or options for mediating among the competing perceptions of the generic issue-spheres in modern society." These spheres are recognized as "the opportunity/privilege issue-sphere and the sacred/profane issue-sphere." Kilson goes on to assert that, historically, the opportunity/privilege issue-sphere has been the main area of concentration for public intellectuals, mainly because "situations and problems relating to the opportunity/privilege gap emerged first as sources of national crises."

For African Americans, issues of segregation, civil rights, and colonialism are examples of opportunity/privilege matters beginning as national crises. I argue that black scholars in the Howard community were public intellectuals who responded to these issues through scholarship, other writings, and their public outreach and activities within the African American community. They responded also through associations with other scholar activists and with both national and global organizations, forming loosely configured networks of national and international black public intellectuals. The global networks they committed to largely addressed the issue of developing Pan-African linkages in order to challenge segregation, colonialism, and global racism and to unite under a common commitment to a shared cultural past, both real and imagined. Howard intellectuals were public intellectuals because of their role as scholars who were simultaneously activists, concerned in particular with issues of race and class.

Furthermore, Howard scholars were organic public intellectuals, who arose from the structures of segregation and who grew to challenge that oppression from within. Although these public intellectuals in many cases had received degrees from leading white universities, they were more organic intellectuals than traditional because they were more than mere academics. They were scholar activists grounded in a segregated black America. They dealt with the dual challenge of operating as second-class citizens and intellectuals. This sense of a double consciousness, which haunted Howard public intellectuals and most other black scholars, was heightened as they grappled with the knowledge that, despite their own inner struggles with segregation and the impact it had on their lives, their responsibility was to focus their work and public activities toward uplifting the race. This idea properly designated many of these scholars as "Race Women and Men."[2]

The media through which Howard black public intellectuals articulated their thought were as diverse as the scholars themselves. The black press provided an important outlet of expression, with newspapers such as the *Pittsburgh Courier* and the *Baltimore Afro-American;* black journals such as the *Journal of Negro Education, Phylon, Crisis,* and *Opportunity;* and other journals such as V. F. Calverton's radical journal the *Modern Quarterly.* Other outlets included participation in organizations such as the NAACP, the National Urban League, the National Negro Congress, the Pan African Congress, the Black Britain Intellectual Collective, the American Society for the Study of African Culture, the American Negro Leadership Conference on Africa, and the black churches. Those who found religious institutions especially conducive outlets for their work were faculty members in the school of religion, including Benjamin Mays, Howard Thurman, William Stuart Nelson, and of course Mordecai Johnson.

Yet, these intellectuals and their contemporaries in the Howard community were not relegated to just one sphere of influence, even though they spent a considerable amount of time in the black public sphere. The black public sphere—though defined, in the United States, largely by segregation and, globally, by colonialism and imperialism—was not confined exclusively to black American relationships. It was also closely and intimately connected to other races, including Africana peoples outside the United States, white scholars of varying ethnicities, and other scholars abroad.

The relationships in this public sphere fully integrated all black life, transcending all lines of class, gender, and degrees of blackness. Even within this landscape of influence, although not completely integrated by law or by custom, black public intellectuals at Howard and beyond found varying ways, through political activism and other modes of less direct activism, to challenge and chip away at the color barrier, which had so many in a quagmire. In doing so and in fighting the daily struggles for academic recognition and personal respect, they were not immune to the ever-present double consciousness that plagued them then, and that still plagues black public intellectuals today.

Martin Kilson, who interacted early in his career with many Howard scholars such as E. Franklin Frazier, in further discussing the role of the public intellectual established a typology for examining black public intellectuals, past and present. In this typology Kilson denoted two distinct phases of black public intellectuals, the Proto–Public Intellectual phase and the Formative stage. According to Kilson, the Proto–Public Intellectual phase occurred in the period between World War I and the 1960s. This phase was defined "by the ethnic boundary or racial boundary limitation on the 'public arena' available to the first cohort of Black Public Intellectuals." Kilson distinguished the Proto phase of black Public Intellectuals: "With few exceptions, those who could function as Public Intellectuals during the era between the two World Wars and into the post-war period had mainly the Black population and a sliver of the White population available as a 'public arena'—as, that is, a 'public market' for projecting a Black intellectual's view of moral, ethical, and political options for guiding American society and life."[3]

The second stage Kilson mentions in the evolution of black Public Intellectuals, the Formative stage, extends from the late 1960s to the early 1970s. At this juncture in their development, black public intellectuals witnessed the expansion of a white market. Kilson argues that in this stage the transformation of the public intellectual in black was now a "full-fledged" and "mature Public Intellectual one." Kilson's model is useful as a means through which to note where Howard scholars fit in the overall evolution of the black public intellectual. Furthermore, his identification of four typologies of black public intellectuals as well as his examination of certain dynamics and characteristics will prove useful in understanding the thought, public activities, and overall historical significance of Howard public intellectuals.

Many members of the Howard intellectual community were held in high regard by black communities all over the United States, and these intellectuals were in great demand as lecturers and speakers. As black public intellectuals, many spoke on various issues of the day in public forums such as churches and other institutions, and in public media such as the black press and black journals. Furthermore, many of these individuals continued to function as public intellectuals long after their careers ended at the Capstone. They spoke on issues such as segregation, black leadership, events at Howard, and countless others. Some, of course, did not feel entirely comfortable in their role as public intellectuals. One significant example of this was Abram Harris. A gifted economist and scholar, Harris intimated to one of his colleagues that he basically felt uncomfortable addressing the public and making public speeches, signifying his ambivalence about his role as a public intellectual.

On the other hand, one of the most gifted orators (along with Mordecai Johnson and Thurman) was Benjamin Mays, who spoke at various black churches and on numerous occasions. For example, in 1938 Mays, then dean of the school of religion at Howard, spoke at the homecoming services of the Third Baptist Church in D.C. He spoke on "The Stupidity of Man" and continued to address the similar theme of man's disobedience to God and his determination to go his own way. For Mays this was a theme he often wrote and spoke about, and in many ways he connected it to his secular and sacred issues in his public intellectual roles of theologian, minister, preacher, and intellectual.[4]

Mays was a prolific scholar and lecturer. He was very active as a public intellectual while at Howard. Indicative of this public role, particularly on a global scale, Mays expressed gratitude in his autobiography, saying that while serving as dean of Howard's school of religion in the years between 1936 and 1939, he "was permitted to attend four World Conferences, three in Europe and one in India." Although he left Howard to assume the presidency of Morehouse College, Mays maintained close contact with many of Howard's professors, remaining active with individuals such as his good friend President Johnson. During his time at Howard, he produced a number of very important articles and books on numerous aspects of the problem of race and religion in American life. Among the most important of his pieces was one in the *Journal of Negro Education* entitled "The Color Line around the World."[5]

Black public intellectuals at Howard and those who were part of the informal network of the national and international black intellectual communities all were active in a variety of spheres. One prime example is the coalition between black political leaders, scholar activists, and other black professionals in forming a chapter of the American Friends of the West Indies Federation. Congressmen Adam Clayton Powell and Charles C. Diggs were the two main proponents of the chapter, forming it in 1958 in D.C. The organization was created on the heels of the celebration of the new West Indies Federation, started on April 22, 1958. This entity was formed under the inspiration of Mrs. Una Morrison Staples, a native of Jamaica, who believed that West Indians residing in the United States "should organize themselves in an effort to support the newly formed organization." The formation of the American Friends of the West Indies Federation was significant primarily as a public issue, because it demonstrated the support offered and the concern felt by black American scholars and political leaders for the affairs of the West Indies in particular, and for the Caribbean in general. It also indicated that the support of black American public intellectuals of varying sorts went beyond imagined cultural identifications and sympathies and was evidenced tangibly through the formation of and participation in similar such entities.[6]

As it evolved, the American Friends of the West Indies Federation won significant approval from Congressmen Powell and Diggs. Powell's wife had West Indian roots, as did Diggs's family. Both representatives planned to be at the federation's inaugural ceremonies. Diggs planned to organize a chapter in Detroit as Powell had organized a chapter in New York City. Congressman William L. Dawson of Chicago was out of town when the district chapter was organized, but he expressed "a desire to organize a similar chapter in Chicago." The group appointed a nine-member organizational committee headed by Howard University history professor Rayford Logan. In May 1958 the group planned a mass meeting to "formally organize the group" and to hear reports from Congressmen Powell and Diggs concerning the celebration held in the West Indies. The first informal meeting was held in the office of Congressman Powell in the House Office Building. In addition to Logan, many others attended this gathering including Una Morrison Staples, attorney Bedford Lawson, Mark Watkins, and L. R. Haselwood, who was president of Howard University's Caribbean Association.[7]

During the golden years of Howard University between 1926 and 1970, the black public sphere placed Howard intellectuals in contact with a number of U.S. presidents, especially since the university was situated in close proximity to the White House, Congress, and the Supreme Court. On June 9, 1965, for instance, President Lyndon Baines Johnson served as the Commencement Day speaker at Howard University. Some argue that he gave one of the most significant speeches of any U.S. president to a group of African Americans. Prior to LBJ, U.S. presidents such as Franklin D. Roosevelt had also spoken at Howard.[8] In some cases, Howard's public intellectuals maintained close contact with the presidential administration and many of its major players. In cases where Howard public intellectuals did not play a significant role with particular presidential administrations, they were at the forefront in analyzing the effects of certain policies affecting black America. For example, Howard public intellectuals took more

direct involvement in the affairs of the Franklin Delano Roosevelt administration during the 1930s and 1940s.

During the heyday of the New Deal (1933–1939), many Howard public
intellectuals were influential consultants to, and influenced the activities
of, the Black Cabinet. These advisers included the Howard social science
collective centering around Bunche, Frazier, and Harris. Although not
official cabinet positions, the Black Cabinet served as an advisory board
organized by President and Mrs. Roosevelt, with the direct involvement of Mary McCleod Bethune, noted educator and founder of Bethune
Cookman College and the National Council of Negro Women. The Black
Cabinet brought the importance of black America to the attention of the
Roosevelt administration, while simultaneously amassing black political
talent to strategize for necessary and beneficial social policies. Bethune, a
regular speaker and presence at Howard University, lobbied the National
Youth Administration so stridently on behalf of black youth during the
Roosevelt administration that she earned a full-time staff position as an
assistant. Bethune and other black leaders such as Bunche, Frazier, and
Harris advised the president and the first lady on the concerns of black
America, primarily the quest for civil rights.[9]

Numerous Howard public intellectuals were very active in civic and
civil rights organizations such as the NAACP and the National Urban
League, and Howard intellectuals were in close contact with many prominent black leaders, ranging from Walter White to Malcolm X. Although
there were many scholar activists and public intellectuals included in the
sphere of what could be called national black intellectualism, the three
most prominent figures that scholars at Howard had close contact with
were W. E. B. Du Bois, Carter G. Woodson, and Charles S. Johnson.

In a segregated and colonized world, community was very important for
black scholars across the country, as well as those who were transnational
in their scholarship and travel. As is true today, but perhaps more so then,
the black scholars making up this "national community" knew of each
other and corresponded often, staying in frequent contact. In addition to
cooperation between and personal friendships maintained by individuals,
it was also common for these intellectuals to debate intensely and to disagree. Evidence indicates that black scholars shared in a unique quandary:
how to cope with the tremendous burden of operating in a segregated and
colonized world further complicated by their state of double consciousness. Finally, as predominantly men, the dimension of gender often complicated their uncertain racial landscapes and there ensued problematic
relationships with many black women public intellectuals as well as with
mainstream white women intellectuals. For all of the uncertainty of black

public intellectuals during this period, there is certainty that, despite these constraints, they were committed and productive in their scholarship and their activism, both domestically and abroad.

Members of the Howard University community were indeed actively engaged with the black community. Sterling Brown, "the maker of community of academia," for example, was also successful in developing community and solidarity among members of the local Washington black community. This interaction with various classes beyond Howard's walls represented the epitome of what a public intellectual was during this time. Brown's schedule was very busy as he functioned in a number of roles and influenced countless individuals and groups, including Arnaud Bontemps and others.[10] In March 1939, for example, the Harlem Cultural Committee, a group dedicated to studying "the cultural needs of the Harlem community," extended an offer to Brown to participate in a conference in April of that year. Specifically, Secretary Marian Minus asked him to chair a panel on literature. Literary luminaries such as Richard Wright, Countee Cullen, Roi Ottley, and Minus would serve on this panel. Although the conference was later postponed until May 6, Minus still asked Brown for his participation. In 1941 Brown was invited by then Fisk University president Thomas Jones to participate on a program, "An Evening with Negro Writers," where he would share the stage with fellow black public intellectuals Alain Locke and Langston Hughes. In 1963 Brown was contacted by Maurice Lawrence, international president of the Duke Ellington Jazz Society, about gaining significant support to have jazz legend and native-born Washingtonian Duke Ellington awarded an honorary doctorate degree. In addition to being an expert on African American literature, Brown was a connoisseur of jazz music and had among his circle of friends and acquaintances many notable musical and artistic giants. Brown was committed to many worthy causes, which is evident by his instrumental involvement in securing Duke's honorary degree award. These activities of public intellectual work meant Brown and other Howard scholars participated in matters that affected black America. These scholars championed many causes, even those that seemed on the surface symbolic but that took on a larger public and social significance with each public appearance, lecture, and occasion of outreach.[11]

In 1958, the Howard social science department sponsored a lecture by distinguished black intellectual W. E. B. Du Bois. Prior to 1958, on two occasions, Du Bois had considered becoming a professor at the Capstone. On this occasion, in the twilight of his career, Du Bois was brought to the university to speak to Howardites on the issues of the day. A major figure involved in bringing him to Howard on this occasion was Rayford Logan.

An editorial in the *Baltimore African American* lauded Howard's social science department for bringing the "distinguished sociologist, author and scholar" to the campus.[12] The editorial commented that Du Bois was a "controversial figure," noting that the State Department "has consistently refused to issue him a passport to travel abroad for international conferences in recent years." The editorial offered that the treatment of Du Bois by the State Department "is more of a reflection upon the narrow concepts of the Department than it is upon Du Bois." In an accurate illustration of the function of education, the editorial contextualized Du Bois's coming to Howard:

> The primary purpose of an educational institution is to educate and it is impossible to obtain a well rounded education by looking at only one side of a sphere. Any institution of higher learning which shies away from a man because he is the object of controversy is hardly worthy of the name. Education itself is a never-ending battle between conflicting ideas and opinions, the validity of which is determined by examination, and experimentation, not by popularity of the ideas advanced.

Although conceding the views of critics that Du Bois was pro-communist, the editorial illuminated that Du Bois had maintained consistency in his battles against colonial exploitation. "It is difficult to determine where his love of communism begins," the editor declared, "and his hatred of imperialism ends." Gathering information from Du Bois's speech and other writings, the editorial concluded that "he sees in socialism not a panacea for all the world's evils, but a force in being capable of coping with, if not destroying, the imperialism, which he has fought so vigorously during the greater part of his 90 years." In analyzing Howard's role in hosting Du Bois, the editorial spoke in glowing terms of both Howard and Du Bois:

> There are a number of compelling reasons why Howard University had no choice but to invite Dr. Du Bois to their forum. As one of the pioneers in founding the Niagara Movement and the NAACP, he helped to crystallize the spirit which has brought the race a long way in its struggle for citizenship. As a founder of the Pan-African Conference, his writings fired the imagination of the young . . . leaders whose courage has brought about the evolution of several independent nations with more to follow.

In conclusion, Du Bois was portrayed as "a scholar and thinker" and "one of the darker men the White man fears." Howard students, in the words of the *Baltimore African American,* "were entitled to see and hear a man while he is still among us." For many it may have been one of the last times to witness Du Bois's brilliance in person as, a few years later, he renounced his U.S. citizenship and embarked on his exodus to Ghana, where he spent the remaining years of his life. He died on the eve of the historic March on Washington in 1963. Whether he was liked or disliked, loved or hated, Du Bois had a huge following. To invite this complex and controversial figure to Howard in the late 1950s at the height of the Cold War was a consistent sign that whatever disputes and disagreements Howard intellectuals (including President Mordecai Johnson) had experienced with Du Bois, they recognized that the global black movement for freedom was larger than any one personality or figure. Significant impact for this movement required a marshaling of the truth to the people, regardless of the consequences. This example of inviting Du Bois to speak demonstrates firsthand that there were definite times when personal idiosyncrasies among public intellectuals at Howard took a back seat to the common good of the race and to attaining social progress.

Dr. Carter G. Woodson was another important member of the national black intellectual community with whom many Howard scholars maintained close contact. The relationship between Woodson and Logan was particularly complicated. At times they showed great respect for one another, and at other times they were in tremendous conflict. Logan worked alongside Woodson in the Association for the Study of Negro Life and History (ASNLH). In fact, Logan understood how much Woodson loved, coveted, and protected the ASNLH. Despite personality conflicts and disagreements, these two maintained a healthy respect for each other. Both were very prickly men who wrestled constantly with the dilemma of being black, male, and intellectual in the segregated academic world. They both met huge obstacles in securing funding for research, and in garnering respect from the mainstream academic establishment.

In 1945 Logan wrote a significant profile of Woodson in *Phylon*. This assessment was all the more interesting because Woodson was still alive, and most reflections about other scholars are published posthumously. In revealing the real Woodson, Logan spoke of a man whose existence was unknown to many. Concerning Woodson's decision to return to his life work as scholar instead of remaining a dean at Howard, Logan wrote, "Dr. Woodson could no longer remain deaf to his calling." Describing Woodson's lifestyle, Logan offered this interesting assessment:

> He came back to Washington and made his headquarters at 1538 Ninth Street, N.W., where he lives, edits the *Journal,* and carries on the other multitudinous activities of the Association and of the Associated Publishers. . . . There he lives in an almost Spartan existence. For

breakfast he has some fruit juice which he prepares himself. For lunch he usually eats raw fruit. After a full day's work in the office, however, he enjoys a hearty dinner followed by a long stroll. He usually retires early. As a consequence, despite his seventy years, he appears hale and hearty. He is as erect as a soldier and appears to be taller than his five feet, eight and a half inches. He neither smokes nor drinks. Romance has apparently played little part in this bachelor's life. In one of his rare bursts of confidence, Dr. Woodson told the writer of one love affair. While he was vacationing some years ago in a New Jersey resort, he saw a young lady whose face seemed familiar. Approaching the charming person, he inquired politely, "Haven't I met you some where before?" "I should think you have," the lovely lady replied, "you proposed to me once."[13]

The relationship between Logan and Woodson is a significant indicator of public intellectual work. Several aspects are important, the first being their association and working relationship with each other and other black scholars. Second, Woodson surrounded himself with individuals who believed and supported his work with the ASNLH and the *Journal of Negro History*. The association between Woodson and Logan is an example of how prominent black public intellectuals at Howard formed networks with other prominent black scholars nationwide, building a sort of loose community of similar figures, who on occasion participated in organizations with overlapping concerns and issues.

Undoubtedly, there was a complicated academic and political relationship linking black public intellectual giants Carter G. Woodson and W. E. B. Du Bois. They obviously shared significant admiration and appreciation for one another, but there was also evident intellectual jealousy and competition for resources. One example can be seen in the two men's competing ideas for an Encyclopedia Africana. A number of Howard public intellectuals were caught in this web, as scholars such as Sterling Brown and Rayford Logan were asked by both men to assist in their projects.

In 1931 Woodson asked Brown to become a member of his staff because of his "knowledge of the Negro in literature and grasp of things in general." Du Bois also solicited assistance on his Encyclopedia Africana project from the Howard collective, including Miller and Logan. The creation of an encyclopedia documenting the experiences of black men and women in America had been resurrected in 1931 by Dr. Anson Phelps Stokes, president of the Phelps Stokes Fund. On November 7, 1931, Phelps Stokes called a meeting "to consider the possibility of publishing, with the help of the Phelps Stokes Fund and other foundations, groups and individuals who may be interested [in an] Encyclopedia of the Negro." Among the twenty-five individuals in attendance, half were white. African American public intellectuals in attendance at the initial meeting were Fisk professor of literature and former executive secretary of the NAACP James Weldon Johnson, and, from Howard University, President Mordecai Johnson, professor of mathematics and sociology Kelly Miller, and literature professor Benjamin Brawley. This meeting, characterized as a gathering of the "liberal" establishment, also included Eugene Kinckle Jones representing the National Urban League and Walter White representing the NAACP.[14]

Missing from this first meeting were the nation's two most influential black male intellectuals of the twentieth century; neither Woodson nor Du Bois was invited. Du Bois reported that this was because of his criticism of the Phelps Stokes Fund's reports on education in Africa. Du Bois heavily criticized the fund's promotion of industrial education, a type of education championed by Booker T. Washington and emphasizing the development and utility of practical skills for black Americans, as this was opposed to Du Bois's method of leadership training, which advocated the development of the critical faculties of black Americans. A second meeting concerning the encyclopedia was held on January 9, 1932, and this time Du Bois and Howard philosopher Alain Locke were invited. Woodson was yet again left out. Obviously miffed at this continued omission, Woodson continued his independent efforts to create an encyclopedia for the Negro.[15]

By the time of the third meeting on March 12, 1932, a board of directors had been selected and incorporated. African American leaders appointed to the board included Tuskegee principal Robert Russa Moton who was named vice president, Professor Benjamin Brawley, Atlanta University president John Hope, writer James Weldon Johnson, and Du Bois. Friction between Du Bois and Woodson ensued when Du Bois took on greater responsibilities with the Phelps Stokes project. Du Bois noted in his autobiography that the same year he returned to Atlanta University, he was appointed editor-in-chief of the project. Hearing the news, Woodson was deeply scarred and hurt. On May 30 and June 6, 1936, in the pages of the *Baltimore Afro-American*, Woodson expressed his resentment that Du Bois, Brawley, and others had been selected and were involved with the Phelps Stokes Fund project. Woodson asserted that if Du Bois accepted the post then he would be a "traitor to his race." Woodson was very skeptical of any project designed to reflect the exploits of the black race that was headed and funded by whites. He believed that the encyclopedia should be "a task which only the colored man himself can do." He felt that whites could not write black history authoritatively due to the fact that they did not "live and work among them [blacks]." Woodson was also affected adversely because he had already been researching and writing toward producing an encyclopedia, well before 1932, and he attributed the fact that he had been omitted to this.[16]

Howard public intellectuals who had cordial relations with both Woodson and Du Bois, including Wesley and Logan, were drawn into this dispute between the two, a particular case within a larger issue where various black scholars were pitted against each other for scarce resources and positions. Although such a project was surely a significant example of the public intellectual work being undertaken by black scholars, the encyclopedia generated serious animosity and bickering among those vying for limited opportunities to promote their own research agendas. The irony of the entire situation was that, despite Du Bois's selection as editor-in-chief, the encyclopedia was never published, mainly because of a lack of support both financial and otherwise. What was published in the end was essentially a bibliography entitled *Encyclopedia of the Negro: Preparatory Volume with Reference Lists and Reports,* which came out in 1945.[17]

Around the time of Woodson's death in 1950, Du Bois offered his own account of the encyclopedia project. Indicating that the project was one Woodson "left unfinished," Du Bois mentioned that it was an idea he himself "had toyed with in 1909, securing as collaborators Sir Harry Johnston, Flinders Petrie, Giuseppe Sergi, Albert Hall and Franz Boas. . . . But my project never got beyond the name stage and was forgotten."[18] Du Bois acknowledged that, sometime later, Woodson "took up the idea as a by-product of his Journal; but few knew of his project at the time." Du Bois states that in 1931 the Phelps Stokes Fund "projected an *Encyclopedia of the Negro,* but invited neither Woodson [n]or me to participate," but then a group of influential black leaders, namely, Moton of Tuskegee and Hope of Atlanta "protested and finally we were both invited." Du Bois mentions that he attended the "subsequent meetings but Woodson refused" even "after I and many others talked to him and begged him to come in."

Woodson gave two reasons for his refusal. First, the presence of a "white enterprise forced on Negroes" was unacceptable to him. Second, Woodson "had himself already collected enough data eventually to make an encyclopedia." Du Bois admits he and colleagues moved on without Woodson, but this was not "because we were unwilling to have him work on the encyclopedia." In fact, Du Bois states they were "eager." The reasoning behind the decision reflected, from Du Bois's perspective, the knowledge "that one man and especially one man with a rather narrow outlook which had been forced upon him, could not write a scientific encyclopedia of sufficient breadth to satisfy the world."

In the end, the Phelps Stokes Fund was unable to acquire the necessary funds, and Du Bois believed this was because of his position as editor. The project concluded with "the publication of only one thin preliminary volume." Du Bois reflected that Woodson "left the kernel of a great work" that "would be a magnificent monument to his memory, if this were to be made the basis of broad rewriting and extension and published as a memorial to his life work."

Yet, despite the very political nature of the circumstances surrounding the project, Du Bois, though critical of Woodson's professional and personal differences as both historian and individual, offered a measured tribute to him upon his death. Du Bois observed that, "As a historian, Woodson left something to be desired." Characterizing Woodson as "indefatigable in research," a fact reflected in a number of solid historical works, Du Bois also stated that some of Woodson's other books (whose titles he chose not to mention at the time) "were not of so great value." In characteristic Du Boisian style, echoing a similar critique of Woodson by Logan, he concluded with a critical and honest assessment of his colleague:

> Indeed his service to history was not so much his books as his editorship of the Journal, which brought into print some of the best scholars in this branch of history. On the other hand, Woodson himself lacked background for broad historical writing; he was almost contemptuous of emotion; he had limited human contacts and sympathies; he had no conception of the place of women in creation. His book reviews were often pedantic and opinionated. Much of his otherwise excellent research will have to be reinterpreted by scholars of wider reading and better understanding of the social sciences, especially in economics and psychology; for Woodson never read Karl Marx. . . . The passing of Carter Woodson leaves a vacuum hard to fill. His memory leaves a lesson of determination and sacrifice which all men, young and old, black and white, may emulate to the glory of man and the uplift of his world.

To be sure, Woodson and Du Bois evidenced a similar dilemma of invisibility as was experienced by other African American intellectuals of their time, which prompted many to become quite frank about their desire to maintain control of their public activities, including projects with which they were involved and scholarship they conducted. In 1936 Woodson expressed his inability to serve as an adviser for the Federal Writers' Project that Brown was directing. He cited two major reasons. The Federal Writers' Project was a federally commissioned project designed to document the experiences of blacks who were former slaves or who had recollections about their family during slavery. Woodson conveyed that his first reason for choosing not to join the Federal Writers' Project was his reluctance to allow his "name" to be "officially" used as adviser. He stated that he had "no time to give to matters beyond the work of this office," meaning the ASNLH, the association he had founded. Woodson added that he did not "permit my name to be connected with organizations or efforts to which I have no time to give attention."[19]

Perhaps Woodson's second reason for refusing to be an editor on the project is more telling, indicative of his own ambivalence toward being a black public intellectual in a segregated world. It is strikingly similar to sentiments expressed by others of his cohort. This was his evident distrust of politicians, governmental representatives, and philanthropic entities that had failed to support Woodson's efforts with the association, and in his eyes those who had sought to hinder its further development. With this understanding in mind and his remembrances of his unpleasant affiliation with the Howard University administration and with President Durkee, Woodson warned Brown of the possible consequences of openly associating with him on such a project, now that Brown was placed in charge of it. Added to Woodson's reluctance was his further understanding that the project was not only very time-consuming but evidently also tightly monitored. Woodson wrote to Brown, "The other reason is that, it will be inadvisable for you to use my name in connection with your project. You probably owe your position to the interracial magnates and job-holding politicians, who are inalterably opposed to the work of the Association for the Study of Negro Life and History. To remain on friendly terms with them, you had better keep away from the undersigned. He is considered a dangerous Negro."[20]

To demonstrate the fact that his refusal was nothing personal and that he still held Brown in very high regard, Woodson informed Brown that, at the recent annual meeting of the ASNLH, Brown had been selected to join the editorial board of the *Journal of Negro History*. In this capacity he would join the likes of Rayford Logan, Lorenzo Greene, Lawrence Reddick, Luther P. Jackson, and W. Allison Davis, as well as Woodson. Soon after that Brown became a member of the staff. The fact that Woodson selected Brown to join the board of the *Journal* indicates his respect for the mind and thought of the Howard literary and social critic and, more pointedly, indicates his trust in him as well.[21]

Howard's black public intellectuals also had consistent contact with Charles S. Johnson, another influential member of the country's impressive crop of black public intellectuals. Johnson had become president of Fisk University by 1947. In 1944, before the end of World War II, he had established the Race Relations Institute at Fisk to confront the race problem on a global scale. His institute was held every year on a different aspect of the race problem.[22]

The actual groundwork for the institute began with a 1942 partnership between the Rosenwald Fund, the American Missionary Association, and the social sciences division at Fisk University, of which Johnson was chairman. The institutes became a public policy vehicle of sorts—an annual event where scholars and experts were invited to present their research and to discuss matters of public policy import. Patrick Gilpin notes that lecturers and discussion leaders for the institutes were chosen from academics and intellectuals, from "community, minority-group, and regional and national organizational leaders," and from among "national and international personalities in human relations." Participants at the Race Relations Institute included "a cross section of the leadership in middle-class America" and "represented churches, schools, community organizations, governmental agencies, labor, management, organized minorities, and many other segments of the population." Gilpin adds that those who participated in the annual institutes "came with a common interest in improving race relations."[23]

In addition to asking many of Howard's professors—such as Charles Hamilton Houston and Sterling Brown, for example—to participate in the activities of the institute, Johnson also established significant personal and professional relationships with these intellectuals, which went beyond mere scholarship. It was through relationships such as these that a great deal of mentoring occurred in the national and global black intellectual community. Charles Johnson was a great conduit for facilitating the sense of community among black intellectuals across the nation and around the world. His institute—held every year on a different aspect of the race problem—provided a consistent intellectual space and repeated opportunities for Howard professors to demonstrate their scholarly expertise before a wide public audience. In a letter to Sterling Brown, Howard's own "maker of community," Johnson shows how the informal network of black intellectuals provides a sense of support and encouragement despite the dilemmas posed by segregation. In 1928 he wrote:

> I was remarking to [Countee] Cullen the other day that I felt that your poetry has shown the most distinctive and superior contribution of any of the younger writers since 1926. It seems to me that there is a great struggle, even among the most brilliant ones of that earlier period, 1922–1926, against going to seed. I wondered if it is to be the fate of many of them to flash early and die. One hope lies in getting in contact with the actual source material and in keeping abreast of the best that is being done in the world of letters. You have a distinct advantage here and, unquestionably, you are using it.[24]

Johnson considered Brown not only a trusted friend but a valuable poet and social critic of America. In this capacity Johnson deemed Brown not just a mere poet, but more a conveyer of ideas whose poetry and social criticism contributed mightily to his desire to improve race relations and increase interracial understanding in America.

* * *

The pages of the black press and black periodicals provided a valuable outlet for black public intellectuals, who were often shunned by the white mainstream journals and newspapers. Black newspapers such as the *Pittsburgh Courier,* the *Chicago Defender,* and the *Baltimore Afro-American* as well as black periodicals such as the *Crisis* and *Phylon* allowed black public intellectuals such as those of the Howard collective a chance to promulgate their voices and scholarship, uninhibited by the debilitating nature of segregation and overt racism. As it is today, in the first decade of the twenty-first century, many members of the national and global black intellectual communities operated and networked within the same circles. They knew of each other and undoubtedly read one another's works. Many of the same names appeared repeatedly in these various publications, which indicates how, in one sense, segregation did promote community among black intellectuals, not only on the local level but also on national and international levels. These publications helped to anchor black public intellectuals, especially those of the Howard community, as pioneers of nascent forms of black, African, and Africana studies and what can be called Africana policy studies.

A number of Howard scholars had close contact and involvement with a number of civil rights organizations, most notably the NAACP. For example, among his many other activities, Frazier had frequent contact with NAACP secretary Walter White. Frazier was on one occasion in 1934 notified that the board of directors had appointed him to serve on a Committee on Plan and Program "to consider the future program of the Association in light of changing national and world conditions." The committee members, chaired by Abram Harris, were said by White "to spend a week at the National Office," charged with the goal of "making an analysis of the work, which has been done in the economic, political, civil rights and other fields during the past twenty-five years." On another occasion Frazier was asked by White to serve as director of a study designed to examine the Harlem Riot of 1943. In response to White's inquiry, Frazier stated, "I can say that you can say that you may suggest my name," adding he was "certain" that, "if the offer is made, arrangements can be made for me to be absent from any duties here," at Howard.[25]

Other correspondence between Frazier and White dealt with public issues. Concerning White's troubles with trying to control and censure Du Bois on the subject of segregation in the pages of the *Crisis,* he confided in Frazier and asked for advice. White also asked Frazier's opinion on the issue, as a representative of younger black public intellectuals, and asked for "any suggestions as to action or policy," adding that he would be "grateful for your advice and opinion."

I very much wanted to talk with you and to get your advice as to what should be our attitude in the present situations with regard to the *Crisis*, Dr. Du Bois and the whole issue of segregation. My own experience, especially during these last few years, convinces me that instead of letting up in the fight on segregation we have got to battle evil more vigorously than we ever have before. I do not see how we can turn back the clock, and any acceptance of segregation or any let-up in our fight for full integration of the Negro into every phase of life on precisely the same basis as anyone else would, in my opinion, be definite turning back.[26]

In addition to Frazier, others being considered to serve on "an editorial board of young, intelligent, uncompromising individuals," and in "the preparation" of material for syllabi, were "Charlie Houston, Abe Harris, Rayford Logan and John Davis."[27]

In addressing White's inquiry, Frazier explained that he would not address the NAACP's plans to institute the adult education classes on political, cultural, and legal subjects. Instead he offered that "I shall confine my comments on Du Bois' position on segregation."[28] Although he confessed to not having "read very closely Du Bois' recent pronouncements on the segregation issue," Frazier offered his assessment of what he perceived to be "two distinct attitudes toward the existence of segregation and discrimination." Addressing Du Bois's positions, Frazier offered that "what Du Bois has said concerning segregation as a natural social phenomenon is nothing new." Frazier's impression was that Du Bois "belonged to the group that believed in doing something about segregation." Addressing the statement that "all the fight that has been put up against segregation has been futile," Frazier's answer was, "That may be so." But he went on to say, "It is conceivable that institutions and social arrangements can not be affected by human effort." He added that the same view could be applied to Communists. Frazier made an attempt to distance his own position, as offered "last summer at Amenia," from some of Du Bois's comments. He added the following:

There is another aspect of Du Bois' recent statements that should be met. From what I have read of Du Bois recently, the Negroes in the United States would simply regard the situation as hopeless and attempt to do nothing about it. Some of the things which Du Bois says are reminiscent of Garvey's nationalistic movement; but Du Bois is not as thorough-going and consistent in his scholarly gestures in the direction of Negro nationalism as Garvey. Du Bois seems, to me, to be simply engaging in intellectual play. It seems to be a confession, on his part, of the failure of his entire philosophy, and that since he is too old or is afraid to risk his livelihood in coming out in favor of Communism or the destruction of competitive capitalist society as the only solution to the Negro's problem, he has sought refuge in a tame and harmless racialism. As Du Bois envisages racial separateness, the Negro would lock himself up within the ghetto and there let his petty social elite parade as the leaders and the upper class in the Negro group.

Distinguishing his own comments at Amenia the summer before, Frazier articulated to White that he himself "advocated the conscious development of nationalistic sentiment." Frazier stressed that his opposition "advocated . . . development of morale, group solidarity, and efficient opposition to the walls of racial segregation and prejudice." And he added that he "did not envisage this as an end." He continued:

> I did not envisage a Negro ghetto, stratified according to bourgeois society. I was advocating a revolutionary nationalism that is the development of racial solidarity as a cohesive force among a people who were exploited by the White master class in this country. Such a program might have appeared paradoxical in as much as the intellectuals and the possessors of influence and what little money we have to become the leaders of the program; but this is the very thing which is happening in Poland today among the Jews who have a much larger, a wealthier and a more influential bourgeois element among them.

Always complex in his views, Frazier wished "to add another word." Characterizing the NAACP as "a militant organization," he argued that it had no other choice, it "must be a militant organization." He clarified, "My present criticism of it is that what was radical and militant twenty years ago is not radical and militant today." Offering his suggestion on a future plan of action, Frazier proposed that "Militancy on the part of an organized minority can prevent segregation and other forms of ostracism from becoming fixed in the mores of the country. Therefore, instead of sitting down, contemplating philosophically the phenomenon of segregation as DuBois advocates, the N.A.A.C.P. ought to become more militant and enlist every form of strategy to break down the walls of segregation."

Issues of militancy and segregation versus nonviolence and integration continued to be paramount for Howard public intellectuals well into the civil rights era, and Frazier remained deeply involved. In 1961, for example, Howard University's Cramton Auditorium was host to one of the most engaging political debates of that time. Fifteen hundred people crammed into the auditorium to hear a debate on the pros and cons of segregation. The debate, titled "Segregation or Integration," showcased Nation of Islam minister Malcolm X and Bayard Rustin and was moderated by E. Franklin Frazier. Rustin was speaking in favor of integration and Malcolm X was speaking in favor of segregation. The *Tri-State Defender* reported that Malcolm X and Rustin "spoke eloquently and were armed with a mass of historical facts as well as logic and reason."[29]

The audience was brought to a "stilled shock" as Malcolm made a heavy attack against "so-called Negro leaders." Malcolm uttered, "The Black man in America will never be equal to the White man, as long as he attempts to force himself into his house." He continued by characterizing "the real problem" as being "that the anemic Negro leader, who survives and sometimes thrives off of gifts from White people, is dependent upon the White man [to] whom he gives false information about the masses of Black people." In response to Malcolm's statement, Rustin received cheers when he retorted, "[Y]ou say America as presently constituted is a sinking ship, and Negroes should abandon this ship for another called 'Separation' or another state. If this ship sinks what possible chance do you think your 'separate' state would have?"

In rebuttal to Rustin, Malcolm retorted, "We Muslims have isolated ourselves from the White man long enough to analyze this great hypocrisy and begin to think Black, and now we speak Black. We care nothing for the White man's love, but we do have his respect because we demand it. You students must do the same."

Following "the somber impact of Mr. X's continued reference to history and his many sharp criticisms of current practices," one Howard faculty member commented that "Howard will never be the same. I feel a reluctance to face my class tomorrow." In summarizing the day of intense debate, Howard president James Nabrit Jr. observed that "this discussion has been a very thrilling experience because Howard is dedicated to the task of making young people think. We appreciate the opportunity to host such lively cross-currenting."

In addition to serving as moderators and lecturers for events addressing public issues of a domestic nature surrounding civil rights and segregation, Howard public intellectuals participated in more sustained networks in organizations dealing with more global concerns. Perhaps the most active and influential international organization of African, Caribbean, and African American intellectuals was the American Society for the Study of African Culture (AMSAC).

Following the Afro-Asian Conference in May 1955 in Bandung, Indonesia, a meeting that highlighted the nonalignment concerns of various African and Asian nations in the Cold War world, a group of francophone black intellectuals calling themselves the Société Africaine de Culture (SAC) organized what became known as the International Conference of Negro Writers and Artists in Paris in 1956. Alioune Diop, the Senegalese-born editor of *Présence Africaine,* depicted this gathering as a second Bandung of sorts. Diop was a francophone intellectual of considerable measure himself, and he interacted with Howard public intellectuals such as Logan during the 1950s. *Présence Africaine* was a literary journal that critiqued colonialism. It was formed by the francophone intellectuals who created the Société Africaine de Culture. This group consisted of an impressive network of the major intellectuals and scholars of African descent of the day.[30]

The American organization, AMSAC, showcased the most active members of the global black intellectual community and connected the Caribbean, African, and African American intellectual communities in both material and spiritual ways. For the initial conference, organizers invited a number of African American artists, writers, and intellectuals to participate. These included Horace Mann Bond, Howard professor and ambassador Mercer Cook, John A. Davis, Thurgood Marshall, James Baldwin, and Duke Ellington. Those African American intellectuals in attendance formed the American Society for the Study of African Culture. AMSAC was jointly founded by Africans and African Americans in an attempt to create a deeper understanding and appreciation of the connection between the cultures as well as the contributions of both overall to the diaspora. Through annual international conferences and luncheons, attendance at official events, and other intellectual functions, AMSAC connected these global intellectuals in face-to-face meetings, where African, Caribbean, and African American scholarship and culture was on display. Also, through media such as the AMSAC newsletters, this global black intellectual community was intimately interconnected. Furthermore, the black press—as it has always done with the global black intellectual community—facilitated dialogue and transfer of knowledge and cultural activism as it highlighted and covered activities of AMSAC and other related groups. To be sure, although AMSAC's central motivation was the preservation, promotion, and sharing of intellectual and cultural knowledge of peoples of African descent, the group was also very politically active in supporting and promoting civil rights in the United States, the overthrow of colonialism and imperialism in Africa and the Caribbean, and the independence of African nations.[31]

Among the group of African intellectuals who participated in AMSAC functions can be found the names of Nnamdi Azikiwe, Kwame Nkrumah, Jomo Kenyatta, Julius Nyerere, Tom Mboya, Frantz Fanon, Leopold Senghor, Sekou Toure, and countless others. The group also included many of the most active members of the national black intellectual community, and many notable Howard University professors such as Frazier,

Hansberry, Cook, Logan, Wesley, and Franklin. Other notable black intellectuals in the group included John Henrik Clarke, Martin Kilson, Langston Hughes, and Thurgood Marshall.

AMSAC's annual international conference was a significant event both for this organization and for the global black intellectual community. On April 11–13, 1963, Howard University hosted the fourth international conference. At a luncheon of ambassadors from various African nations, AMSAC president John A. Davis announced that the conference would deal with the theme "Southern Africa in Transition." Also at the luncheon were Ambassador Julius M. Uochi of Nigeria, Congo Chargé d'Affaires Joseph Pongo, and Howard University president James M. Nabrit. The conference was slated to deal with important aspects of independence in African nations south of the Sahara and specifically featured discussions on challenges and problems to independence in areas such as the Portuguese territories of Mozambique and Angola, the Congo, South Africa, southwest Africa, northern and southern Rhodesia, Nyasaland, and the High Commission Territories. A number of significant African leaders were scheduled to be in attendance. "This conference will not only consider the problems of each specific area," President Davis stated, "but will discuss and evaluate the techniques being used in the present struggle." Among these techniques were passive resistance, armed force boycott, propaganda, collective international action, and regional Pan African action via groups such as the Pan-African Freedom Movement for east, central, and southern Africa. The AMSAC conference at Howard came on the heels of the "precedent-setting" conference of the American Negro Leadership Conference on Africa, which had met only a few months earlier in New York. That particular groundbreaking conference "voiced the colored people's concern about United States policy in emergent African countries." The conference had addressed troubled areas on the continent including Mozambique, Angola, the Congo, South Africa, and other areas. Participants had included Howard public intellectuals such as Logan, and they had focused on examining U.S. foreign policy in emergent African countries.[32]

Many noted African leaders were either educated in the United States and Britain or made speaking appearances at universities such as Howard. African independence leaders Kwame Nkrumah, Sekou Toure, and Patrice Lumumba were among the many African political intellectuals and statesmen who graced Howard's campus during its golden years. Speaking at AMSAC's third annual international conference in Philadelphia in 1960 and reading a paper titled "The Historical Aspects of Pan-Africanism," Rayford Logan mentioned a debate at Howard University on February 10, 1943, where Nkrumah had "derided the mandate system and demanded the independence of all Africa at the end of the war." Known as an authority on African affairs, Logan was also a noted authority on the mandate system, having written his dissertation on the subject. Logan's speech was timely, as AMSAC's third international conference was focused primarily on "the historical development of Pan-Africanism in which Negritude has played such an important part." Forty papers were given at the conference and were eventually included in an edited book titled *Pan-Africanism Reconsidered.*[33]

In noting the Western influence on members of the global black intellectual community, Logan spoke of how "great libertarian principles" such as the Declaration of Independence and the Magna Carta had "influenced in varying degrees the ideas of African nationalists." Further describing the effect of Western thought on the activities of these global scholar activists, Logan observed:

> Many of them also absorbed some of their ideas, directly or indirectly, from Greek and Roman philosophers; Bodin, Descartes, Voltaire, and Rousseau; Milton, Locke, Hobbes, Burke and Mill; Marx; Jefferson and Lincoln. Nehru . . . . Eric Williams . . . are all Oxford men. . . . Nkrumah, Azikiwe, George Padmore, Jones Quarterly, and other Africans studied in the United States and Nkrumah studied also in England. . . . Jomo Kenyatta studied in London and Tom Mboya spent a year at Oxford. Julius Nyerere is a product of Edinburgh University; Dr. Hastings Banda of Fisk University, the University of Chicago and Edinburgh University. Dr. Du Bois received his doctorate from Harvard University in 1895 and Dr. Woodson in 1912. Leopold Senghor is a graduate of the Sorbonne.[34]

The important influence of Western thought on the makeup of these scholar activists is apparent. It suggests that members of the global black intellectual community shared ideas and learned from each other. These scholar activists exchanged ideas on subjects as diverse as the meaning of freedom, independence, and activism as it concerned peoples of African descent in various areas in a world that was for a long time segregated, colonized, and under the control of a Cold War. Historian Brenda Gayle Plummer notes in her influential book *Rising Wind* that Howard scholars such as Frazier, Locke, Houston, and others were very active among both national and global networks of black intellectuals on issues as diverse as the Italo-Ethiopian crisis and other anticolonial struggles.[35]

Among the global activists who were educated in the United States was Nnamdi Azikiwe, the first prime minister of Nigeria. He was a very important figure in the global black intellectual community and had extensive ties to Howard. Azikiwe was educated for a time at Howard and was close to a number of professors who had a tremendous influence on him. Alain Locke was one professor of note who developed a very close relationship with him. In a 1945 letter to Azikiwe, Locke expressed sheer excitement as he stated, "I cannot tell you how often we think of you here, and of the pride that we have, as friends of yours, in your success and more importantly, in your steadfast and courageous leadership of the young African movement."[36]

Various Caribbean intellectuals played huge roles in the global black intellectual community between the years 1929 and 1970. Among those connected with the Howard intellectual community in some fashion were C. L. R. James, George Padmore, and historian of the Caribbean Eric Williams. While Padmore was a student for a brief period at Howard, Williams was active in the Howard community and served as a professor from 1941 to 1945. At Howard, Williams was prolific as a scholar and published numerous works, including many important articles on the role of the Negro in the Caribbean. Williams served as professor of social and political science and also chaired the research committee of the Anglo-American Caribbean Commission, which was a wartime organization created in 1943 and dedicated to coordinating American and English defense policies for the Caribbean. Williams's classes were said to be "so large that no classroom, no auditorium, was adequate accommodation, and the Chapel had to serve as classroom." Because Caribbean studies textbooks were inadequate and biased, Williams was known to compile works to assist him in his teaching. Perhaps the most important work that Williams published during his tenure at Howard was his seminal work, *Capitalism and Slavery*, which came out in 1944.

Williams not only influenced other public intellectuals but was shaped by them as well. One of the best examples of this mutual influence was the relationship he had with Bunche, Frazier, and Harris. Historian Kenneth Janken, in his biography *Rayford Logan and the Dilemma of the African American Intellectual*, asserted that Logan characterized the relationships among Bunche, Harris, Frazier, and Williams as those of a Marxist clique. Logan was said to have often disagreed with the group over the determining factor of strife in America and the world. Williams, Harris, Frazier, and Bunche adhered to class as the main issue dividing America and the world while Logan and other Howard professors stood on the premise that race was the deciding factor.[37]

Also in 1944, following a recent trip to the West Indies, Williams shared with Dean J. St. Clair Price his observations of the relationship between Howard and the West Indies:

> I feel that Howard University has an important role to play in West
> Indian life. Of this role it is only as yet dimly conscious. With the

overcrowding of English and Canadian universities, and as a result of closer ties between the West Indies and the United States, the number of West Indian students at Howard is likely to increase. I am convinced that Howard should consciously embrace this opportunity.[38]

Later in 1944, in a similar letter to Mordecai Johnson, Williams affirmed his earlier observation, saying that "The people of the Caribbean take as much pride in Howard University as if it were located in the Caribbean. . . . It is no exaggeration to say that in the West Indies one would find as enthusiastic and as successful a group of alumni as Howard can boast in any section of the United States." Williams went on to appraise the Pan-African consciousness of the Caribbean people. "The people of the Caribbean are vitally aware of the American Negro," he wrote. "They are keenly aware of men like Carver, Du Bois, . . . outstanding papers and personalities." Howard public intellectuals—namely, Logan and Frazier—paid a significant amount of attention to matters affecting the Caribbean, Latin America, and other areas of the African diaspora including Brazil.[39]

It is unclear to what extent C. L. R. James was active in the Howard University intellectual community. He was a very prominent global public intellectual who arrived in the United States in 1938 and also spent time in various Marxist and Trotskyite intellectual circles in London. Along with African political intellectuals Kwame Nkrumah, Jomo Kenyatta, and fellow Caribbean contemporary George Padmore, he was very active in the black intellectual network in London. Although James's relationship with Howard is not clear, he maintained a correspondence with Locke. James first opens one letter, for example, with the friendly greeting, "My dear Locke." James mentions having seen Locke "that day in 1951 on Sixth Avenue with my little son" and continues that his recent book on Herman Melville "would be our next medium of communication." James hoped his book would interest Locke "not only as politics but also as criticism." Further seeking Locke's support, James closed the letter by stating "as one who did not grow up in the U.S., and was not educated here, I am anxious that American scholars should discuss the book. I believe that you with your British experience and with your wide circle of friends and acquaintances can recognize the need for this in the discussion of a book to which I have given many years."[40] Evidence of correspondence between Locke and James is significant for several reasons. One is that it further demonstrates how Howard public intellectuals were both aware of and in communication with other black public intellectuals operating in national and international networks.

* * *

In addition to Williams and James, another significant scholar activist in this group was Haiti's Dantes Bellegarde. In 1931 Locke praised Bellegarde, saying, "Certainly no Haitian representative has been more warmly received and admired by American Negroes, and we deeply treasure the fraternal regard in which you have held us."[41] Bellegarde was very active in the Pan-African congresses of the early twentieth century. In fact, he was in attendance at the 1927 congress in New York. At this particular conference, he denounced U.S. Haitian policy as being racially motivated. He believed that the United States treated black Haitians differently than it did members of other nations. In a speech translated by Rayford Logan, Bellegarde argued that the United States was determined to demonstrate Haitian inferiority so as to further counteract demands for political equality by African Americans. The 1927 congress, at the urging of Bellegarde, passed a number of strident resolutions calling for an end to the U.S. occupation of Haiti.[42]

The relationship between Bellegarde and Logan extended back to these days where they both served on the Pan-African congresses. Kenneth Janken described Bellegarde as "the elder statesman [who] became Logan's mentor in Caribbean affairs." In 1926 Bellegarde invited Logan to Haiti to investigate the U.S. occupation there. Based on this trip, Logan wrote a number of magazine articles on the research he had gathered. For example, "The Haze in Haiti" appeared in the *Nation* in 1927, and "The New Haiti" appeared in *Opportunity* in April of that same year. In these pieces Logan, reflecting the influence of Bellegarde as his mentor, criticized America's occupation as an example of complacency, racism, and hypocrisy.[43]

From Logan's work on Haiti and earlier work on African colonies in the 1920s and 1930s, Logan was characterized as a strong proponent of Pan-Africanism and a brilliant and evolutionary scholar. Janken argues that three themes are apparent in Logan's works on Africa and Haiti. "The indigenous opposition to American or European imperialism," Janken argued, "is grounded in severe colonial abuses; the Western powers have an obligation to correct the injustices they have perpetrated, principally by training the various indigenous peoples in self-government; and power in Africa and the diaspora ought to be exercised by an appropriately civilized (western) indigenous middle class."[44]

On September 11, 1930, Bellegarde made perhaps the most important speech of his life. At the eleventh assembly of the League of Nations, he criticized the United States for its dangerous foreign policy goals. Bellegarde felt very strongly that American foreign policy posed a threat to the preservation of world peace. His speech was covered by the *New York Times:*

There was no doubt in his mind, Bellegarde said, that the United States "today controls the affairs of the world" and that Europe is "especially menaced in its economic life . . . and seeks to resist domination. . . . If Europe succeeds, then let Latin Americans beware, especially because the United States is already turning their direction and its trade with them is developing fast. . . ."

Mr. Bellegarde's quarrel was with the American policy, which he held was chiefly responsible for the mutual lack of confidence between the United States and Latin America, handicapping their trade and causing the latter to see "the shadow of a dreadnought behind each yankee dollar." . . . Until the American military occupation of Haiti has ended, he declared, fear and mistrust of the United States would continue among Latin Americans.[45]

In an assessment of Bellegarde, Howard professor Mercer Cook characterized the diplomat as being one who "courageously proved that American domination and the ruthless manner by which that domination was being achieved constituted a direct menace to European and Latin American security."[46]

The writings of Bellegarde over the period 1938–1957 evinced uneasiness about the apparent uncertainty of the rise and influence of Negritude and Marxism among younger black, Caribbean, and African intellectuals. At this point in his career, it seems, he was functioning as a "statesman" of sorts and was less active than in his younger years. He did not relinquish or retract his earlier views, however, and took the liberty to consistently raise those arguments again and again. In the twilight of his career, Bellegarde acted as an arbiter for border conflicts between the Dominican Republic and what is now known as Haiti. He took the opportunity to make countless public lectures throughout Canada and the United States. Also, while in the United States, Bellegarde took on a number of visiting professorships, most notably at Atlanta and Howard. He received honors from all over the world for his lifetime of service in diplomacy and international relations. Among the countries to honor him were Cuba, the Dominican Republic, Venezuela, Mexico, Canada, Chile, Brazil, and the United States.[47]

* * *

Mercer Cook, professor of Romance languages at Howard, was unique in that he served as a public intellectual in the academic arena, the political arena, and in various organizations within the global black intellectual community. Skilled in a number of languages, particularly French, Cook held council with some of the most noted African independence leaders such as Leopold Senghor and others. Cook played a central role in the intellectual community at Howard University and also in the global black intellectual community. Cook was the first ambassador from the United States to be assigned to the new Republic of Niger. Established on August 3, 1960, Niger was, as Cook put it, "a poor country with great potential, its people proud, but friendly toward the United States." Cook added that the United States could "cement its relationship with the government and people of Niger by extending to that country greater economic aid."[48]

In his diplomatic role in John F. Kennedy's administration, Cook worked extensively on behalf of newly independent African nations. He served as an intermediary between the United States and many African political intellectuals and leaders during a critical time in U.S.-African relations. The time of Cook's appointment coincided with a heightened sense of paranoia in the United States and around the world concerning the consequences of the Cold War. Public intellectuals such as Cook were vital to maintaining good relations with independent Africa. Cook was vital also in maintaining important ties between African peoples and African Americans. The coverage in the black press of the activities of Cook and other global black intellectuals served to connect black communities in the United States with their counterparts in Africa, the Caribbean, and around the world. Also, Cook and other members of the global black intellectual community in the Cold War climate established significant alliances with other oppressed groups among peoples of color.

On his return from Niger, Cook assessed the impact of President Kennedy's actions concerning the trouble at Ole Miss involving James Meredith, who integrated the institution on October 1, 1962. Cook believed that the Kennedy administration's "firm stand. . . . in getting James Meredith admitted to the University of Mississippi caused Africans to view Americans with added respect. . . . The showdown at 'Ole Miss' won President Kennedy and the United States Government a massive following in Niger." Furthermore, Cook added, such a response elicited "undoubtedly the same [reaction] in most of the newly independent African countries."[49]

Cook had a close relationship with the celebrated African writer René Maran. In a piece titled "René Maran (1887–1960)," Cook distills his personal assessment, characterizing Maran as "a kind of literary godfather to countless Africans and West Indians."[50] Maran was said to have "encouraged them with his counsel, his contacts, and above all, by his example." Cook concluded that "French Negro literature would have been something quite different if René Maran had not blazed the trail." Cook asserted that Maran possessed a "feeling of kinship with American Negroes" and discussed his relationship with other black intellectuals. Cook viewed Maran as closely connected with many African American intellectuals:

Despite all kinds of pressures and preoccupation, he tried to keep informed on developments in U.S. race relations and Negro writing. He maintained close personal contact with people like the late Carter G. Woodson, Alain Locke, and Charles S. Johnson. Numerous Afro-Americans still alive can testify to the warm hospitality extended them in the Maran apartment. And in many of his articles, the author of *Batouala*—who, incidentally never visited the States—told French readers about our struggle for civil rights.

In his tribute, Cook included the text of a letter that Maran had written him regarding Ralph Bunche and his winning the Nobel Peace Prize:

> Bunche, winner of the Nobel Peace Prize! It has been a long time since I have felt a joy so complete, so profound. Please offer to him all my compliments, all my congratulations. Both come from the heart of a man devoid of envy, and who has sacrificed his life to his race. And thank him for having given all of us the greatest comfort that we can enjoy. . . . A victory won by one of us is a victory for all. Bravo, Bunche! He's a good fellow. Really one! All my friendship . . .

In addition to other black, African, and Caribbean intellectuals, the public sphere of black public intellectualism at Howard and beyond included also a circle of important white and Jewish scholars. Among the most notable of these that influenced the Howard community were Melville Herskovits, Gunnar Myrdal, and Robert Park. Herskovits taught at Howard for a brief time and had close relationships with a number of Howard professors, especially Alain Locke. Myrdal spoke at Howard in 1944, at the time of the publication of his famous and very controversial work on the American race problem, *An American Dilemma*. Park headed and trained a group of black scholars in the Chicago School of sociology. Among the scholars he trained and whose work and orientation he influenced were Howard professor E. Franklin Frazier and Fisk professor and president Charles S. Johnson.[51]

In an article in *Phylon* titled, "An American Dilemma: The Racial Theories of Robert E. Park and Gunnar Myrdal," author R. Fred Wacker states that Gunnar Mrydal observed that the race conflict was grounded in the ignorance of whites—who were gradually coming to an understanding of the tremendous social costs of segregation, which he characterized as an "irrational and illegal caste system." On the contrary, Wacker characterized the Chicago view of race relations as espousing that group conflict reflected a natural competition for "jobs, space, and status." A discussion of Myrdal and Park is important to any discussion of Howard public intellectuals because it demonstrates two of the divergent views on race relations during the mid- to late 1940s and 1950s that influenced the thinking of many at Howard.

Race was such a stranglehold issue that it not only tied into conflict prominent black scholars such as Woodson and Du Bois but also ushered white and European scholars such as Park and Myrdal into heated debates, prompting intense ideological conflicts between them. Myrdal attacked Park and the Chicago School because the Chicago School view on race was in direct competition with his view. Both vied for paramount status among scholarly experts on the so-called Negro problem. In 1939,Park, supported by the work of students such as Frazier and Charles Johnson who were beginning to use neo-Freudian ideas in their work on racial dilemmas, suggested to Myrdal that anyone who was to undertake a serious study of American race relations had to understand psychoanalytic approaches to prejudice, particularly as they applied to the condition of African Americans in the United States.[52]

Although Myrdal involved a number of Howard scholars (including Ralph Bunche and Abram Harris) in working on his 1940 study of race relations, his own work overshadowed the others' research and he garnered more of the credit for the entire project. With their immeasurable contribution they deserved to be given larger roles, for Howard public intellectuals contributed mightily to the important analysis that the study elicited. The larger American dilemma for Howard public intellectuals, as well as other black scholars, was that both segregation and the dilemma of race continued to serve as tremendous barriers against their full recognition and involvement as American citizens and prominent scholars. Furthermore, the stigma of race continued to haunt Howard public intellectuals long after the work of Park, the Chicago School, and Mrydal became grounded in public consciousness. Another irony is that although Myrdal (a Swedish economist) and Robert Park (a white sociologist) are still common names in the research of theories involving race and race relations, many of the Howard public intellectuals remain either obscure, unknown, or greatly undervalued and underappreciated.[53]

* * *

Howard's black public intellectuals operated within a large network of scholars and organizations in the United States and around the globe despite the constraints of segregation at home and colonialism abroad. To be sure, their scholarship addressed matters of broad public concern, which in turn reflected their advocacy of such issues as equality, civil rights, and an end to colonialism and segregation. Many of Howard's public intellectuals were involved in organizations ranging from the domestically centered NAACP to the globally minded AMSAC. These public intellectuals also reached out to the greater public through publication of articles and other pieces in the black press. Many lectured and spoke at various black churches in the Washington community and around the country. Abroad, the Howard public intellectuals—in efforts ranging from their work at the Pan-African congresses in the early twentieth century to their participation in organizations such as the American Negro Leadership Conference on Africa—demonstrated their Pan-African concerns and identification. They worked alongside African and Caribbean intellectuals on U.S. soil, as well as internationally on the African continent, in Europe, and in Asia. Howard public intellectuals were not singular or uniform in voice or in terms of outreach. The support and public outreach of these intellectuals was as individual as the personalities and research interests of each scholar. However, a common thread running through their work—in advocating freedom and equality for people of African descent and especially in challenging segregation at home and abroad—was a tie that bound them together as black public intellectuals.

CHAPTER FIVE

Bridging Theory and Practice

Africana Policy Studies and Black Studies Institutes

OWARD UNIVERSITY FUNCTIONED AS A prototypical black studies institute. Howard public intellectuals contributed research in various areas of Negro, early Africana, and African studies, including the nascent field of Africana policy studies, developed by the group Michael Winston characterizes as "the policy research nucleus." Their advocacy of various domestic and international institutes and organizations promoted an early transnational black studies during the postwar period after World War II and the Cold War of the 1950s and early 1960s.[1]

Howard intellectuals' somewhat ambivalent support of black studies coincided with their active involvement in the formation of various research institutes—from the early 1930s and 1940s to the Black Power era of the late 1960s and 1970s. What are some of the characteristics and components of Howard's nascent black studies institute? The following analysis provides a framework for examining the structure of contemporary black studies institutes and situates the Howard model as a comparative prototype. Successive institutes and current black public intellectuals were modeled to mirror Howard and its public intellectuals.

There were evident relationships between Howard intellectuals and those whom Martin Kilson, Robert Boynton, and others call "the New Black Intellectuals," or black public intellectuals. Many stellar scholars who were not incorporated into the contemporary media-driven black public intellectual collective were mentored and influenced by Howard scholars. Even as we look at the Howard group, our definition and understanding of what constitutes a black public intellectual needs expansion. For one, Howard scholar Ethelbert Miller argues that Henry Louis Gates used the model of the Howard community to formulate his model of the "Dream Team" at Harvard. This assertion, which Gates readily admits, is not surprising considering the close relationship over the years between Harvard and Howard, not only in the production of black studies intellectuals but also in the development of Negro and black studies as they evolved in the late 1960s.[2]

Unmistakably, Howard intellectuals played a vital role in creating the fields of Negro, African, and early Africana studies, as well as in pioneering Africana policy studies, despite the tremendous constraints placed in their way by racism and segregation. Both black men and women were significant members of the Howard University intellectual community, although historians have consistently emphasized the men above the women, a fact that has hampered an accurate representation of the community. Black women scholars and administrators left an indelible mark on the shaping of Howard University as a cathedral of intellectual excellence. For instance, historian Merze Tate contributed significant studies over the years of her tenure at Howard. Similarly, historian Lorraine A. Williams provided important leadership for the history department while producing seminal scholarship in Pan-African studies. Bibliophile Dorothy Porter contributed to intellectual debates at Howard while spearheading the impressive collection of Moorland-Spingarn Research Center.[3]

In ascribing to the role of scholar activists, Howard public intellectuals promoted research in transnational black studies while they also demonstrated the varieties of black public intellectualism beyond the ebony tower. To be sure, these scholar activists were a driving force in the nascent movements to establish African, African American, and Africana studies in the United States. They were central to the political movements such as civil rights, African and Caribbean independence, and anti-apartheid that served as backdrop and source material for these studies.

In developing what can be called Africana policy studies, a group of professors at Howard tailored much of their research to practical ends, whereby they influenced policymakers and policy decisions around figures, events, and movements pertaining to the evolving African New World in North America, Europe, Africa, and Latin America. These professors—whom Howard historian Michael Winston in his article "Through the Back Door: Academic Racism and the Negro Scholar in Historical Perspective" calls the "policy research nucleus"—promoted pioneering research on the effects of existing policies on African Americans and peoples of African descent around the globe. Winston included in this nucleus Rayford Logan, Sterling Brown, Ralph Bunche, E. Franklin Frazier, Abram Harris, Charles H. Thompson, and Charles Houston, primarily because they dedicated a significant amount of research and advocacy to developing policy studies as they affected Africana peoples the world over.[4]

Although those named by Winston certainly fit within this group, more Howard public intellectuals—whether individually through their independent research, in collaborations with one another, or in terms of service on policy-related matters—contributed to the development, implementation, and evaluation of policies concerning Africana peoples globally. These intellectuals can be considered as laying foundations for a nascent Africana policy studies at Howard. The nucleus developed and proposed cutting-edge research designed to fill the voids in the existing scholarship on peoples of African descent. Their research evidenced practical policy recommendations, organizations, and activities, which added flesh to the theoretical constructs. Though underappreciated by policy officials, these scholars, through their research and activism, held sway in many middle-class circles and organizations in black communities in the nation's capital, around the United States, and all over the world.

Howard intellectuals developed a de facto black policy studies institute. This institute never materialized in the manner that contemporary think tanks developed. It was not a uniform school of thought. Nevertheless, through the applicability of their research on various subjects of interest to the black community, these thinkers made substantial strides in impacting the development, implementation, and evaluation of public policy. According to Charles Henry, during the 1930s, Bunche, Harris, and Frazier as well as other Howard colleagues "produced a body of work that broke sharply with the preceding generation of black scholars and contributed to a paradigm that remained dominant until the sixties." Theirs was a class-based paradigm. Colleagues like Locke, on the other hand, concentrated on culture as the focus of paradigm formation and analysis (Locke developed a theory of cultural pluralism).[5]

Even with public policy connections, the Howard group evidenced a variety of research and public stances. For instance, Sterling Brown became a man of the people, as a significant poet, cultural critic, and scholar speaking for and consulting with groups as diverse as the Washington chapter of the National Urban League and the New School for African Thought.[6] E. Franklin Frazier, conditioned by his disciplinary training under Robert Park, impacted public policy primarily as a sociologist writing on Negro youth, juvenile delinquency, and the Negro family. In some instances, ideological differences between these scholars hampered the degree and frequency with which they could collaborate on policy projects.

Despite its impressive array of intellectuals, there is debate whether Howard ever developed a definite discipline of black studies. The university's potential to impact the public policy field was weakened by a lack of sustainable resources allocated to the social sciences. However, Howard intellectuals certainly impacted the study of race and public policy analysis. For example, the activities of this group included research (particularly by Alain Locke and Sterling Brown) on segregation and discrimination in America. Frazier, Bunche, and Harris produced important policy research on the implications of New Deal policies on African American life in the nation's capital as well as around the country.[7] Scholars such as Merze Tate and Rayford Logan published probing research and critical commentaries on American foreign policy abroad, notably concerning African decolonization, Latin American independence, and New Guinea's self-determination. Frazier, Brown, Locke, Thompson, and Bunche developed considerable policy research and critique examining the state of black culture and institutions, including the black community, black middle class, the black family, adult education in the black community, and civil rights organizations.[8]

Furthermore, they were also influential in creating and maintaining numerous black think tanks in America and around the world during the mid- to late twentieth century. These include the Institute of the Black World, Fisk University's Race Relations Institute, the International Society for the Scientific Study of Race Relations, the Research Institute for the Study of Man, and others.[9] Even today the imprint of the intellectual community at Howard can be seen in a number of existing think tanks, such as those associated with universities including Harvard's W. E. B Du Bois Institute and the Institute of African American Research at the University of North Carolina–Chapel Hill, as well as those functioning independently in the public and private sectors, namely, the Joint Center for Political and Economic Studies, founded primarily by Howard public intellectuals.

In examining the historical legacy of the Capstone's policy group, it is important to analyze the models and assessments advanced by Howard scholars. Undoubtedly, Frazier's approach to Africana policy studies was influenced by his commitment to the Chicago sociological school of thought. Contemporary scholars have raised serious questions regarding the applicability of Frazier's research methodology to issues affecting black America. Most apparent is the heated debate over Frazier's research on the black family, including the manner by which his research led to the Moynihan report, which, undergirded by its black pathology thesis, has remained a public policy scourge for most black studies scholars.[10]

Similarly, Alain Locke's research on black music as a social indicator represents seminal subject matter for black policy studies. In addition to his work on black music, his edited work *When Peoples Meet* that appeared first in 1942 (reissued in 1946) evidences his critical approach to culture and policy issues, which could be called cultural pluralism and which he often characterized as "culture contacts."[11]

As Howard functioned as a research institute, its public intellectuals engaged in various efforts to establish a fully functioning black studies entity during the golden years from 1926 to 1970. Kelly Miller, Alain Locke, and others worked to build a sense of community around this notable collection of black scholars, mainly attributed to the leadership of Mordecai Johnson, Howard's complicated and visionary first black president. Their efforts were driven by their goal to marshal and mobilize a community of scholars that would be dedicated to the advancement of the Negro in America and around the world.

Miller and others attempted to link the American Negro Academy to Howard, and they achieved some measure of success. Many of the Howard intellectuals were among the ANA's exclusive membership, as historian Alfred Moss argues. As Logan and Winston note, the ANA had even more of a central connection to Howard than may be fully understood, because from 1895 to 1897 Alexander Crummell taught at the Capstone, and it was during this time that he formed the exclusive academy in D.C. Howard's board of trustees also allowed the ANA to hold meetings on the Howard campus throughout much of the first decade of the early twentieth century (before the academy's demise). Despite the lack of a formal sustainable connection between the ANA and Howard University, the ANA's intellectual impact carried forth as its Howard contingent worked diligently to establish the Howard University Center for the Study of the Negro. Important among the center's components was the interdisciplinary nature of many of the scholars involved in this collective, including E. Franklin Frazier, Rayford Logan, Alain Locke, Kelly Miller, Charles Thompson, and others.

Two other institutional arms of Howard's de facto policy institute were the development of Charles Thompson's *Journal of Negro Education*, established in 1932, and the *Journal of Religious Thought*, founded by the dean of the school of religion, William Stuart Nelson, a theologian and successor to Benjamin Mays. Both the *JNE* and the *JRT* proved to be essential in the making of this community, and they still exist as viable scholarly journals. The *JNE* was a medium whereby Howard intellectuals and their contemporaries, members of the national and global black intellectual communities, from W. E. B. Du Bois to Preston Williams, could publish much of their work. Thus they could contribute research to the development of African American, African, African diaspora, and Africana studies as well as policy research. The *JNE* published annual yearbooks that focused on various aspects of American race relations and issues of concern to blacks at the time, including segregated education and health care issues.

Additionally, by establishing annual institutes, convocations, and conferences, the school of religion mined the areas of African American religious studies, black theology, and other derivatives. Two major conferences—a 1944 institute on Christianity and American race relations and a 1969 gathering examining black theology—demonstrate a continuity of thinking whereby the *JRT* functioned as the publication vehicle for Howard's public theologians, focusing on the study of race relations, religion, and black theology. *The Christian Way in Race Relations*, edited by Nelson and published in 1948, as well as a black theology special summer supplement in the *JRT*, published in 1969, reflect the critical role of black religious thought at Howard.

Other aspects of the virtual Howard black studies institute were the conferences that Howard scholars both developed and hosted, including the History Series and Social Sciences Series, and the Institutes of the School of Religion, just to name a few. Howard as a nascent black studies institute invited a number of important guest speakers to campus, everyone from Du Bois and Richard Wright to Mary McLeod Bethune, and others. Howard scholars also had an informal speakers' series in place, which allowed them to undertake various speaking engagements in the greater Washington, D.C., area, around the country, and throughout the world. These examples contribute to the argument that the Howard University intellectual community functioned as an impressive and significant nascent black studies institute.

In addition to developing the *Journal of Religious Thought*, Howard also promoted what could be called an early form of black church studies, and African American religious studies, through the work and activity of scholars such as Howard Thurman and Benjamin Mays. According to Lawrence Carter, Thurman and Mays asserted a sort of "theology of race relations," which was given a voice in annual convocations seeking to address various issues of black clergy and the black church vis-à-vis mainstream society.

Black church studies during the golden years at Howard were furthered by the efforts of the school of religion in developing an annual institute of religion. Organized by Dean William Stuart Nelson, this institute of religion met at Howard from 1944 to 1948 to discuss the role of religion and Christianity in addressing the social ills prevalent in post–World War II America. Even though Mays left to become the president of Morehouse College in 1940 and Thurman moved to San Francisco in 1944, their impact on these institutes was felt both in their participation in subsequent institutes and in the groundwork they laid for black church studies scholarship and the mentoring of young scholars in the school of religion.

Their pioneering work provided a strident critique of Christianity's inability to properly address prevalent social inequities of the day—namely, racial segregation, sexism, and classism. These scholars were forerunners of post-1960s black liberation theology. In fact, many of the notable pre–Black Power Christian intellectuals were working or studying at Howard University in the school of religion during some portion of its golden years. Mays and Thurman constructed a bridge of black religious thought, spanning from their day to the time of Howard black theologians such as J. Deotis Roberts, who, with his contemporaries, moved the discussion of black religion from merely challenging mainline white Christian church studies to advancing a self-defined black theology.

By their research, public intellectual activity, and activism, Howard religion scholars connected Christianity and theological and religious research to the immediate concerns of the surrounding black communities of Washington, D.C., the United States, and even around the world. The global nature of their theological and religious research helped promote black studies abroad. In this way, they incorporated traditional religious studies into the framework of African American and Africana studies.

Howard scholars were affiliated with, participated in, and heavily influenced the formation and activities of various institutes and research centers around the nation and the world. On May 23, 1931, at Virginia Union University, while discussing the merits of a speech made by Dr. Gordon Blaine Hancock at Columbia, Rayford Logan in the pages of the *Baltimore African American* suggested that "there be made a coordinated study of the Negro." He went on to argue for the establishment at Howard of "an institute for the study of Negroes." The paper reported that the institute should have, on faculty, "both leading anthropologists and psychologists, in an impartial attempt to discover the contributions of the Negro to civilization." Logan added that there should also be created a "chair of abnormal psychology for the study of the deluded Negro."[12]

The quest to establish such a center or institute for the study of the Negro took on many forms at the Capstone, especially during its golden years. There are many connections between Howard, its public intellectual collective, and the ANA. It must be noted that a number of black women intellectuals, such as Anna Julia Cooper, were also affiliated with the ANA.[13] The attempt to situate Howard as the home of the ANA was furthered by the efforts of professors Alain Locke and Rayford Logan in the late 1920s and early 1930s, and it continued as mathematics and sociology professor Kelly Miller devised the framework for the National Negro

Library, which also incorporated a very definite institute component in its structure.

Howard professors (namely, Sterling Brown) also promoted what historian David Roediger calls, in regard to black intellectuals, the nascent field of whiteness studies. In 1941 Otto Klineberg, professor at Columbia University, sent an invitation to Sterling Brown, Howard poet and cultural critic, concerning his participation in the Institute of Race Relations event taking place in New York City. The institute was sponsored by the American Friends Service Committee and the Committee on Race Relations. Klineberg's letter indicated he had repeatedly contacted the very busy and sought-after Brown about confirming his participation in the institute. Klineberg requested that Brown "give one morning lecture on Negro Literature, and an evening's readings from your own poems." Here, as many others had both before and after him, Klineberg recognized Brown's central role as the authority on Negro literature in America and as the folk poet laureate of America—even if the nation's literary leaders did not recognize him as one of the country's great poets. Klineberg expressed to Brown "his wish" that "we had more of your time so that we could hear something also about the Negro in 'White Literature' or something along those lines." In many ways, this statement by Klineberg points to Sterling Brown's influence on whiteness studies as well as on black studies.[14]

In fact, Brown and many black scholars at Howard—including, among their contemporaries, figures like James Baldwin, James Weldon Johnson, C. L. R. James, and others—were the pioneers of whiteness studies. Brown, in his writings, for example, examined white characters in Negro literature (a version of the white image in the Negro mind, before Mia Bay and George Frederickson's pioneering work on those subjects), among other related subjects.[15] Brown, like Du Bois, was noted for characterizing white America as possessing "a jaundiced view of life behind the Veil." In this sense, Brown struggled to correct misrepresentations of black racial identity in relationship to mainstream American society. Brown countered evident misrepresentations "by providing authentic views of Black life by lifting the Veil for all to see clearly and steadily the humanity of Negro people." In short, these "authentic views" of quintessential black cultural identity were best epitomized in Brown's estimation from the perspective of black folk culture.[16]

As they confronted racist scholarship (as Jacqueline Goggin writes of Carter Woodson), black public intellectuals at Howard and elsewhere also engaged in and began to define the subject of whiteness and its impact on the development of blackness—as well as the result of what Locke and Frazier often called "cultural contacts." Therefore, it stands to reason that the Howard group influenced a very real form of whiteness studies in a time (the post–World War II and early Cold War eras) when the meaning of whiteness and race took on new definitions and greater significance. As within other areas of study involving race, the consummate public intellectual Brown and virtually all the members of his Howard cohort are now forgotten, even though they were forerunners who contributed mightily to the development of these disciplines, which still engage academic and public discourse and still connect and apply academic theory to socioeconomic challenges and realities in surrounding communities of this nation, particularly those of urban areas.

Finally, Klineberg requested of Brown a bibliography of sources dealing with black literature and race. He sought to arrange a public dialogue befitting of a public intellectual of Brown's stature. "Perhaps if you are not too tired," Klineberg suggested, "we can work in an informal discussion of the material" dealing with white literature "during the afternoon." In addition to influencing whiteness studies, Sterling Brown (as Fahamisha Patricia Brown correctly notes) also influenced the area of black literary studies. As one of Brown's most noted pupils, Houston Baker has taken and legitimized black literary studies as a significant academic field.[17]

Howard scholars played a vital role in the establishment and functioning of the American Council of Learned Societies (ACLS) Committee on Negro Studies. This effort arose from liberal white intellectuals' emerging concern about race and black history. The work of Melville Herskovits with the Committee on Negro Studies is one example of this changing climate of racial understanding on the part of liberal white intellectuals. Other examples of the climate change include the emergence and influence of the New Deal's slave narrative project, the Farm Security Administration, and critical scholarly analyses of race relations such as John Dollard's classic study *Caste and Class in a Southern Town*. Historian Robert Harris Jr. notes that ACLS's "designation of its Committee on Negro Studies in 1941" was designed for the purpose of "anchoring both the Black scholar and the study of Afro-American life and culture in American scholarship." Furthermore, "the Committee on Negro Studies was developed as a counterweight to the Carnegie Corporation study of the Negro" led by Gunnar Myrdal. While Myrdal was developing his project in 1939, ACLS secretary Waldo Leland "suggested that Melville Herskovits . . . organize a Conference on Negro Studies." The ACLS was basically competing with the Social Science Research Council (SSRC), which served "as an informal advisor" for Myrdal. Also, philosophically speaking, the ACLS believed that it held a more "humanistic perspective" to the study of the Negro in America than the SSRC.[18]

It was anticipated that the Conference on Negro Studies "would naturally" attract and "include Black scholars working in the field of Negro Studies." The only problem posed to Herskovits and the organizers was where to hold the meeting in Washington, D.C., where the ACLS head-quarters was located. The challenge was to find housing and dining for an interracial gathering of scholars. Herskovits, who had taught at How-ard University in 1925, finally decided to contact former colleague Ralph Bunche about having the conference at Howard. Bunche took care of all the arrangements—and it is ironic and strange that, although Herskovits depended upon Bunche's position and hospitality to secure Howard as the site, "he [later] opposed inviting him to join the Committee on Negro Studies" because he felt that Bunche's level of productivity had declined in the intervening years and, he thought, this justified his exclusion.[19]

The Conference on Negro Studies was held at Howard University on March 29 and 30, 1940. Twenty-three scholars attended the conference, and almost half of those were black, including Howard scholars. The "pur-pose" of the conference "was to allow a small group of scholars to exchange information on the state of research and to suggest measures to stimulate and improve the study of the Negro . . . mainly through interdisciplinary cooperation." This goal was achieved, as the scholars in attendance repre-sented various different disciplines: physical and cultural anthropology, history, political science, sociology, economics, psychology, philosophy, literature, and the arts. In total six scholars presented research on topics such as Latin America, African cultural survivals, and African economics. One of the four black scholars who presented their research was histo-rian Lawrence D. Reddick, who at the time was the curator of the New York Public Library's Schomburg Collection. Reddick "raised an issue that became the committee's nemesis." He called for the committee to wage a battle against the racial bias inherent in American scholarship, which diminished the importance of studying African Americans and worked to deny recognition and support for black Americans.

The attendees recommended that a permanent body be formed to carry on the work started at the conference. The permanent body would above all be charged with the goals of promoting interdisciplinary research in Negro studies. It would also be given the duty of removing barriers to Negro students conducting research in the area, creating accessible micro-film centers, publishing important interdisciplinary work, and organizing a panel to function as a clearinghouse for funding initiatives. To carry out these duties a standing committee was formed, which included Herskov-its as the chair, Reddick, Sterling Brown, Lorenzo Turner, Otto Klineberg of Columbia, and others. The committee had the function of "serving as a developmental panel," by which "to encourage research and teaching in an emerging field." The first task facing the committee was to develop a report on the status of Negro studies. Out of the eight selected to serve on the committee, Brown, Reddick, and Turner were the only blacks.[20]

Howard intellectuals played a central role presenting research and informed scholarly commentary at various academic institutes throughout the nation. Many members of the Howard intellectual community were frequent and active participants in another major initiative designed to promote the study of race and public policy, Charles S. Johnson's Race Relations Institute at Fisk University. This institute was formed in the fall of 1942 as a result of a collaboration between the Rosenwald Fund and the American Missionary Association. Fisk's Charles S. Johnson, as Patrick Gilpin writes, "brought an impressive record of public service, research and publication to the task." He took great pains to amass the nation's best and brightest researchers on various aspects of the black experience, making a great effort to highlight and include many of the nation's most impressive black scholars, such as Howard's talented tenth, including Sterling Brown, Charles H. Houston, and others.[21] His Race Relations Institute functioned as a public policy forum where issues such as equal education and segregation in general were discussed, debated, and couched as strategy. The RRI functioned in the same way that the *Journal of Negro Education* functioned as a policy journal, and the Howard University network of scholars operated as a policy institute. The three formed a close-knit policy nexus for black America during the Jim Crow and Cold War era.

In addition to being involved in the Institute of Race Relations at Columbia, in Charles S. Johnson's Race Relations Institute at Fisk, and on the ACLS Committee on Negro Studies, Sterling Brown (as many of his colleagues at Howard) was also involved in promoting African studies and African American studies on a transnational and international scale.

In 1943 Dr. Fernando Ortiz was named director of an International Institute of Afro-American Studies. This institute was established "during a recent session of the First Inter-American Congress of Demography in Mexico City." A writer for the *African American* reported that the likelihood of "American racial prejudice" was believed to have "thwarted an attempt to set up this organization in the United States." Adding to the challenges offered by the American race problem, the reporter noted, "opposition from the delegation from Argentina" also blocked any chance of such a group being established in America. Members of the institute's executive committee included Howard's Alain Locke, as well as Melville Herskovits and Arthur Ramos. Sterling Brown was also a very active and influential member of this group as evidenced by his correspondence with Ortiz.

Even in the 1940s, then, members of the Howard University community of scholars were aware, as other black scholars across the nation and around the world, that black studies and its related offshoots were global phenomena, and they were active in making those international connections. Through their research and their participation in international forums, seminars, and institutes such as the International Institute of Afro-American Studies, they helped forge the path for the future disciplines of African diaspora studies and the like.[22]

Following the Conference on Negro Studies at Howard in 1940, Howard public intellectuals continued their efforts to establish a nascent form of the discipline at the university, as well as to establish associated contacts in international and domestic contexts. The committee continued the work of the 1940 conference and even extended its work transnationally. In a letter to members of the Committee on Negro Studies, Herskovits enclosed a letter from Jorge A. Vivo, editor of the Mexican society's proposed journal, *AFROAMERICA*. Herskovits indicated that he had contacted Vivo, "accepting the invitation to be a member of the Editorial Committee." He also noted that "the title of the journal will not be unfamiliar, since it was the one tentatively agreed on at the Washington meeting with Professor Ortiz and others."[23]

The enclosed document, which Herskovits referred to as dated October 24, 1944, evidenced that Vivo had asked him to "become a member of the Editorial Committee of *AFROAMERICA*, the review of the International Institute of Afro-American Studies." The document also named Fernando Ortiz as the director of the institute, and Herskovits and Alain Locke as contributors, along with Carlos Basauri of Mexico, Auguste Remy Bastian of Haiti, Arthur Ramos of the United States, and Julio le Riverend of Cuba. The official title of the journal was to be the *Journal of the International Institute of Afro-American Studies*. It would be published twice a year, in Spanish, English, Portuguese, and French. The document also mentioned that the journal would contain sections dealing with doctrinal issues, reviews of books and articles, and notes and news. Besides Herskovits on the editorial committee, there were also Locke, Ortiz, Richard Pattee of Puerto Rico, Jean Price Mars of Haiti, Ramos of Brazil, and Vivo of Mexico. Finally, there was a listing of "collaboredores," which included Aimé Césaire of the French Antilles, and Howard scholars Eric Williams of the British Antilles, E. Franklin Frazier, Sterling A. Brown, Rayford Logan, and Charles Wesley. Other notable leaders and intellectuals forming a part of this group were Du Bois, Woodson, Charles S. Johnson, Lorenzo Turner, and Walter White. There were also representatives from Argentina, Brazil, Canada, Colombia, Cuba, Ecuador, Haiti, Mexico, Perú, Puerto Rico, the Dominican Republic, Uruguay, and Venezuela.[24]

* * *

While there are many examples of individual members of the Howard faculty participating on committees and in conferences dealing with global black studies, other examples abound detailing more institutional support and appreciation for such studies. Howard continued to position itself as a top-notch research center as can be seen in its efforts to build its library collections in African diasporan studies. For example, the acquisitions of "a gift of sixty-eight volumes of the works of Cuban authors" in 1943, which were "presented to the Howard University Library" by Dr. Paul G. Menocal, mayor of Havana, indicates the obvious attempt by President Johnson and others to amass valuable material on the global black experience. This particular collection certainly does not stand alone among Howard's acquisitions, but it represents the commitment made by the university to Latin American studies and its ability to garner such important resource materials.[25]

The acquisition of materials such as the Cuban collection was a step toward creating the National Negro Museum and Library at Howard, a project that Kelley Miller had championed since the 1920s. Miller had envisioned that the museum would function as a research center and institute, whereby scholars at the Capstone (which Miller believed should be the National Negro University) would produce significant scholarship and inform, educate, and engage the black community of D.C. on important issues facing it. Half of the vision involving the building of an important collection of materials on the global black experience was firmly accomplished. It is demonstrated in the legacy left in the form of the Moorland-Spingarn Research Center, one of the most extensive research repositories of materials on the Africana experience in the world. The research center was formed in 1973 from the Moorland-Spingarn Collection of materials on the black experience.

Kelly Miller's initial dream of a National Negro Museum and Library was revived in 1979. Opening on February 10, 1979, the Howard University Museum contained "more than 150 artifacts, rare documents, and illustrations from the United States, the Caribbean, and Africa." Michael Winston, then director of the research center, characterized the museum as "a teaching museum, a museum of Black history." The museum's initial exhibit showcased themes of American slavery, the abolitionist movement, the Civil War, Reconstruction, and the black family during slavery. It even included belongings of antislavery leader Frederick Douglass—namely, his spectacles.[26]

Despite such an auspicious museum opening, however, Miller's institute, though supported by Logan, Locke, and other public intellectuals at Howard, just fizzled out, requiring Howard faculty to travel elsewhere to promote black studies via institutes and forums. The reasons for this are still not fully understood, though two major reasons for its demise can be attributed to the untimely deaths of Miller in 1939 and before him the unexpected death of the other leading advocate of the museum and institute, English scholar Benjamin Brawley. Furthermore, there was a continual shortage of funds because of the inability of President Johnson and the Howard intellectuals to identify and secure alternative sources of funding.[27]

Miller and the other scholars had intended the National Negro Library and Museum to be an institute as well. In a document entitled "The Origin of the Idea," Miller laid out the original plan and program for the library and museum. In a section entitled "A Bureau of Research," Miller noted that "a program of research" should be created "in connection with the Museum and Library" and "should be encouraged and related to it." The proposal also addressed the problem of the possible duplication of research, stating that "various studies now being conducted by individuals could be correlated in planning and operation so that duplication of efforts would be avoided and as far as possible cooperation obtained."[28]

The document detailed the "widespread movement" that had begun in American universities "about ten years ago for the promotion of research." As a result of this effort, various "institutes for research were established at several universities." Two of the most prominent were at the University of North Carolina–Chapel Hill and the University of Virginia. It was noted that, as a result, "faculty activity in productive research has been stimulated and the research and scholarly atmosphere of these universities have been strengthened." It was also indicated that books and pamphlets "are also representative of research influence." Miller asserted that "similar results can be expected at Howard University."[29]

He believed that if such an institute could be created, and with emphasis on this aspect of the work, such an effort would result in "a complete transformation [in] faculty attitudes and university program." Miller concluded with a powerful statement of the feasibility of establishing the library and what it could accomplish:

> The pursuit of knowledge in its research point of view and contributions to knowledge would be added to the dissemination of knowledge. One of the objectives of the Institute would be the promotion of the investigation and study of the life, art, history, and ethnology of the Negro and Negroid peoples. Projects which would comprise the program of the Institute would be submitted for determination to an Institute Council. It is hoped that funds can be secured for the financial support of these projects. The state legislatures have made research grants to these universities and the foundations have made appropriations toward the research program. It would certainly seem that

appropriations for research could be reasonably requested from the Congress of the United States and foundations as a part of the Museum and Library project. The world still awaits the great works of Negro authorship and the publication of researches in ethnology, anthropology, folklore, art, history, music, government, sociology, economics, and education. A real university must stimulate research and make it possible.[30]

In this effort to establish a Negro Library and Museum, to function also as an institute, Kelly Miller sought the support of countless scholars at Howard, scholars around the country, and other influential Americans both black and white. Beyond Howard's campus, Miller had the support of such prominent individuals as J. A. Gregg, bishop of the AME Church, Channing H. Tobias, and Hebert Putnam, a librarian at the Library of Congress, among others. Miller's support garnered beyond Howard's campus evidenced the growing public appeal for his idea of a Negro Library and Museum.

He also had the support of President Mordecai Johnson. In July 1938, Johnson expressed to Miller that he was "glad to note the vigorous interest, which you are continuing to take in relation to our collection of books, art objects, etc. by and about the Negro." Johnson went on to state that he had asked Professor Brawley, chairman of the University Committee on the Library, "to recommend a special committee, which will give vigorous attention to the form and promotion of this project." In August 1938, Johnson appointed a special committee for the project and asked that Miller "accept membership on this committee" and to work with Brawley and others. Others who served on the committee included Charles H. Thompson, Frazier, Harris, Wesley, Bunche, Charles Eaton Burch, Mays, Locke, Logan, and Nabrit.[31]

Miller's proposal called also for the creation of a Howard University Press, which "would have as its purpose the publication of monographs and studies, which grow out of the work of the Museum and Library." It was understood that the press would have its own editor, director-manager, and board of directors. Eventually, the press came into existence but not as a part of the proposed Museum, Library, and Institute.[32]

By November 1938 Miller could hardly contain his enthusiasm and excitement as the idea of the National Negro Library and Museum was launched. In a letter to Professor Guy B. Johnson, he stated that he was "delighted beyond expression at the action of the Howard trustees in adopting the proposal." He confided, "My dream of a quarter of a century is now on its way to consummation," and he went on to thank Johnson "for furthering the project through your committee." He ended the letter with a triumphant expression of hope and belief that "all forces and factors within the university, as well as friends everywhere, who are interested in the cause of higher education of the Negro will rally to support . . . the National Negro Library and Museum, now that the undertaking has been launched."[33]

The implications of Miller's death in 1939 and Brawley's death in 1938 as well as an illness that came upon President Johnson were far-reaching and devastating to the movement for the National Negro Library and Museum. It is well documented in his papers that Miller had considerable support for this effort before fate seemingly took it all away. Another letter to Johnson, written before Miller's death, evinces his sorrow, as support for his project lost momentum:

> Since the death of Dr. Brawley, concurrent with the illness of the President last February, the movement has been at a standstill during the past four months. The Committee has been without a head and consequently wholly unable to proceed. The misfortune of such a delay which circumstances made inevitable must be apparent to you. The sudden halting of promotion and solicitation at this time is most unfortunate. To let the iron cool after it has been heated to the melting point jeopardizes the success of the entire project.[34]

Correspondence between Brawley and Miller indicates that the initiative had been making great progress, and it would probably have continued to do so. Had the two lived, it is more than a remote possibility that the institute would have lived and functioned fully because of its support from President Johnson and many of the other public intellectuals of Howard, who served on the committee.

Also, as it intended, such an institute could have coordinated the research efforts of many scholars at Howard. Such an institute could have allowed Charles H. Thompson's *Journal of Negro Education* to focus even more than it did on segregation and inequality in higher education. Had Miller's idea come to fruition, Howard would have been the first major black college and university to have such a research institute, thereby preceding Fisk University's Race Relations Institute by three years. As it stands, however, with the deaths of Miller and Brawley, so died the movement and a considerable opportunity for Howard to become the leading intellectual center in the entire country, with the National Negro Library that Miller envisioned.[35]

There were other attempts to establish a Center for the Study of the Negro or related institutes at Howard. In 1928 Rayford Logan, then at Virginia Union University, in a letter to Alain Locke argued that "Dr. Johnson broached the subject of a center for the study of the Negro as you suggest."

Logan had conveyed to Johnson "that the idea had been germinating in my mind for some time." He ended the letter by saying that, "if such men as you and Dr. Johnson sponsor it, I am sure that we shall see its fruition."[36]

In 1940 Logan, by then at Howard, informed Dean Charles H. Thompson of the College of Liberal Arts that an institute on Latin American affairs should also be established at Howard. Logan's interest in Latin American studies went back to a master's thesis he had written on the mandate system in Haiti, and to the influence of one of his mentors, Haitian diplomat Dantes Bellegarde. To the importance of establishing an institute on Latin American studies, Logan argued:

> I feel that the question of Latin America will continue to be of such vital importance to all Americans and especially to colored Americans that an Institute on Latin American Affairs some time during the next school year would be extremely valuable to the University Community. Such an Institute would serve not only to show our continued interest but also to remind scholars and the general public that the problem of the Negro should not be ignored. In the event that such an Institute should be held, the committee sponsoring it would most assuredly welcome the cooperation of the Committee on Cultural Relations with Latin America.[37]

Although the institute Logan was referring to was more like a onetime event, it nevertheless signaled the apparent interest on the part of Howard intellectuals in having some kind of intellectual forum in which to discuss important scholarly and policy issues of the day. Whereas the momentum to establish a freestanding institute for the study of the Negro had died with Miller and Brawley, Howard intellectuals continued to find other outlets for their institute-minded energies. In 1943, for example, Alain Locke became a member of the board of directors of the African Academy of Arts and Research. This entity sponsored a series of programs "designed to better acquaint the American public with African culture and way of life." Its first project was slated to be an African dance festival at Carnegie Hall on December 13, 1943, with Eleanor Roosevelt as the "guest of honor and speaker."[38]

Interest in establishing institutes to support scholarship by, about, and of relevance to black people continued after leadership at Howard passed from Mordecai Johnson to James Nabrit in 1960. Johnson, in 1926, had nurtured the vision of assembling a stellar intellectual community. From 1926 until his retirement in 1960, he had worked steadily to achieve that vision. When Nabrit, a fellow Morehouse alum, took office after Johnson, he continued to emphasize intellectual development. This was illustrated in his Charter Day address when he indicated that "the primary mission of Howard University is intellectual."

In 1965 Nabrit proposed the establishment of the Howard University Center of Human Rights, which paralleled the university's mission and the initiatives by several members of this intellectual community to establish various institutes, both at Howard and around the country. In a letter to Logan, Nabrit mentioned his "purpose to establish at Howard University a research and teaching center, which for purposes of exploration, I am calling The Howard University Institute of Human Rights." Nabrit understood that "there are many aspects of this idea, which must be explored before funds are sought to bring it into being." He offered his "conviction . . . that given a sound proposal the means to make it a reality on this campus will be forth coming." Articulating his reasons for the need of such an institute, Nabrit offered, "One can think of few, if any, more important needs in a university setting than that of defining what we commonly call human rights, of describing the limits to which these areas might be widened. It is difficult, moreover, to think of an institution of learning whose history and character better fit it to undertake such explorations as these than Howard University." To set this idea in motion, Nabrit appointed a committee and asked Logan to serve as chairman, expressing his "hope that I may have a favorable answer from you not later than Tuesday July 5."[39]

There are other examples of Howard intellectuals participating in institutes around the country, and giving of their scholarly and professional expertise. In 1934 public intellectual Horace Mann Bond, writing for the Associated Negro Press, published a writeup in the *Pittsburgh Courier* of a speech by Charles Thompson before members of the Swarthmore Institute of Race Relations. "In a scholarly analysis of the legal status of the separate Negro school, Dr. Charles H. Thompson of the Howard University department of education attacked the theory of separate schools for Negroes." Bond states that Thompson "analyzed the arguments for and against separate schools and called attention to the fact that the separate school meant not only the classification of Negroes as inferior beings" but also the presence of "inferior accommodations for Negro children" wherever they existed. Bond noted that Thompson openly deprecated "the growth of segregation in northern communities," citing the Berwyn case "as an example of rank discrimination whose partial solution was not final." In his address Thompson had also mentioned the "numerous court cases brought by Negroes to defend their right to equal opportunity." Bond noted that, in Thompson's view, these cases served as "evidence of the need for even more recourse to the courts." Thompson had pointed out that many of these cases, which were understood to have been brought by Charles

Houston and the law school at Howard, had been successful. Thompson had further stated that "the Negro must learn to use the legal avenues of defense against inequalities found in separate schools." Thompson had ended his speech with a firm proposal, stating that "the gross deprivation of opportunity inflicted upon Negro children could be stopped if Negroes appealed to the courts."[40]

Members of the Howard University intellectual community were particularly active in adult education policy and its application in black communities in the Washington, D.C., area. The formation of an adult education program at Howard was highly significant for many reasons. Because of its connecting the university to the community and its emphasis on an overwhelmingly black population, this initiative's theoretical aims and practical application added to the efforts of the policy research nucleus and further established Howard as a base for what can be called Africana policy studies. The work of Howard intellectuals with respect to adult education represented a significant contribution to policy studies because research conducted on the education of African American adults was a significant area of concern among the black middle class in both D.C. and elsewhere. Furthermore, the area of adult education combined theory from African American studies with the practice of developing and implementing programs in the community to address critical educational needs among the African American adult population in the nation's capital.

On September 27, 1952, the *Baltimore African American* published a story that showed Howard University launching an adult education program. At its inception, it was reported, this program consisted of twenty-eight courses, "designed to meet the needs of the adult population" of Washington, D.C., under the rubric of the New Classes Division, which would begin its first year of instruction on October 6. Dr. John Lovell, director of the New Classes Division, stated that "the program's faculty will be made up of some of the outstanding teachers in their respective fields." Among the professors who were to teach in the program were Sterling Brown, Dr. Frank M. Snowden Jr., and Warner Lawson, dean of the school of music.[41]

In addition to the efforts of these professors, Alain Locke contributed greatly to the development and furtherance of adult education and related policies during his tenure at Howard. Eugene Holmes, Locke's colleague in philosophy at Howard, said that "Professor Locke's contributions to the field of adult education in America have not always been well known." Writing in the *Journal of Negro Education* in the winter of 1965 about Locke's contributions to the field of adult education, Holmes wrote, "Locke's immersion into the burgeoning American Adult Education movement began in 1924, when he was a delegate to the first Conference called by Carnegie Foundation president, F. P. Keppel, . . . [Locke] continued in the movement for the remainder of his adult life."[42]

Holmes explained that Locke was elected as the first "Negro" to serve as president of the Adult Education Association of America in 1945–1946. He characterized Locke's greatest contributions to the adult education movement as being "the publication of *The New Negro*" and "his editorship of the *Bronze Booklets*," mini-histories that documented the "problems and cultural contributions of the Negro." Holmes continued, "Alain Locke perhaps deserves the honor of being one of the first Negro educators to recognize the intrinsic value of adult education, which [simultaneously provided] a scientific basis for" the study of all adults. This would function "as a vital instrument for their social advancement." Holmes concluded that "Dr. Locke remained an ardent supporter [and] an active participant" in the adult education movement. Locke contributed articles "frequently" to journals of associations that dealt with the subject such as the *Teacher*, the *Howard University Record, Survey Graphic, Progressive Education*, the *Journal of Adult Education*, and the *Adult Education Journal*. Some of the titles of Locke's articles give the range of subjects he explored: "The Talented Tenth," "Negro Education Bids for Par," "Minorities and the Social Mind," "Types of Adult Education—The Intellectual Interests of Negroes," and "Education for Adulthood.[43]

Howard's adult education program, a pioneer in the concept of institutionalized lifelong learning for African Americans, covered many fields of study, such as business, music, art, reading, writing, speaking, and "select improvement." Courses included bookkeeping, shorthand, typing, speech, sewing, music appreciation, and "journalistic writing." Professor Sterling Brown offered a new course focusing on folk music and jazz. The *African American* described Brown as "long recognized as an outstanding authority in Negro art and culture." Brown was further praised for "his many years of research and personal contacts," and for amassing "an extensive library of recordings, manuscripts, and other documents in these fields." It was further noted that Brown made available many of his personal documents to the students taking the course.[44]

With regards to policy studies, Charles Wesley, while at Howard, became the pioneer in the study of Negro labor. Historian Francille Wilson argued that "Charles Harris Wesley's pathbreaking study, *Negro Labor in the United States, 1850–1925: A Study in Economic History,* charted a new direction in African American social science and historical research." Few others had devoted as much of their research to this important subject as Wesley did during his career. Wesley's contemporaries, sociologists Charles S. Johnson and E. Franklin Frazier, characterized the work as "a paradigmatic model of scholarship." In a 1940 Charter Day address, Frazier described "Wesley's work as the most pivotal in the institution's history," arguing that scientific social research began at Howard with the publication of *Negro Labor.* Wilson stated that, in this important work, "Charles Wesley constructed a methodological framework, which allowed him to critique racialist scholarship and popular stereotypes of Black workers' experiences and capabilities in terms, which most white scholars would consider not only 'objective' and 'scientific,' but persuasive and exhaustive." Wilson argued that Charles Wesley's work "anticipated the 'new social history' and the 'new labor history' by nearly half a century." She further lauded the book's "sophistication" and its "methodology and complexity of argument," making it a seminal text for those who studied African American labor history. Wesley's *Negro Labor* is noted for its thorough treatment of the black presence in the organized labor movement and included a methodological framework that infused the scientific analysis of the impact of black workers on American labor with the concept of racial vindication.[45]

Wesley was by no means alone in the pioneering of significant research in areas of black studies with policy implications. Howard had a long tradition of providing forums for the preparation and discussion of significant research by its emerging scholars. In the 1920s, for example, Howard's studies in social sciences and history in a series of institutes paved the way for black studies to enter into the twentieth-century scholarly realm.

Charles H. Thompson's efforts in educational policy as it related to civil rights and civil rights policy were also important precursors of Africana policy studies. Although trained primarily in the field of education, Thompson researched and wrote extensively on race relations, civil rights, and employment. In 1932, Thompson entered into probably his most significant contribution to the Howard intellectual community and the most important contribution of his scholarly career when he created the *Journal of Negro Education.* The *Journal* earned the reputation of being one of the most thorough and incisive publications of its time. According to Richard Kluger, Thompson's founding of the *Journal* was a major feat, for he had virtually no income to get it off the ground. He had only enough money to pay the printing bills and postage for correspondence regarding its operation. Fortunately, President Johnson and Howard University provided invaluable office space and paid about one-third of the education professor's salary for serving as the journal's editor.[46]

The *Journal* was launched as a means through which to record and document the conditions of Negro schools, and it served as a channel to analyze the consequences of segregated education. In comparing Thompson's *Journal* to the *Crisis*, Kluger noted that the *Journal* took up the mantle left by the demise of that organ. He characterized the *Journal* as "far less polemical than *The Crisis* had ever been" but observed that it "served a similar purpose: to inform, to arouse, to inspire." Michael Winston argued that Thompson's *Journal* represented "the most important scholarly medium dedicated to analyzing the public policy of segregation," and he further characterized it as "the best single source of information about the status of segregated schools and shifts in the legal strategies adopted to destroy segregation."[47]

In terms of its contribution to Africana policy studies, the *Journal* was significant in that it provided the research and forum that contributed to the NAACP's ultimate success in the *Brown v. Board of Education* decision of 1954. This legal victory was in large part because of the collaboration between Thompson's *Journal*, Howard social science intellectuals such as Kenneth Clark and John Hope Franklin, and legal scholars such as Charles Houston, Thurgood Marshall, and James Nabrit. In addition to addressing the policy of segregation, the *Journal* also provided the major medium of scholarly publication for many of Howard's intellectuals because of the lack of opportunities to publish in most mainstream white academic journals. Scholars such as Logan, Bunche, Brown, and even other black public intellectuals such as Du Bois used the *Journal* as a forum to publish works that were not discipline-specific but more focused on the ongoing dilemma of race.[48]

Howard never amassed the full financial and administrative support to establish an institute on black issues as Charles Johnson did at Fisk, so scholars such as Kelly Miller and Alain Locke struggled to find adequate resources to support their scholarship. With no sustained institutional structure, Howard scholars used its social science and history studies series to promote the research on campus that they could not promote through a fully functioning and ongoing research center or institute. Part of the reason Howard never established such a center was due to academic racism and the ongoing stigma against black scholars and their research. This left no support for vehicles such as institutes to fully support the activities and work of these public intellectuals, the kind of research and activities that their white counterparts readily received and often took for granted. Additionally, administrative intransigence, personality conflicts, and egoism as well as disciplinary allegiances were to blame as well, precluding the formation of a physical space to match the level and scope of an interdisciplinary research center. In essence, the campus and the greater

Washington, D.C., public sphere operated as Howard's de facto Africana culture and policy studies institute.

Despite this dilemma and the lack of a long-standing institute to its credit, the conferences attended, symposiums organized, lectures given, organizations affiliated with in consultant capacities, and the scholarship produced by the Howard community all had a tremendous impact on forthcoming generations of intellectuals. Although Howard was unable to establish a self-supporting black studies institute, the work and influence of Howard intellectuals represented such an institute virtually—without the formal name and building to show for it but with both influence and prestige, such that other black intellectuals benefited from the groundwork laid by the Howard group in the 1960s and onward.

Once foundations and philanthropic agencies became more interested in matters of race and research, black intellectuals began receiving greater funding for black studies, especially in the late 1960s and 1970s. Black intellectuals such as James Turner, John Blassingame, and others, who were beginning their graduate careers, sought out the advice and the example of Howard intellectuals to demonstrate what their programs and institutes might look like. Modern institutes that have borrowed from Howard's model include the Joint Center for Political and Economic Studies in Washington, D.C.; Cornell University's Africana Research Center; the Institute of the Black World in Atlanta, Georgia, which was initially affiliated with the Martin Luther King Center for Nonviolent Social Change; the William Monroe Trotter Institute, at the University of Massachusetts in Boston; the Institute for Research in African American Studies at Columbia, New York; the Institute of African American Research at the University of North Carolina–Chapel Hill; and countless others.

Despite its obvious influence on other institutes, however, a number of challenges directly affected Howard's inability to establish a sustained and independent institute comparable to Fisk's Race Relations Institute. Among these challenges was the need to interact with a Congress that controlled the purse strings and was willing to appropriate only a limited amount to a black school. A second reason could be that Howard's alumni base, unlike its predominantly white counterparts at institutions such as Harvard, did not possess the means nor the wherewithal to endow such an academic venture. Few foundations at the time were interested in supporting research on black studies, and the ones that were—including the Rosenwald Fund, which funded Fisk's Race Relations Institute—were not interested in supplying significant support for multiple research centers that would conduct research on black studies or race relations.[49]

Another major way in which members of the Howard group influenced and promoted the development of black studies was through their individual and collective influence, and their nurturing and mentoring of succeeding generations of black scholars. Those still alive from this group have passed down this intellectual legacy to the current crop of new black public intellectuals. Sterling Brown influenced so many of his students both in and out of the academy, including Michael Thelwell, Amiri Baraka, Houston Baker, ntozake shange, and Haki Madhubuti. He also inspired many others, including Henry Louis Gates Jr., the modern-day maker of community in academia and the genius behind the formation of the Harvard Dream Team. Rayford Logan mentored and laid the groundwork for some of the academic giants, such as the late John Blassingame, who brought the modern black studies movement to fruition at Yale and other college campuses. William Leo Hansberry was greatly influential in the intellectual and personal development of scholars such as Chancellor Williams, also a Howard history professor, and others such as John Henrik Clarke and Nnamdi Azikiwe, the first prime minister of Nigeria who named an African studies institute in Nigeria after Hansberry.[50]

There were those such as historians Woodson and Hansberry who formed and maintained active institutes outside of Howard, ones that still function today. Frazier and Hansberry used their intellectual and organizational skills, which could have been used at Howard, to form other domestic and international institutes and centers such as the Institute of African Studies (IAS) founded in 1959 at Columbia University and what is now the Africa-America Institute (AAI) founded in 1953 in New York. These institutes promoted African education as well as the emerging discipline of African studies.

The central role Howard scholars played in the formation and development of these institutes further legitimizes these scholars as public intellectuals and pioneers of black studies and Africana policy studies. The creation of these institutes reached out beyond academia and impacted public discourse, even helping to influence civil rights and African independence movements by generating intellectual activism on an array of issues. Hansberry's designation as the "prophet without honor" could be taken to apply to many members of this impressive intellectual community.[51]

The school of religion and the public intellectuals who composed it, for example, were influential in their contribution to research institutes in the United States and around the world. Prior to coming to Howard in 1934, Benjamin Mays had worked with Joseph Nicholson in New York to publish the pioneering work in black church studies, *The Negro's God*.[52] Mark Chapman contributed to a larger work examining the contributions of black religious intellectuals such as Howard Thurman to the development of what he calls a theology of race relations. Chapman notes that, from 1944 to 1948, the Howard School of Religion held regular gatherings at the

Institute of Religion (1944–1948) where black Christian intellectuals discussed Christianity and race relations in America, emphasizing Christianity's role, applied and embodied by believers, in solving America's racial problems. Mays and other black religious contemporaries such as Thurman also understood that the race problem, though unique to America, was not solely an American invention or problem—it had international implications as well. Chapman notes that numerous important essays from these institutes were published in *The Christian Way in Race Relations* (1948), edited by William Stuart Nelson, Mays's successor as dean of the Howard School of Religion.[53]

The policy studies nucleus at Howard pioneered a type of scholarship that promoted not only African American and Africana studies but also scholarship connecting African American studies with policy studies in origination, implementation, examination, and evaluation. Simply put, the Howard group forged what can be called Africana policy studies, or the study of policies that affect peoples of African descent all over the globe. From studies of the New Deal to critiques of apartheid in South Africa, to comparative studies of race relations in Brazil and the United States, Howard scholars examined and challenged existing policy research and policies representing people of African descent. The research of this nucleus was domestic, transnational, and international in nature, content, theory, and practice. Domestic studies included Ralph Bunche's critique and evaluation of civil rights organizations, and Frazier's critiques of the black middle class, black intellectuals, the black church, and the black community as a whole. Frazier spent considerable time examining how modern race relations worked throughout the world. This research had significant implications for policy analysis.[54]

The major problem these scholars faced in gaining recognition from the mainstream policy and political leaders for their research was the same problem they had encountered in gaining respect and legitimacy from the academic mainstream. Racism and the concomitant devaluation of their intellectual ability and policy astuteness were still powerful forces militating against their success. Much of the research undertaken by this nucleus of thinkers could have and should have been taken more seriously and used to inform and transform failing policies and situations in need of significant policy research and remedy. No better scholars examined the nexus between theory and policy—between research and actual conditions, not just for black America but for all of America—than the Howard group.

The Howard group understood what the famed and often highly praised New York Public Intellectuals recognized.[55] For conditions in society to change for the better, both the scholarship produced on social issues and the scholars involved must be invested in research and deeply concerned with appreciating and valuing the subjects under study. By valuing these subjects as human beings and then finding critical and effective ways to transform their community, researchers might inform viable policies and solutions that would improve the quality of life for those targeted groups (in this case, Africana marginalized populations), and for all groups. Too often, Western scholarship in the academy has centered on how far the research and the researcher can be removed from the subject. However, as Charles H. Houston believed, to produce effective policy research, one must know one's subject and his or her condition well enough to properly find and develop the correct policy prescription. Policies can be effective only if the research behind them is well informed and sensitive to the condition of those most affected. This does not mean that the research should be biased or driven by sentiment rather than hardheaded analysis of the data. It should always remain critical.

On the question of black intellectuals, E. Franklin Frazier established the first major social critique in the post–World War II era, even before Harold Cruse's famed and controversial *Crisis of the Negro Intellectual*.[56] Of all his pathbreaking and controversial works, Frazier's "Failure of the Negro Intellectual" was one of the most important examinations of the black intellectual class. Ironically, it has also been one of the most ignored and least studied. In this article Frazier asserted that black intellectuals had failed to assume the pluralistic orientation that would promote a strong racial identity as well as self-respect. Frazier argued that blacks should not do away with their organized social life, which had sustained them prior to integration, but should be able to integrate that within the wider American community. This appeared to be Frazier's understanding of assimilation and integration. The article rejected a complete dissolution of black culture and an uncritical adoption of mainstream white cultural values and mores. Instead, Frazier asserted that, in adopting a pluralistic philosophy, black intellectuals and black culture itself, in being integrated into American society, would become a distinctive part of a diverse whole. "There has been an implied or unconscious assimilationist philosophy," Frazier emphasized, "holding that Negroes should enter the mainstream of American life as rapidly as possible, leaving behind their social heritage and becoming invisible as soon as possible. This has been due, I think to the emergence of a sizable new middle-class whose social background and interest have determined the entire intellectual orientation of educated Negroes."[57]

Frazier strongly believed that many black intellectuals had not properly examined the assimilationist problem for the black middle class, of which many were now a part despite, in some cases, their working-class origins. Clovis Semmes argues that, among middle-class blacks, "Frazier saw an uncritical acceptance of American values and ideals." He added that, according to Frazier, "the failure of the Black intellectual also found its basis in social organizations . . . [and] in this case was the result of a structure of dependency on White economic support." Because of this dependency, Frazier believed that white philanthropy had historically played a huge role in training the black intellectual class. This assertion is interesting, considering that Frazier and his cohort of black sociologists trained by Robert Park at the Chicago School of Sociology were products of this same system, as were many other Howard scholars and their contemporaries.[58]

A question arises as to how Frazier and his Howard cohorts and other contemporaries reconciled this apparent double consciousness that was exhibited as they examined their education and training in light of their peculiar condition as black public intellectuals. Perhaps one of the most harrowing of the paradoxes was that, even though many of them (as was the case with Frazier) were educated at elite institutions by scholars among the most renowned in their fields, they were denied entry into the faculties of elite—and even middling—white universities. White philanthropists' lack of full support to black intellectuals and their research meant that the Howard scholars and their contemporaries had to cope with the schizophrenic nature of being black public intellectuals in a segregated world where they were treated as second-class scholars and citizens. And to be sure, as Frazier notes in his examination of the black bourgeoisie, although the black elite and black masses provided much of the support for intellectuals such as Frazier, on the other side of the coin there was a strange self-hatred felt by many toward black intellectuals. Many tried to internalize this self-hatred and attempted valiantly—in some form or fashion, privately, publicly, or with some combination of the two—to make sense out of this dilemma of the black intellectual.[59]

Frazier in his pioneering book *Black Bourgeoisie* demonstrated the effect that cultural hegemony had on black intellectuals, which in turn was also found in the larger black middle class. Frazier indicted the black intellectual class for participating in their own devaluation and for not expanding their worldview beyond the boundaries of the United States to include the problem of race relations around the world. He noted that black American intellectuals could learn a great deal from their African nationalist contemporaries. Frazier could speak on this group with authority because—as a result of participation in a number of organizations, such as the American

Society for the Study of African Culture—he had gained a good under-standing of the contributions and condition of African scholars.[60]

On the question of assimilation, Frazier observed that "they [Black intellectuals] have failed to study the problem of Negro life in the broad framework of man's experiences in this world. They have engaged in petty defenses of the Negro's social failures but more often they have been so imbued with the prospect of integration and eventual assimilation that they had thought that they could prove themselves true Americans by not studying the Negro."[61] Ambivalent as ever on the issue, as were many of his contemporaries, Frazier offered the hope that the attainment of a greater and more critical consciousness could save the Negro intellectual from the fate of continued marginalization. He advised that "the Negro intellectual should not be consumed by his frustrations." He added that any other black intellectual like himself "must rid himself of his obsession with assimilation" and "must come to realize that integration should not mean annihilation, self-effacement, the escaping from his identification."[62]

The totality of Frazier's work made a tremendous contribution to the development of African studies in the United States. As one of the found-ers and the eventual president of the African Studies Association, Frazier helped, in this respect, to institutionalize the discipline of African stud-ies.[63] In terms of scholarship, Frazier is best known for research on various institutions within the black community and for his controversial stances on the presence of African survivals in the aftermath of slavery.

Historian Michael Winston sheds new light on the subject. He notes that Frazier and Melville Herskovits, instead of being bitter enemies, were in fact friends despite their heated debates. Actually, Frazier's research on the African contexts prior to the 1950s functioned to provide "historical 'background' for the study of Black American institutions, especially the family."[64]

As a scholar of African Studies, Frazier often wrestled with blending his scholarship and activism, as did many of the Howard group. Frazier had two sides as a scholar. In one sense, he was very "cautious," even characterizing European imperialism as just a phase in "the expansion of Europe." However, he was also more activist. This Frazier also "saw clearly the connection between White supremacy in the southern United States and its kindred political and economic institutions in Asia, Africa, and the Caribbean."[65]

Frazier became a member of the Council on African Affairs in 1941 at the insistence of then council executive director Max Yergan. This signaled his early attempt to synthesize scholarship and activism—as the 1960s black studies movement did—and also illustrated the tremendous amount of recognition black intellectuals and activists gave to Frazier's knowledge and interest in the evolving condition of the African continent. Yergan justified his invitation to Frazier, saying the "particular desire on the Council to have you join [is] not only because of your general interest in Africa, but in order that the Council may have the benefit of your help in formulating and carrying out our program of research and publication." This statement was significant because Yergan was aware that Frazier was one of the most vocal black public intellectuals who offered strident criticism of the United States' policy of acquiescence to European imperialism. In many ways, it was due to the research and activism of Frazier and other members of the global black intellectual community that the United States altered its policy and began to support African decolonization movements.

Other members of the Howard community of scholars, including Logan, Mordecai Johnson, Bunche, and Locke were early members of the Council on African Affairs. Many of them left the group as it became increasingly more radical and as the McCarthy crackdown tightened in the 1950s.[66] Logan, Hansberry, and other members of the Howard community, also significant contributors to African studies, were compelled on a more personal level by research and personal beliefs to support African decolonization efforts. One important reason for their support was their relationship to many Africans such as Nnamdi Azikiwe, who were their students at Howard and who would later become critical figures in the decolonization movements. And Frazier, in this matter, was more than an elite intellectual. "Although he frequently insisted that he was a 'scientist' of society, no more, no less," Winston argues, "E. Franklin Frazier was far from an 'ivory tower' academic. He succeeded in keeping his academic and political interests separate most of the time, but in the case of Africa he was clearly committed to decolonization and the development of independent African states long before he began to write professionally in this area."[67]

In keeping with his engagement with African decolonization, Frazier was appointed chief of the Division of Applied Social Sciences of UNESCO at the headquarters in Paris. In this role, Frazier had the responsibility "to organize seminars at the research institutes supported by UNESCO in Africa." While he was in Paris in the 1950s, Frazier also became a member of the American Society for the Study of African Culture. As a member of this organization, he and other Howard intellectuals such as Hansberry interacted with their African counterparts in the society, who were also members of the global black intellectual community, including Alioune Diop, the editor of the group's journal *Présence Africaine*. This contact, experience, and interaction with African political intellectuals in the Society would provide further insights for Frazier's harsh critique of the black intellectual class in "The Failure of the Negro Intellectual" and in *Black Bourgeoisie*.[68]

In 1954, following his return from Paris, Frazier, along with his colleague Rayford Logan, more fully established Howard's African studies program. Here, Frazier "began to teach courses on Africa in the department of sociology, including one on social change in Africa." Beginning in the early 1950s and continuing to the time of his death, "Frazier's contributions to the relatively new field of African Studies included a modest number of research articles on urbanization and social change in Africa, the impact of colonialism on African social forms and personality, and African education." In addition to these contributions, Frazier's *Race and Culture Contacts in the Modern World*, published in 1957, along with other works during this period, established him as a major contributor to the development of modern African studies.[69]

Howard University also had a tremendous influence in the founding and shaping of the nation's most influential black think tank, still presently in existence, the Joint Center for Political and Economic Studies, in Washington, D.C. This is the premier public policy think tank for African Americans, founded in 1970, five years following the passage of the 1965 Voting Rights Act and two years after the assassination of Dr. Martin Luther King Jr. As a consequence of the Kerner Commission report indicating the presence of two Americas, Joint Center biographer Juan Williams noted, white think tanks in the post-*Brown* era provided "little help to Black politicians in the way of ideas specifically crafted to help them cope with a history of disadvantages."[70]

> Two centuries of isolation and virtual exclusion from meaningful participation in the political process have resulted in a lack of interest, background, and training in practical politics on the part of the Black community. Thus there is frustration and disenchantment among Negroes[,] which has led to the advocacy of separatism, confrontation, and violence rather than participatory democracy as the more effective means of achieving the Negro's legitimate goals in our society.[71]

Many militant black activists staunchly disagreed that an organization such as the Joint Center could be effective in transforming American society in the way they envisioned. "To these militants," Juan Williams wrote, "the Joint Center was merely a sop." They viewed "the institution" as "merely a midwife for White efforts to increase the number of moderate accommodationist Black politicians." One of the founders of the Joint Center, Howard alumnus Kenneth Clark, however, held a clear vision of the role that a trained corps of black politicians could play in aiding black Americans and the nation as a whole to carve out viable routes to black progress. In a 1967 conference on the future of the civil rights movement,

Clark commented that "Elected Negro officials are now the only civil rights leaders who are representative of the aspirations, the desires, and the quest for answers posed by their constituents, and who are elected by their people to speak for them."[72]

An institute of black elected officials was convened in D.C. in 1969 to provide direction for growing black political movement consensus in the nation. The institute was spearheaded by noted social psychologist Dr. Kenneth Clark, Howard law professor Frank Reeves, and attorney Vernon Jordan. At the institute Clark, Jordan, and Louis Martin, among others, drafted a proposal to form an institute for black political education. Twelve African American leaders supported Dr. Clark's urging for a more permanent organization. In collaboration with Howard University and his Metropolitan Applied Research Center (MARC), Clark submitted to the Ford Foundation the proposal for development of the center.[73] The proposed center had broad and specific goals, seeking to empower black political participation through training of black elected officials and educating the general public about public policy matters. Williams noted, "Essentially, the Joint Center's creation was confirmation by nationally prominent Black leaders of the inherent potential of the American political system."[74]

By 1970 white foundations had begun to take an interest in black issues, reversing their longtime neglect under pressure of the civil rights movement and growing racial conflict, and in April 1970 the Ford Foundation awarded the grant to Howard and MARC to establish the Joint Center for Political Studies. In addition to having roots at Howard, the Joint Center's major initial financial backing came from the Ford Foundation.[75] The role of the Foundation in supporting the initial efforts of the founders of the Joint Center must not be underestimated. It was understood that forming an organization for black politicians would pose tremendous problems. Ford Foundation officials saw that there was great difficulty in forming "a guild of Negr[o] elected officials—a trend precisely opposite to an integrated leadership community, which men of reason continue to seek." Despite this concern, however, they placed their full support behind the effort.[76]

Frank Reeves, a significant political activist and a Howard law professor, became the center's first executive director. He legitimized criticisms from militants who argued against focusing energies on politics by stating that a decided concentration had to be placed on politics so as to improve "the conditions in the ghettoes against which we rebel." Reeves and other black leaders equated black progress and black power with increased black political participation and presence in the highest offices of American government.[77]

Much of the Joint Center's success and stability can be attributed to the political genius of Louis Martin and to the longtime president of the center, Eddie N. Williams. Martin was selected by Clark and the other founders to assist in establishing this important political entity because of his political savvy. (The *Washington Post* dubbed Martin the "godfather of black politics.")[78] He had years of experience as adviser to a number of U.S. presidents, including Kennedy, Lyndon Johnson, and Jimmy Carter. Martin was the unanimous choice to become the think tank's first chairman of the board of governors.[79] Eddie Williams succeeded Reeves as head of the Joint Center in 1972, when Reeves found himself in ill health. Prior to coming to the Joint Center, Williams had been vice president for public affairs at the University of Chicago. Martin persuaded Williams to take the position (he regarded the recruitment of Williams as one of his life's best decisions).[80]

The role of Howard intellectuals in creating black, African, and Africana policy studies has been critical. Racism and segregation worked to thwart the efforts of Howard public intellectuals to promote these areas of studies. The involvement of Howard public intellectuals in organizations and institutes outside of Howard aided them in promoting their agendas with regard to black, African, and Africana policy studies. Lastly, their work at Howard in creating institutions to support their scholarship in these areas were significant, even though they experienced tremendous difficulty in gaining support and legitimacy for their efforts.

CONCLUSION

O N JANUARY 9, 2002, THE *Washington Post* published an article by
columnist Courtland Milloy entitled "D.C. Should Find Ways to
Attract Black Scholars." In this piece, Milloy spoke of the controversy involving several members of Harvard's Dream Team, including
renowned black studies professors Cornel West and Henry Louis Gates
Jr., who were leaving for Princeton and other universities due to a heated
controversy with then Harvard president Lawrence Summers. As we now
know, West left, returning to Princeton, while Gates remained as chair of
Harvard's famed W.E.B. DuBois Institute for African and African American Research. Milloy likened the situation "to a bidding war for star ath-
letes" and found it "a remarkable turn of events to see some Black people
being valued for their brains as others have been for their brawn." He
then turned to a brief discussion of members of the Howard intellectual
community, citing a familiar 1950s photograph of Charles Drew, Sterling
Brown, E. Franklin Frazier, Rayford Logan, James M. Nabrit Jr., and Alain
Locke, affectionately known as the "Big Six." Milloy cited this photograph
in order to provide "a reminder that a concentrated Black brain trust is
nothing new." He continued:

> Still, few of those brilliant old-timers ever came close to receiv-
> ing the fame and fortune of the Harvard crew. Nor could they have
> dreamed that such a powerful African American studies department
> could ever exist in the heart of the Ivy League. But when all is said and
> done, after the thrill of watching Harvard's young professors execute
> their Black power plays wears off, what remains is a Black community
> still very much in need of a more rigorously focused academia.

All the more ironic is Milloy's next statement, which poses a paradox for a
city that was home to such an impressive collection of intellectuals, a city
to which they gave their lives, lived them out, and in which they became
eloquent and noted scholar activists. Milloy observes:

Wouldn't it be nice if institutions of higher learning such as Howard or the University of the District of Columbia—or even a coalition of area colleges—were able to attract more of the best Black minds to deal with the acute problems facing Black America. Surely no place could use such a dedicated assembly more than Washington, D.C., with its symbolic value as a nation's capital still struggling to live up to its ideals.[1]

What a paradox that the situation described by Milloy is that of the nation's capital, and that the Dream Team is not in D.C., where the Howard scholars labored and lived, but instead nestled exclusively at Harvard, away from the city where many argue the Howard scholars helped to create a Black Renaissance to rival that in Harlem.

In a 1993 article entitled "The Dilemma of the Black Intellectual," Cornel West posited a telling contrast between black intellectuals of the post–World War II world and those of his generation. West argues that there were more and better intellectuals in the post–World War II generation than in his own generation. West describes the situation clearly as an intellectual heir to the legacy of the Howard group and their contemporaries:

> Prior to the acceptance of Black undergraduate students to elite white universities and colleges in the late sixties, select Black educational institutions served as the initial stimulus for potential Black intellectuals. And in all honesty, there were relatively more and better Black intellectuals then than now. After a decent grounding in a Black college, where self-worth and self-confidence were affirmed, bright Black students then matriculated to leading white institutions to be trained by liberal, sympathetic scholars, often of renowned stature. Stellar figures such as W. E. B. Du Bois, E. Franklin Frazier, and John Hope Franklin were products of this system.[2]

West depicts the condition and circumstances of black public intellectuals in the generation before his own and links their experiences with the predominantly black institutions they attended as undergraduates and subsequently served as faculty, because of the discriminatory nature of white institutions at the time. West states that there was a significant number of these intellectuals and further hints that they were arguably as capable as—if not more capable than—current black intellectuals, despite the restraints they faced with segregation and discrimination.

The late John Hope Franklin, a scholar from the generation of which West speaks, offered a more probing critique of academic racism in his revealing piece "The Dilemma of the American Negro Scholar." In this important work, Franklin, a member of the Howard intellectual community for a number of years, argues:

> The dilemmas and problems of the Negro scholar are numerous and complex. He has been forced, first of all, to establish his claim to being a scholar, and he has had somehow to seek recognition in the general world of scholarship. This has not been an easy or simple task, for at the very time when American scholarship in general was making its claim to recognition, it was denying that Negroes were capable of being scholars. Few Americans, even those, who advocated a measure of political equality, subscribed to the view that Negroes—any Negroes— had the ability to think either abstractly or concretely or to assimilate ideas that had been formulated by others. As late as the closing years of the nineteenth century it was difficult to find any white persons in the labor or business community, in the pulpit or on the platform, in the field of letters or in the field of scholarship who thought it possible that a Negro could join the select company of scholars in America.[3]

Franklin's examination of the dilemmas and challenges facing black scholars during his era and in prior generations is illuminating. It highlights the very experiences that were faced daily by members of the Howard community in their professional lives.

There are many similarities and differences between black public intellectuals operating in the era of legal segregation and those who operate today. Black scholars active in a segregated and colonized world included John Henrik Clarke, Dorothy Porter, Anna Julia Cooper, Charles S. Johnson, Horace Mann Bond, and many of the Howard intellectuals. The current group of black intellectuals is substantial and growing and includes the likes of Toni Morrison, Henry Louis Gates Jr., Gerald Early, Glen Loury, Cornel West, bell hooks, Derrick Bell, Adolph Reed, Michelle Wallace, Michael Eric Dyson, Lani Guinier, and countless others.

The list of present-day black public intellectuals presents an important cadre that operates in a more integrated public sphere. In contrast, their black public intellectual predecessors were very active in a very large black public sphere that also allowed for significant contact and interaction with white scholars, foundations, and global scholars and entities. Although there were obvious restrictions facing these scholars, they were arguably more productive or as productive as the current group. Both groups of scholars had advantages and disadvantages during their eras, but neither should be discounted or ignored—as has been the case with the group represented by the Howard University intellectual community and their contemporaries. The public spheres for the two eras are indeed different and yet still linked. Although the intellectuals were unique in each era, they are still connected.

Jerry G. Watts, in an important 1989 article entitled "Dilemmas of Black Intellectuals," argues that "the status of the Afro-American Intellectual community has changed drastically during the last twenty years."[4] Watts affirms that, "As a result of the civil rights movement and urban uprisings of the 1960s, . . . predominately white universities began to open their doors" more readily "to Black scholars," although this trend had been gradually set in motion in a token way in the 1940s and 1950s. Hiring of a significant number of black scholars "occurred together with substantial increases in the numbers of Black students admitted into predominately white colleges and universities." Watts argues, while being careful of "not overstating this number," that this reality "brought a new range of occupational options for the Black academic elite."

In this way, with the creation of a post–Jim Crow black intellectual elite with more opportunities for access and funding than their predecessors, a number of other trends emerge that are important in understanding the current group of black public intellectuals. These trends connect the two groups but also distinguish them from one another. One of the major issues is the increasing level of bourgeoisification of black public intellectuals in this new era. Although it is true that current black public intellectuals make salaries and obtain grants that their predecessors never dreamed of, the concept of bourgeoisification is nothing new to black intellectuals, particularly since the term was coined by E. Franklin Frazier, in a preceding generation at Howard.

There are characteristics that differentiate these two intellectual groups from one another and some that inevitably connect them. For instance, both groups wrestle with an elevated status of sorts, but because of the nature of segregation and colonialism, black intellectuals of the 1930s through the 1970s, at Howard and elsewhere, were more intimately connected to the social realities facing the black masses than their counterparts today. Those in the Howard community during its heyday were in many cases grouped together for a long time on only a few university campuses, which allowed for the formation of cadres and community. Furthermore, for the Howard group, the bourgeoisification label did not fit them to the level and degree as it does the current group of black public intellectuals.

However, Howard intellectuals to a large degree did ascribe to certain attitudes and behaviors akin to those of the black bourgeoisie as defined by Frazier, namely, the obsession with status. Today, with greater access, financial possibilities, and demands placed on the celebrity intellectual, black public intellectuals have been forced to create a type of community that, while real, is more amorphous, more loosely connected, and less concentrated than was the case with the Howard group and its contemporaries. Contrary to the views expressed in much recent literature, current intellectuals are not the pioneers and innovators of discussions about race; the Howard group and their contemporaries of the late 1920s to early 1970s are still credited with this academic discourse.

Watts argues that the generation of black intellectuals who were active in the days of the Howard group "recognized that employment at white colleges was impossible for them," although a small few gained entry in the intervening years.[5] "This restricted access to American academia," Watts states, "did not stifle their ambitions, though it did, in some cases, hinder their intellectual production." Watts believes that the "absurdity and irony of their condition" was "highlighted" by the fact that several (notably, Frazier) were elected to the highest offices in their professions. However, many (such as Frazier, Du Bois, Logan, and others) were never offered permanent positions in predominantly white colleges and universities.

Watts characterizes the generation of black public intellectuals that followed Frazier's group as a "transitional" group. In this group, he places John Hope Franklin, John A. Davis, and St. Clair Drake, although he would argue that in their transitional mode they were also contemporaries in a large sense with Frazier and others. These transitional scholars, Watts contends, "began their careers while academic compartmentalization was strictly racist, only to have the doors of white academia open to them later. . . . Black scholars who entered graduate school during the 1960s formed the first generation of Black academics that saw employment in predominately white universities as a viable option."

Watts argues that the recent flight to predominantly white universities by many of his generation's black public intellectuals "has been devastating to the predominately Black college." Whereas black public intellectuals such as Howard president Mordecai Johnson, Charles Hamilton Houston, and others perhaps contemplated what a post-segregated academy would look like, they probably never envisioned the brain drain of black talent that has occurred. Nor could they have imagined the absence of black community on many predominantly white campuses, which either have isolated their black faculty or have relegated them to black studies departments and programs that are continually fighting for existence. The concept and reality of community among black scholars and public intellectuals was never a utopian situation during the era of the Howard group as intense debates occurred alongside collegiality and respect. However, the increased opportunities afforded current black public intellectuals has not translated into a greater sense of community. The result is, in fact, a less cohesive constituency coming together to promote black studies. Today, alongside greater wealth and access to resources, there is just as much bickering and infighting as there was in the era of the Howard group, when members experienced bitter infighting because of competition for scarce resources and scholarly opportunities.

During segregation and its aftermath, prestigious white universities barred many competent black faculty from serving full-time on their faculties, except for minor stints they might serve as visiting professors. On the rare occasions that these universities allowed black scholars to serve on their faculties, they hired only a token few. White universities did not begin to open their doors until the black studies rebellions of the late 1960s and early 1970s, which established these programs and departments.

This time and generation in which many of today's black public intellectuals came of age and were attending many of the nation's elite universities was due in large part to the early successes of federal affirmative action initiatives. Despite this gradual trend, however, the presence of black scholars on faculties at leading white universities was challenged by university administrators who regularly questioned the efficacy of black studies as a discipline, always keeping their legitimacy in question. The more things change, the more they stay the same.[6]

The irony of the matter is that many black scholars of the pre–World War II and postwar era received their graduate degrees from either Ivy League institutions or other elite American universities. Yet they were not offered full-time posts on their faculties. Segregation might have been overt only in the Deep South, especially in academe, but American racism stretched over the entire country and, I would argue, was actually more institutionalized in the North. Robert Bruce Slater writes, "Prestigious universities such as Harvard, Yale, Princeton, Stanford, Duke, and the University of Chicago faithfully observed the custom of racial exclusion. After the Civil War, for a period of almost 100 years, distinguished Black academics such as Carter G. Woodson, Alain Locke, E. Franklin Frazier, and Rayford Logan were not acceptable as scholars at America's great institutions of higher learning."[7]

Slater notes that for approximately three hundred years, "America's leading institutions of higher learning observed a strict racial taboo against the hiring of Black faculty." Beginning in the 1940s, there occurred a gradual movement of black scholars into predominantly white universities as "the academic rules that restricted appointments to members of the white race began to change." Not until the early 1990s, however, did a greater influx of black scholars join the faculties of leading white universities and become sought-after commodities, thus creating the reinvigorated and market-driven black public intellectual.[8]

An even greater paradox is that today, in an era with the first African American U.S. president, Barack Obama, those same elite institutions of higher learning that denied opportunities to Du Bois and Frazier are competing heavily for the services of top intellectual talent and seeking to form dream teams. With Jim Crow visibly gone and integration supposedly at work, the once beleaguered black scholar has now become a public celebrity who garners significant fame and fortune for many of the nation's elite universities. All this occurs as universities vie to outbid one another for the services of black scholars, not a common occurrence in the days of Alain Locke and William Leo Hansberry.

What is interesting is that, while the "bidding wars" continue, the state of black studies is still uncertain—and in many respects even threatened. The memory of the early black intellectual pioneers such as the Howard group is lost; they are forgotten and not fully appreciated by the elite universities or even many of the black scholars who now function as the intellectual vanguard. What is to blame for this trend? It causes us to reexamine Cruse's *Crisis of the Negro Intellectual*, Franklin's "Dilemma of the American Negro Scholar," Frazier's "Failure of the Negro Intellectual," and Cornel West's subsequent "Dilemma of the Black Intellectual" in order to uncover the link between the scholars in the generation of the Howard community and those operating today in a post–Jim Crow America.

Public intellectuals in a segregated and colonized world interacted and engaged with the segregated black public in unique ways. The Howard group traveled extensively, both nationally and internationally, to conduct research, attend conferences, form institutes, and encourage scholarly organizations. At the same time, they published extensively and developed tremendous global reputations as scholars and activists.

To ponder what impact they had on the larger integrated public of today is an impossible task. However, to say that they were ineffective would be to propound a falsity of the worst kind. With less, they arguably did more; under tremendous sociopolitical constraints they continued to speak truth to power and reach out to all areas of the black public sphere, including both the black middle class and the black masses. True, many fashioned themselves on the elite educations some of them obtained, but all were intimately connected with the harsh social realities experienced by the black masses. In many ways they experienced increasing levels of the consequences of racism in America. For even though they were scholars, they were first and foremost black, whether they appropriated labels or not. And with this knowledge came the understanding of how they fit within the American social order. William Leo Hansberry has been characterized as "the prophet without honor." I would argue that this label should be broadened to include the Howard group and most black scholars of their generation, be they male or female.

Discussions of the phenomenon of the origins and heyday of the public intellectual often begin and end with Alfred Dreyfus and the New York Intellectuals. This was a group of Jewish writers, artists, and intellectuals who operated in the 1930s, 1940s, and 1950s in the heart of New York City. Included in this group were individuals from about three different generations of scholars, including first-generation scholars Philip Rahv, Lionel Trilling, Dwight MacDonald, and Sidney Hook; second-generation scholars Irving Howe, Daniel Bell, Seymour Martin Lipset, Nathan Glazer, Alfred Kazin, and Saul Bellow; and third-generation scholars Norman Podhoretz, Philip Roth, Norman Mailer, and others. The group reflected considerable diversity of thought across a wide spectrum, and it catalyzed the political role of the public intellectual in American culture in some ways comparable to the Howard group.[9]

In his pioneering yet controversial book *The Last Intellectuals,* Russell Jacoby offered the thesis that the cultural frontier of the public intellectual has now passed and that this type of intellectual is now dead. Obviously, Jacoby failed to adequately consider the impact of black public intellectuals in his analysis, and particularly the role of the Howard community. This book seeks to address that omission, centrally provoking a renewed debate about the exact role of the black public intellectual in twenty-first-century American and world society. Although relegated to the margins of the academic and policy worlds, Howard public intellectuals yet impacted these publics in such a way that they and their work changed the nature of scholarship and public engagement by scholars. Part of the problem up until now has been that they and their work were relegated to the dust bin of history. My goal has been to revisit and evaluate their contribution, the public debate surrounding their continuing legacy, and the challenging model of public intellectualism that they left for current and future generations.

There is an interesting point of comparison and contrast between the New York Intellectuals and the Howard intellectuals, for they were living and working during approximately the same historical time frame. The nation's capital, during the New Deal, was the home of domestic and international power politics. Moreover, as Walter Fluker and Catherine Tumber argue, Washington, D.C., was "the Civil Rights Movement's center of gravity," and Howard's black public intellectuals such as Howard W. Thurman, Charles Houston, Abram Harris, Mordecai Johnson, Alain Locke, and E. Franklin Frazier conversed and interacted with the likes of Mary McLeod Bethune, Nannie Burroughs, A. Philip Randolph, W. E. B. Du Bois, and other national black leaders.[10]

In 1990, about a decade after Jacoby's work, Robert Boynton offered a revisionist interpretation to the death knell of the public intellectual. Boynton argued for the presence of a new public intellectual who would recover this important tradition. Left out altogether from Jacoby's discussion of the public intellectual—and functioning only as a brief side note in Boynton's work—was the public intellectual activity of many prominent African American scholars of the pre–World War II and post–World War II world. The most notable omission was—and continues to be—those who formed the intellectual community at Howard University during the middle part of the twentieth century.

The Howard University intellectuals operated from the late 1920s to about 1970 and paralleled and rivaled the activity and work of the New York Intellectuals. Furthermore, if one goes with contemporary definitions of the public intellectual (as an intellectual who is highly engaged with the public), then it must be argued here that the Howard intellectual community represents more closely the true meaning of what a public intellectual is and, thus, provides a more edifying model for what one should be in the future. In fact, the Howard group was more engaged with its public than are many contemporary black public intellectuals, even though its public was more limited than the public inherited by its intellectual heirs. Despite this, the contributions of this group of scholars to American and world intellectual communities cannot be underestimated. The Howard group, with all its constraints, proved very cosmopolitan, very active on both national and global scales. Taken altogether, the volume and quality of their scholarship, the breadth and depth of that scholarship, their contributions made as activists both in the United States and abroad, as well as their service as part of governmental bodies and institutes in the United States and abroad, all demonstrate the successful and effective public nature of these scholars. What's more, they formed a solid community, a community of scholarship at Howard, with black scholars in the United States and abroad, and with white scholars and scholars in Europe, on the African continent, and around the world.

There are many differences between the Howard public intellectuals and the new black public intellectuals, which distinguish one group from the other. First of all, the current group has more access to financially well-off white institutions than did the Howard group. While some members of the Howard group did gain the opportunity to teach on one-year stints at white institutions, they for the most part were not offered tenured positions. A small few, such as John Hope Franklin and Abram Harris, gained the opportunity to teach at white colleges and universities for more than a brief period. Second, current black public intellectuals have many more options in terms of venues to work and ways in which to promote their work. The new black public intellectuals have more access to a white public than the Howard intellectuals because of the benefits of integration. A significant drawback experienced by current black scholars, with a few exceptions as evidenced at Harvard and at conferences, is that they lack, in their professional lives, the face-to-face community that existed at Howard. There is significantly less contact between today's black intellectuals and the black community.

Black studies professor James B. Stewart articulated the need to expand our current notions of what constitutes a "public intellectual." Stewart argued that public intellectuals functioning as "public policy critics and consultants based on detailed knowledge . . . have less popular visibility than *inspirational* speakers, who speak in broad generalities about a lot of different subjects." He affirmed that "discipline based public intellectuals tend to have broader direct impact on the lives of people of African descent than celebrities, but are nonetheless 'public intellectuals,' albeit from the lenses of somewhat different publics." A few contemporary examples of these discipline-based public intellectuals are Ron Brown, Vernon Jordan, and Donna Brazile. Darlene Clark Hine, Manning Marable, Peniel Joseph, and Stephanie Evans are also black public intellectuals who are equally respected as research scholars. As with the Howard group, these different groups of black public intellectuals do not separate their role as thorough research scholars from the articulation of their work to the larger public. Their public intellectualism stems from and is rooted in their disciplinary/interdisciplinary research work. In essence, Stewart advanced the notion that this particular group represented a more direct legacy of the Howard model of public intellectual than many contemporary black public intellectuals such as Cornel West, Michael Eric Dyson, bell hooks, and Henry Louis Gates Jr. Arguably, there is merit to this position as well as those positions that link the Howard group with today's erudite, popular public intellectuals.[11]

The legacy of Howard intellectuals for subsequent generations of black intellectuals can be observed in many ways. One instance is in the integral role played by each of these intellectuals in laying the foundation for and creating institutionalized African American studies at Howard. For the Howard group, their research and identification as scholars to varying degrees evidenced a critical connection between the African continent and the diaspora. In this sense, as much of their research purports, individually and collectively, the discipline of Africana studies owes a tremendous debt of gratitude to their pioneering work. Also, in the area of policy studies, the "policy research nucleus" emphasized the fundamental connection between the world of policy and the world of African American and Africana life and culture. The nucleus thus helped to create what can be called Africana policy studies. It is obvious and deserving of proper recognition that these intellectuals influenced so many other areas of scholarship as well, such as multicultural studies, black men's history studies, black women's history and studies, postcolonial studies, and black literary studies.

* * *

There is much, also, that the Howard group and the current crop of black public intellectuals have in common. The Howard group laid the foundation for the modern intellectuals and in many ways served as models for them. Many argue that the segregated and colonized world hindered the effectiveness of the Howard group, but I contend that, in addressing their public, which was mainly black and included many progressive scholars and lay persons, they were very successful. In contrast, I wonder if the current crop of black public intellectuals have connected as effectively with the black public or are judged successful because of their more integrated audience. Recently, Houston Baker, a Sterling Brown protégé, has responded to this query with a clarion call—in the provocative title of his recent book, *Betrayal: How Black Intellectuals Have Abandoned the Ideals of the Civil Rights Era*. In a manner reminiscent of E. Franklin Frazier's "The Failure of Black Intellectuals," Baker takes to task both Ivy League and neoconservative black public intellectuals for misrepresenting the model set forth by Martin Luther King Jr.[12]

Moreover, members of the Howard community such as E. Franklin Frazier, Sterling Brown, Rayford Logan, and others helped bridge the gap between these two generations and helped inspire many of the black public intellectuals of today, either directly or indirectly. Howard intellectuals left an important legacy, both individually and as a collective, to the current group of black public intellectuals. There is a great need to address the historical omission of this group, including their impact on and presence in academia, as scholar activists, and in relation to matters domestic, transnational, and abroad.

The Howard intellectual community left an important legacy to generations of public intellectuals who came after them, as well as to those yet to emerge. Despite the crippling effects of segregation, the public intellectuals who composed this community contributed significant scholarship, performed valuable and committed activism, and mentored subsequent generations who still are influenced by their work and example. Even through their mistakes and imperfections, the Howard community evidenced what real possibilities can come about if intellectual life becomes more engaged with the concept of community. One important fact that emerges is that, while individuals can influence a community, it is the community that transforms and shapes the individual. In essence, the overarching lesson that we gain from studying the Howard group is that intellectual life cannot exist properly without both the individual and the community working in concert, always searching for elusive answers to life's most pertinent questions. In taking up the mantle of Du Bois's talented tenth and filling that role in such exemplary fashion, the Howard group of intellectuals set the standard for public intellectuals, both black and white. It is hoped that this study has demonstrated the necessity for historians and other scholars to further examine the role, function, and linkages among twentieth- and twenty-first-century black public intellectuals.

NOTES

Introduction

1. The term "talented tenth" represented members of the black professional and intellectual elite, known as race men and race women, and drew attention to their continuous achievements in lifting the race. Black scholar and public intellectual W. E. B. Du Bois popularized the phrase in an article entitled "The Talented Tenth," which appeared initially in September 1903 in a book entitled *The Negro Problem: A Series of Articles by Representative Burghardt Du Bois, Paul Laurence Dunbar, Charles W. Chestnut, and Others* (New York: J. Pott, 1903). Other notable contributors to this volume of essays were Booker T. Washington and T. Thomas Fortune. The concept gained increasing popularity with Du Bois's publication of his landmark book of essays, *The Souls of Black Folk,* in 1903. Du Bois, the first African American to earn a Ph.D. in history from Harvard University and himself a staunch advocate of classical education, believed that the top 10 percent of the black race would serve as the leadership vanguard of the race, elevating the remaining 90 percent by their efforts, achievements, and advocacy. By the early 1930s, Du Bois had revised his earlier pronouncements regarding the role of the black elite in racial advancement, instead advocating a more significant role for the black masses in assuming black leadership and promoting social change within the race.

2. Although heavily focused on black professors and academics, today black public intellectuals, as Grant Farred argues, include those who specialize in the use of "vernacularity," such as artists, musicians, entertainers, hip hop emcees, and so on—anyone with a public platform, influence, and the ability to communicate ideas in the public arena. *What's My Name? Black Vernacular Intellectuals* (Minneapolis: University of Minnesota Press, 2003).

3. For a discussion of the New York Intellectuals, see Hugh Wilford, *The New York Intellectuals: From Vanguard to Institution* (Manchester, England: Manchester University Press, 1995); Neil Jumonville, *Critical Crossings: The New York Intellectuals in Postwar America* (Berkeley and Los Angeles: University of California Press, 1991); Alexander Bloom, *Prodigal Sons: The New York Intellectuals and Their World* (New York: Oxford University Press, 1986).

4. Patricia Hill Collins, "Black Public Intellectuals: From Du Bois to the Present," *Contexts* 4, no. 4 (Fall 2005): 23–24. I agree with the assessments of Collins, Joy James, and Stephanie Y. Evans, who factors in the oft-neglected group of black women public intellectuals, including Anna Julia Cooper, Ella Baker, Mary McCleod Bethune, and countless others. Stephanie Y. Evans, *Black Women in the Ivory Tower, 1850–1954: An Intellectual History* (Gainesville: University of Florida, 2007).

5. Houston Baker, *Betrayal: How Black Intellectuals Have Abandoned the Ideals of the Civil Rights Era* (New York: Columbia University Press, 2008).

6. For a discussion of James H. Cone's treatment of nationalist and integrationist lineages in African American intellectual history, see the introduction in *Martin, Malcolm, and America: A Dream or Nightmare* (Maryknoll, N.Y.: Orbis Books, 1991).

7. A race man was a man of African descent, primarily of the New Negro ilk, who historically sought, albeit imperfectly, to uplift the race. Race men worked and distinguished themselves in their public and private lives for their education and professional status. These men strove to live out an empowered manhood that promoted race pride and encouraged educational achievement in the talented tenth model. That notwithstanding, it is impossible to discuss race men without mentioning in the same breath race women. As they lived out this notion of manhood, race men were not immune to patriarchal conventions of the day, seeking to imbibe those of the mainstream society within gendered black cultural spaces. Despite adoption of patriarchal norms, race women contributed mightily to the nineteenth- and twentieth-century African American freedom struggle. For more in-depth study of the race men/race women phenomenon, see Hazel Carby, *Race Men* (Cambridge, Mass.: Harvard University Press, 1998); Evans, *Black Women in the Ivory Tower;* and Kevin Gaines, *Uplifting the Race: Black Middle-Class Ideology in the Era of the "New Negro," 1890–1935* (Chapel Hill: University of North Carolina Press, 1996).

8. Michael R. Winston, "Through the Back Door: Academic Racism and the Negro Scholar in Historical Perspective," *Daedalus* 100 (1971): 671–701; William M. Banks, *Black Intellectuals: Race and Responsibility in American Life* (New York: W. W. Norton, 1996); Alfred Moss, *The American Negro Academy: Voice of the Talented Tenth* (Baton Rouge: Louisiana State University Press, 1981); Brenda Gayle Plummer, *Rising Wind: Black Americans and U.S. Foreign Affairs, 1935–1960* (Chapel Hill: University of North Carolina Press, 1996); Charles P. Henry, *Ralph Bunche: Model Negro or American Other?* (New York: New York University Press, 1999); Jacqueline Goggin, *Carter G. Woodson: A Life in Black History* (Baton Rouge: Louisiana State University Press, 1993); Kenneth Janken, *Rayford W. Logan and the Dilemma of the African American Intellectual* (Amherst: University of Massachusetts Press, 1993); Genna Rae McNeil, *Groundwork: Charles Hamilton Houston and the Struggle for Civil Rights* (Philadelphia: University of Pennsylvania, 1983); Anthony M. Platt, *E. Franklin Frazier Reconsidered* (New Brunswick, N.J.: Rutgers University Press, 1991); August Meier, *Negro Thought in America, 1880–1915: Racial Ideologies in the Age of Booker T. Washington* (Ann Arbor: University of Michigan Press, 1963).

9. For a discussion of the social history of academic intellectuals, see Thomas H. Bender, *Intellect and Public Culture: Essays on the Social History of Academic Intellectuals in the United States* (Baltimore: Johns Hopkins University Press, 1993); Earl Thorpe, *The Mind of the Negro: An Intellectual History of Afro-Americans* (Westport, Conn.: Negro Universities Press, 1970); Nell Irvin Painter, *Sojourner Truth: a Life, a Symbol* (New York: W. W. Norton, 1996).

10. James E. Turner, *The Next Decade: Theoretical and Research Issues in Africana Studies* (Ithaca, N.Y.: Africana Studies and Research Center, 1984); Fabio Rojas, *From Black Power to Black Studies: How a Radical Social Movement Became an Academic Discipline* (Baltimore: Johns Hopkins University Press, 2007); Peniel Joseph, *The Black Power Movement: Rethinking the Civil Rights–Black Power Era* (New York: Routledge, 2006).

11. Zachery Williams, ed., *Africana Cultures and Policy Studies: Scholarship and the Transformation of Public Policy* (New York: Palgrave Macmillan, 2009).

12. Known as "Harvard's Talented Tenth," the Dream Team was an elite group of black scholars and public intellectuals assembled in the 1990s at Harvard University's W. E. B. Du Bois Institute for African American Studies by literary scholar and department chair Henry Louis Gates Jr. The list of scholars includes Cornel West (philosopher), Elizabeth Brooks Higginbotham (historian with a master's degree from Howard in June 1974), William Julius Wilson (sociologist), Gates himself, Kwame Anthony Appiah (cultural theorist and philosopher), Alvin Pouissant (psychiatrist), Orlando Patterson (sociologist), and Martin Kilson (government scholar). In fact, over the years, Howard professors such as Sterling Brown and Rayford Logan played instrumental roles in helping to establish in 1969 Harvard's Afro-American studies program, which eventually became the Du Bois Institute, home of the highly touted Dream Team. David Gergen, "Harvard's Dream Team," *Newsweek*, March 18, 1996; John Gravois, "'Dream Team' Reassembles in Harvard's Black Studies Department," *Chronicle of Higher Education News Blog*, September 14, 2007. Martin Kilson, also a scholar of black public intellectuals, was instrumental—along with the major force, Nathan Huggins—in establishing and maturing Afro-American studies at Harvard. See Martin Kilson, "From Birth to a Mature Afro-American Studies at Harvard, 1969–2002," in Lewis R. Gordon and JoAnne Gordon, eds., *A Companion to African American Studies* (Malden, Mass.: Blackwell, 2006).

13. David L. Smith, Chet Lasell, Eleanor Holmes Norton, Paula Giddings, Sterling Stuckey, Wahneema Lubiano, and Cornel West, "A Symposium on the Life and Work of Sterling Brown," *Callaloo* 21, no. 4 (Autumn 1998): 1039, 1042, 1067.

14. Darlene Clark Hine, *Speak Truth to Power: Black Professional Class in United States History* (Brooklyn, N.Y.: Carlson Publishing, 1996); Darlene Clark Hine, *Hine Sight: Black Women and the Re-Construction of American History* (Bloomington: Indiana University Press, 1997); Rosalyn Terborg-Penn, Sharon Harley, and Andrea Benton Rushing, eds., *Women in Africa and the African Diaspora: A Reader* (Washington, D.C.: Howard University Press, 1989, 1987); Evans, *Black Women in the Ivory Tower*; Bettye Collier-Thomas and V. P. Franklin, eds., *Sisters in Struggle: African American Women in the Civil Rights Movement* (New York: New York University Press, 2001); Francille Rusan Wilson, *The Segregated Scholars: Black Social Scientists and the Creation of Black Labor Studies, 1890–1950* (Charlottesville: University of Virginia Press, 2006); Pero Dagbovie, *The Early Black History Movement, Carter G. Woodson, and Lorenzo Johnston Greene* (Urbana: University of Illinois Press, 2007).

Chapter One

1. Walter Dyson, *Howard University, the Capstone of Negro Education: A History, 1867–1940* (Washington, D.C.: Graduate School of Howard University, 1941), 442; Jonathan Scott Holloway, *Confronting the Veil: Abram Harris Jr., E. Franklin Frazier, and Ralph Bunche, 1919–1941* (Chapel Hill: University of North Carolina Press, 2002), 45–50.

2. Alain L. Locke (1885–1954, at Howard from 1912 to 1953) was a member of the American Negro Academy, one of the nation's first African American think tanks, with links to Howard. He was appointed to the Howard faculty in 1912 and taught logic and ethics, as well as philosophy, education, English, and literature. A Rhodes Scholar, Locke was fired in June 1925 by President Durkee but was reappointed in 1928.

3. Winston, "Through the Back Door," 698. See also Constance Green, *The Secret*

City: A History of Race Relations in the Nation's Capital (Princeton, N.J.: Princeton University Press, 1967). The January 1936 issue of the *Journal of Negro Education* (hereafter cited as *JNE*) showcased articles by Du Bois, A. Philip Randolph, Ralph Bunche, and others.

4. Logan actually first uses the term in his book, *The Negro in American Life and Thought: The Nadir, 1877–1901* (New York, Dial Press, 1954). Rayford Logan was on the faculty at Howard from 1938 to 1973. He was a historian specializing in the study of Haiti, colonial Africa, and black America. He served as news correspondent for the *Pittsburgh Courier* covering the 1945 U.N. organizational conference. Logan's diaries, located in the Library of Congress, record the challenges of black scholars prior to integration.

5. Wilson J. Moses, "The Lost World of the Negro, 1895–1919: Black Literary and Intellectual Life before the Renaissance," *Black American Literature Forum* 21, no. 1–2 (1987): 61–65.

6. Ibid., 65. He is critiquing Green's *Secret City*.

7. Ibid.; in note 7, Moses mentions that Woodson and Cruse were both "indebted" to Du Bois for developing the concept of the talented tenth. See also Harold Cruse, "Black and White: Outlines of the Next Stage," *Black World* (March 1971): 28; Carter G. Woodson, *A Century of Negro Migration* (Washington, D.C.: Associated Publishers, 1918); Harold Cruse, *The Crisis of the Negro Intellectual* (New York: William Morrow, 1967).

8. Booker T. Washington, known as the Wizard of Tuskegee, was the founder and president of Tuskegee Institute. He advanced the idea of industrial education, advocating self-help and hard work for the race. W. E. B. Du Bois was a leading professor, author, poet, editor, scholar, public intellectual, activist, and Pan-Africanist. He was the first African American to receive a doctorate in history from Harvard, and one of the founders of the ANA. There are several notable works on Du Bois's life, including Manning Marable, *W. E. B. Du Bois: Black Radical Democrat* (Boulder, Colo.: Paradigm Publishers, 2005). David L. Lewis, *W. E. B. Du Bois: Biography of a Race, 1868–1919* (New York: Henry Holt, 1993), which covers the first half of Du Bois's life, was the winner of the 1994 Bancroft Prize and the 1994 Francis Parkman Prize. David L. Lewis, *W. E. B. Du Bois: The Fight for Equality and the American Century, 1919–1963* (New York: Henry Holt, 2000), covers the last half of Du Bois's life, concluding with his death in Ghana in 1963 on the eve of the March on Washington.

9. The most comprehensive biography of Crummell is Wilson Jeremiah Moses, *Alexander Crummell: A Study of Civilization and Discontent* (Amherst: University of Massachusetts Press, 1989). The best history of the ANA is Moss, *American Negro Academy*.

10. Kelly Miller was professor of mathematics at Howard from 1895 to 1907 and went on to serve as department head of sociology and dean of the College of Arts and Sciences. He was a public intellectual, essayist, newspaper columnist, and a prolific academic. He retired in 1934.

11. Carter G. Woodson (1875–1950) popularized Negro history and founded Negro History Week in 1926. He was appointed dean of liberal arts and head of the graduate faculty at Howard in 1919–1920. He published several influential works of black history.

12. At the association's fifty-third annual meeting in New York, on October 3–6, 1968, the organization's name was changed to its current designation, the Association for the Study of African American Life and History (ASALH). For more current information about the work of the ASALH, visit its Web site at http://www.asalh.org.

13. Janette Hoston Harris, "Woodson and Wesley: A Partnership in Building the Association for the Study of Afro-American Life and History," *Journal of Negro History* 83, no. 2 (Spring 1998): 109–19; C. G. Woodson, "An Accounting for Twenty-five Years," *Journal of Negro History* 25, no. 4 (October 1940); Rayford W. Logan, "Carter G. Woodson: Mirror and Molder of His Time, 1875–1950," *Journal of Negro History* 58, no. 1 (January 1973); Charles H. Wesley, "Recollections of Carter G. Woodson," *Journal of Negro History* 83, no. 2 (Spring 1998); Michael R. Winston, "Carter Godwin Woodson: Prophet of a Black Tradition," *Journal of Negro History* 60, no. 4 (October 1975): 459–63; Richard I. McKinney, "Mordecai Johnson: An Early Pillar of African American Higher Education," *Journal of Blacks in Higher Education* 27 (Spring 2000).

14. Pero Gaglo Dagbovie, "Black Women, Carter G. Woodson, and the Association for the Study of Negro Life and History, 1915–1950," *Journal of African American History* 88, no. 1 (Winter 2003). See also Goggin, *Carter G. Woodson;* Jacqueline Goggin, "Countering White Racist Scholarship: Carter G. Woodson and the Journal of Negro History," *Journal of Negro History* 68, no. 4 (Autumn 1983); Darlene Clark Hine, "Carter G. Woodson, White Philanthropy and Negro Historiography," *History Teacher* 19, no. 3 (May 1986); Charles H. Wesley, "Carter G. Woodson—as a Scholar," *Journal of Negro History* 36, no. 1 (January 1951); Rayford W. Logan, "Phylon Profile VI: Carter G. Woodson," *Phylon* 6, no. 4 (1945): 315–21.

15. Harris, "Woodson and Wesley." A revealing portrait of Woodson is given by his colleague Rayford Logan in "Phylon Profile VI." See also Wesley, "Carter G. Woodson—as a Scholar"; Winston, "Carter Godwin Woodson."

16. Janken, *Rayford W. Logan,* 205.

17. E. Franklin Frazier, a 1916 graduate, worked at Howard from 1934 to 1962 as professor and department head. He was a premier sociologist and a staunch supporter of integration and cultural pluralism. Abram Harris was professor and chair of the department of economics at Howard from 1927 to 1945. His research showed a commitment to integrating Marxist principles to resolve challenges facing black workers. In 1950, Ralph Bunche became the first African American to win the Nobel Prize. He was recruited to Howard to start a political science department and was its chair from 1928 to 1950. In 1947 he was appointed director of the U.N. Trusteeship Department and later as undersecretary general.

18. W. E. B. Du Bois, *The Souls of Black Folk,* ed. Henry Louis Gates Jr. and Terri Hume Oliver (1903; Centenary edition, New York: W. W. Norton, 1999), 11.

19. Raymond Wolters, *The New Negro on Campus: Black College Rebellions of the 1920s* (Princeton, N.J.: Princeton University Press, 1975), 78–79; Dyson, *Capstone of Negro Education,* 63.

20. Wolters, *New Negro on Campus,* 79–81; Rayford W. Logan, *History of Howard University: The First Hundred Years, 1867–1967* (New York: New York University Press, 1969), 146.

21. Wolters, *New Negro on Campus,* 80–82; James M. McPherson, "White Liberals and Black Power in Negro Education, 1865–1915," *American Historical Review* 75 (1970): 1364–65.

22. McPherson, "White Liberals and Black Power," 1385.

23. Wolters, *New Negro on Campus,* 73–74.

24. Dwight Oliver Wendell Holmes was a teacher, university administrator, and college president who served at Howard in many capacities, including registrar and dean from 1919 to 1937, when he left to become president of Morgan State College (now University), serving there until his retirement in 1948. Charles Wesley, a pioneer in the study of black labor history, was the third African Ameri-

can to receive a doctorate in history from Harvard. He was professor of history at Howard from 1913 to 1920, then dean of liberal arts and the graduate school and chair of the history department from 1921 to 1942. He helped Woodson build the Association for the Study of Negro Life and History. He was married to Dorothy B. Porter (at Howard from 1926 to 1973).

25. Wolters, *New Negro on Campus*, 85–86; Logan, *Howard University*, 115–16.

26. Wolters, *New Negro on Campus*, 86. William Leo Hansberry was professor of history at Howard from 1922 until his retirement in 1959, teaching that the cradle of civilization was in Africa and that Egypt derived its culture from the kingdoms of Kush and Ethiopia. He was supported by Wesley and Logan, though not by many of his colleagues. He had an important hand in the founding of the African-American Institute, Africa House (a student hostel in Washington), and the All-African Students Union of the Americas. Many important African leaders pushed for the publication of his research, but he was not recognized in America, which earned him the title "prophet without honor."

27. Wolters, *New Negro on Campus*, 86; "A New Course in History at Howard University," *Howard University Record* 17 (1923): 237–39; John Hope Franklin, "Courses Concerning the Negro in Negro Colleges," *Quarterly Review of Higher Education among Negroes* 8 (1940): 138–44.

28. Logan, *Howard University*, 115–16, 171, 208.

29. Benjamin Brawley (1882–1939) was English professor at Howard, and the author of numerous important published works.

30. Logan, *Howard University*, 139–40; Dyson, *Capstone of Negro Education*, 368–69.

31. Dyson, *Capstone of Negro Education*, 368–69, 396–97.

32. Wolters, *New Negro on Campus*, 86, see also 89–91. George B. Hutchinson, "Jean Toomer and the 'New Negroes' of Washington," *American Literature* 63, no. 4 (December 1991): 683–87.

33. Wolters, *New Negro on Campus*, 89.

34. *New York Age*, October 10, 1925; Roscoe Conkling Bruce to Jessie, June 27, 1925, W. E. B. Du Bois Papers, University of Massachusetts.

35. Wolters, *New Negro on Campus*, 111–12. Carl Murphy, founder and editor of the *Baltimore Afro-American* from 1882 until his death in 1922, had served as professor of German and chair of the department from 1913 until 1918. He had left Howard University on bad terms with Durkee.

36. Wolters, *New Negro on Campus*, 108; Alumnus, "Durkeeism," *Baltimore Afro-American*, November 21, August 1, June 27, 1925.

37. Wolters, *New Negro on Campus*, 102. During the 1920s, there were numerous articles that illustrated the troubled economic position of the professoriate. See, for example, "Academic Salaries," *School and Society* 13 (1921): 16–17; Aubrey J. Kempner, "How Professors Live," *School and Society* 12 (1920): 436–41; and Robert J. Aley, "College Salaries," *Educational Review* 59 (1920): 244–49.

38. Thorstein Veblen, *The Higher Learning in America: A Memorandum on the Conduct of Universities by Business Men* (New York: B. W. Huebsch, 1918), quoted in Wolters, *New Negro on Campus*, 102.

39. Wolters, *New Negro on Campus*, 102–3.

40. Ibid., 104–5; "Correspondence of the Salaries Committee," in *Washington Daily American*, December 22, 1924.

41. Locke to Du Bois, summer 1925, W. E. B. Du Bois Papers, University of Massachusetts; Wolters, *New Negro on Campus*, 106.

42. Wolters, *New Negro on Campus*, 103.

43. Ibid., 188–89.

44. E. Franklin Frazier, *Black Bourgeoisie: The Rise of a New Middle Class in the United States* (London: Collier-Macmillan, 1957; New York: Collier Books, 1962).

45. Holloway, *Confronting the Veil*, 36–37.

46. Moses, "Lost World of the Negro," 61–65.

47. Ibid., 65. See also Holloway, *Confronting the Veil*, 40; Janken, *Rayford W. Logan*, 6–12.

48. Wolters, *New Negro on Campus*, 113.

49. James A. Wechsler, *Revolt on the Campus* (New York: Covic, Friede, 1935); Seymour Martin Lipset, *Rebellion in the University* (Boston: Little, Brown, 1971), 158–78; *Washington Post*, May 8, 1925.

50. *Opportunity* 3 (1925): 164; *Baltimore Afro-American*, May 16, 1925; *Washington Post*, May 8, 13, 1925; "Kelly Miller Says," *Baltimore Afro-American*, May 23, 1925.

51. *Chicago Defender*, May 16, 1925; *Washington Post*, May 13, 1925.

52. "Kelly Miller Says," *Baltimore Afro-American*, May 23, 1925.

53. Henry B. Stegall and Miles C. Algood quoted in *Chicago Defender*, May 23, 1925; "Two Congressmen from Alabama," *Chicago Defender*, May 30, 1925; *Dallas Express*, May 30, 1925; *Baltimore Afro-American*, May 23, June 6, 23, 1925.

54. *Messenger* 8 (1926): 46; Alumnus, "Durkeeism," *Baltimore Afro-American*, July 25, 1925; *New York Age*, September 19, October 24, 1925; Wolters, *New Negro on Campus*, 119.

55. "Statement of Trustees," quoted in *Chicago Defender*, August 22, 1925; "Statement of Charles R. Brown," ibid.

56. *Washington Daily American* (clipping, n.d.) quoted in Wolters, *New Negro on Campus*, 120.

57. Logan, *Howard University*, 590; Wolters, *New Negro on Campus*, 121.

58. *Washington Tribune*, December 19, 1925, March 12, 1926; Logan, *Howard University*, 204; Alumnus, "Durkeeism," *Baltimore Afro-American*, August 15, September 5, 1925.

59. B. G. Lowery and Butler B. Hare, quoted in *Chicago Defender*, May 8, 1926; "Statement of Trustees," quoted in Logan, *Howard University*, 233–34.

60. Logan, *Howard University*, 234–35.

61. Alumnus, "Durkeeism," *Baltimore Afro-American*, December 26, 1925; *Washington Daily American*, December 10, 11, 1925; *Baltimore Afro-American*, December 19, 1925.

62. Charles B. Purvis to Francis J. Grimké, May 9, 1921, cited in Carter G. Woodson, ed., *The Works of Francis J. Grimké*, 4 vols. (Washington, D.C.: Associated Publishers, 1942), 4:309–11; J. Stanley Durkee to B. F. Seldon, June 20, 1927, in Dyson, *Capstone of Negro Education*, 397.

63. W. E. B. Du Bois, "Howard and Lincoln," *Crisis* 32 (1926): 7–8. See also Wolters, *New Negro on Campus*, 130.

64. Wolters, *New Negro on Campus*, 132. See also Alumnus, "Durkeeism," *Baltimore Afro-American*, February 8, April 10, May 8, 15, 22, 1926; Michael R. Winston, "Jesse Edward Moorland," in Michael R. Winston and Rayford Logan, eds., *Dictionary of American Negro Biography* (New York: W. W. Norton, 1982), 448.

65. Wolters, *New Negro on Campus*, 132–33; Alumnus, "Durkeeism," *Baltimore Afro-American*, May 29, 1926; *Baltimore Afro-American*, July 3, 1926.

66. Wolters, *New Negro on Campus*, 133; *New York Age*, June 12, 19, 1926.

67. Wolters, *New Negro on Campus*, 134; W. E. B. Du Bois, "Howard and Lincoln," *Crisis* 32 (1926): 167–68; *Messenger* 8 (1926): 167–68.

68. Wolters, *New Negro on Campus*, 134–35; Richard I. McKinney, *Mordecai, the*

Man and His Message: The Story of Mordecai Wyatt Johnson (Washington D.C.: Howard University Press, 1997), 51.

69. McKinney, *Mordecai*, 51, 57; *Baltimore Afro-American*, July 3, 1926.

70. *Baltimore Afro-American*, July 3, 1926.

71. McKinney, *Mordecai*, 56.

72. Ibid., 57.

73. Ibid., 60.

74. Ibid.

75. Jon Michael Spencer, "The Black Church and the Harlem Renaissance," *African American Review* 30 (1996): 454.

76. McKinney, *Mordecai*, 60.

77. Ibid., 56–59.

78. Logan, *Howard University*, 258–65; *Baltimore Afro-American*, October 16, 1926, June 18, July 9, 1927.

Chapter Two

1. McKinney, *Mordecai*, 60–61.

2. Ibid., 254.

3. Johnson's inauguration speech, Appendix B, ibid., 252–54.

4. Ibid., 62. Howard W. Thurman joined the school of religion in 1931. He was professor of theology and the dean of Andrew Rankin Chapel from 1932 to 1944. Benjamin E. Mays was the dean of the school of religion from 1934 to 1940, when he left to become president of Morehouse College (1940–1967). He made the Howard School of Religion into a first-rate institution. He and Thurman became lifelong friends.

5. McKinney, *Mordecai*, 62.

6. Mordecai Johnson, "Autobiographical Statements," undated, 1–2, Folder 15, Box 178–14, Series D (Writings by Mordecai Johnson), Mordecai Wyatt Johnson Papers (Moorland-Spingarn Research Center, Howard University; hereafter MSRC). Quotations in the next several paragraphs are from ibid., 12–13.

7. McKinney, *Mordecai*, 56; Ralph E. Luker, *The Social Gospel in Black and White: American Racial Reform, 1885–1912* (Chapel Hill: University of North Carolina Press, 1991), 2–3.

8. McKinney, *Mordecai*, 57, 60, 61.

9. Ibid., 58.

10. Dyson, *Capstone of Negro Education*, 400.

11. Ibid., 400–401.

12. Logan, *Howard University*, 247–49.

13. Ibid., 247.

14. Ibid., 60–61. See student enrollment numbers cited in Johnson's inauguration speech, in McKinney, *Mordecai*, 258.

15. *Congressional Record*, 69th Cong., 1st sess., 2861, 3000–3001, 12588, 12611; ibid., 2nd sess., 2056, 3017.

16. Ibid., 70th Cong., 2nd sess., 304, 445, 447, 503–5, 559, 606–7, 649–58.

17. McKinney, *Mordecai*, 66–69.

18. Logan, *Howard University*, 257.

19. Ibid., 258–59.

20. Ibid., 265, 268, 269.

21. Ibid., 257.

22. Clifford L. Muse Jr., "Howard University and the Federal Government during the Presidential Administrations of Herbert Hoover and Franklin D. Roosevelt, 1928–1945," *Journal of Negro History* 76, no. 114 (1991): 1.

23. Ibid., 1–2.

24. Ibid., 11.

25. Ernest Everett Just (1883–1941) joined the Howard faculty in 1907 and remained until 1941, serving as head of various departments (physiology, zoology). He was successful in obtaining several prestigious financial grants for scientific research but met with opposition from Mordecai Johnson who wanted him to balance research with graduate teaching.

26. Muse, "Federal Government," 3–4, 12.

27. Ibid., 11.

28. Ibid., 6.

29. Walter Crump to Mordecai Johnson, April 10, 1931, Moorland Papers, MSRC; Muse, "Federal Government," 4–5.

30. For an excellent biography of Charles Hamilton Houston, see McNeil, *Groundwork*.

31. Muse, "Federal Government," 12–13.

32. Ibid., 70–71.

33. Ibid., 72; also McNeil, *Groundwork*. Houston was vice dean of the law school from 1929 to 1935.

34. McKinney, *Mordecai*, 72.

35. McNeil, *Groundwork*, 84.

36. Ibid., 85.

37. McKinney, *Mordecai*, 73; Logan, *Howard University*, 267–68.

38. Winston, "Through the Back Door," 698. For a history of the *Brown v. Board of Education* case as well as the cases preceding it, see Richard Kluger, *Simple Justice: The History of* Brown v. Board of Education *and Black America's Struggle for Equality* (New York: Alfred A. Knopf, 1976); James T. Patterson, Brown v. Board of Education*: A Civil Rights Milestone and Its Troubled Legacy* (New York: Oxford University Press, 2002); Charles Ogletree, *All Deliberate Speed: Reflections on the First Half Century of* Brown v. Board of Education (New York: W. W. Norton, 2004).

39. McKinney, *Mordecai*, 73–74; also Dyson, *Capstone of Negro Education*.

40. William Stuart Nelson began the annual institutes of religion at Howard and developed the *Journal of Religious Thought*. He began as professor of religion in 1925, went on to teach philosophy and then serve as assistant to the president, dean of the school of religion, dean of the university, and vice president. He retired in 1968.

41. Howard Thurman, *With Head and Heart: The Autobiography of Howard Thurman* (New York: Harcourt Brace Jovanovich, 1979), 87.

42. Dyson, *Capstone of Negro Education*, 172–77; Thurman, *Head and Heart*, 87, 130–35.

43. Walter Earl Fluker and Catherine Tumber, eds., *A Strange Freedom: The Best of Howard Thurman on Religious Experience and Public Life* (Boston: Beacon Press, 1998), 2.

44. McKinney, *Mordecai*, 73–74.

45. Benjamin E. Mays, *Born to Rebel: An Autobiography* (Athens: University of Georgia Press, 1971, 1987), 139–41. Information for the next several paragraphs is from ibid., 140–48.

46. Charles H. Thompson was professor of education from 1926 to 1966, chair of the department of education, dean of liberal arts, and dean of the graduate school.

47. Percy Julian was head of the chemistry department from 1927 to 1929. He received his doctorate at the University of Vienna.

48. Eric Williams taught Caribbean history at Howard from 1939 to 1948. He was involved in the Anglo American Caribbean Commission. He was the first prime minister of Trinidad and Tobago (1956–1981).

49. John Hope Franklin was professor of history at Howard from 1947 to 1956, when he left Howard to become the first African American chair of the history department at Brooklyn College. Sterling Brown was a professor of African American literature and folklore at Howard from 1929 to 1969. He authored numerous publications, influenced many generations of students, and received a Guggenheim fellowship in 1937.

50. Chancellor Williams (1905–1992) was the author of a groundbreaking work *The Destruction of Black Civilization* (Chicago: Third World Press, 1974). He received a bachelor's degree in education (1930) and a master's in history (1935) from Howard, and a doctorate in sociology (1949) from American University. He began teaching at Howard after returning from work as a researcher at the University of Ghana and also served as an Oxford University Fellow.

51. McKinney, *Mordecai*, 75.

52. Ibid., 78.

53. See Miles Mark Fisher, "The Howard Years," chapter 5 of Carter, *Walking Integrity*. Fisher provides an extensive list of members of the Howard University intellectual community, an environment in which Mays excelled. For more information on those figures see Dyson, *Capstone of Negro Education;* Thomas C. Battle and Clifford L. Muse Jr., *Howard in Retrospect: Images of the Capstone* (Washington, D.C.: MSRC, 1995); Harry G. Robinson III and Hazel Ruth Edwards, *The Long Walk: The Peacemaking Legacy of Howard University* (Washington, D.C.: MSRC, 1996). For a good examination of the Howard community of scholars during its golden years, see also Janken, *Rayford W. Logan.*

54. Yohuru R. Williams, "John Hope Franklin's Troubled Tenure at Howard University, 1947–1956: Professor of History," *Negro History Bulletin* (July–December 1998). Logan quoted in Michael R. Winston, *The Howard University Department of History, 1913–1973* (Washington, D.C.: Howard University Press, 1973); Interview with John Hope Franklin by Civil Rights Documentation Project, August 9, 1972, MSRC.

55. Williams, "Franklin's Troubled Tenure," 72.

56. Logan, *Howard University,* 247–51; McKinney, *Mordecai,* 77–81; Michael Winston, *Education for Freedom: The Leadership of Mordecai Wyatt Johnson, Howard University, 1926–1960, a Documentary Tribute to Celebrate the Fiftieth Anniversary of the Election of Mordecai Wyatt Johnson as President of Howard University* (Washington, D.C.: Howard University Archives, MSRC, 1976).

57. Logan, *Howard University,* 249–51. See also Charles Jarmon, "Sociology at Howard University: From E. Franklin Frazier and Beyond," *Teaching Sociology* 31, no. 4 (October 2003): 366–68.

58. McKinney, *Mordecai,* 82–83; William A. Darity Jr. and Julian Ellison, "Abram Harris Jr.: The Economics of Race and Social Reform," *History of Political Economy* 22 (1990): 611–27.

59. Janken, *Rayford W. Logan,* 209–10; Logan, *Howard University,* 364–67.

60. Logan, *Howard University,* 83. Lorenzo Turner was an important African American linguist; his research was on the Gullah language in coastal South Carolina and Georgia. He was professor at Howard from 1917 to 1928 and served as a department head for the last eight years.

61. Alain L. Locke to Mordecai Johnson, December 26, 1929, Folder 1 (1927–1929), Box 164–21, Series C, Alain L. Locke Papers, MSRC.

62. Johnson to Locke, April 19, 1935, Folder 2 (1930–1939), Box 164–41, ibid.

63. Benjamin E. Mays, "My View: Thirty-Four Years of Distinguished Leadership," *New Pittsburgh Courier,* July 16, 1960. Quotations for the next several paragraph are from this article.

64. James M. Nabrit was dean of the law school from 1958 to 1960 and then served two terms as president of the university, from 1960 to 1965 and from 1968 to 1969.

65. Willie James Jennings, "The Burden of the Black Leader," *Books and Culture: A Christian Review* (March/April 1998).

66. P. L. Prattis, "Horizon: Dr. Johnson," *New Pittsburgh Courier,* September 24, 1960.

67. Jacob Billikopf to Claude Barnett, April 7, 1931, Folder 1, Box 164–14, Series C, Alain L. Locke Papers, MSRC.

68. Ibid.

69. Johnson, "Autobiographical Statements," undated, Folder 15, Box 178–14, Series D, Mordecai Wyatt Johnson Papers, MSRC.

70. McKinney, *Mordecai,* 83.

Chapter Three

1. Listed in the historiography documenting the dilemmas of black intellectuals one can find Cruse, *Crisis of the Negro Intellectual* (New York: William Morrow, 1967); John Hope Franklin, "Dilemma of the American Negro Scholar," in Franklin, *Race and History: Selected Essays, 1938–1988* (Baton Rouge: Louisiana State University Press, 1989); Cornel West, "The Dilemma of the African American Intellectual," *Cultural Critique,* no. 1 (Autumn 1985); Jennings, "Black Leader."

2. For more on this, see Cruse, *Crisis of the Negro Intellectual.*

3. Mercer Cook was professor of Romance languages at Howard (1927–1970), head of department, and professor emeritus (1967–1970). He was an international diplomat, and ambassador to Niger, Senegal, and Gambia. Quotations in this and the several following paragraphs are from Mercer Cook, "Phylon Profile, XVIII: Ralph Johnson Bunche—Statesman," *Phylon* 9 (1948): 305–6.

4. Ralph Bunche, *A World View of Race* (Washington, D.C.: Associates in Negro Folk Education, 1936), 95–96.

5. Gunnar Myrdal (1898–1987) was a Swedish economist, politician, and Nobel laureate, known for his landmark book, *An American Dilemma: The Negro Problem and Modern Democracy,* that was commissioned by the Carnegie Foundation and first published in 1944.

6. Cook, "Ralph Johnson Bunche," 307.

7. For more information on Locke's tenure at Howard, see Leonard Harris and Charles Molesworth, *Alain L. Locke: Biography of a Philosopher* (Chicago: University of Chicago, 2008), chapters 4 and 5.

8. Ralph J. Bunche, Y. H. Krikorian, William Stuart Nelson, William Stanley Braithwaite, Benjamin Karpman, W. E. B. Du Bois, "The Passing of Alain Leroy Locke," *Phylon* 15 (1954): 243. Locke passed away in New York City on June 9, 1954, and his funeral was held on June 11. A footnote mentions that the funeral orations that compose these remembrances "were collected under the auspices of

the Alain Locke Memorial Committee, 12 Grove Street, New York City, 14." The committee was made up mainly of close friends of Locke.

9. Quotations in this and the next several paragraphs are from William Stuart Nelson, "The Passing of Alain Leroy Locke," 245–46.

10. Quotations in this and the next several paragraphs are from W. E. B. Du Bois, "The Passing of Alain Leroy Locke," 251–52.

11. Sterling Brown cited from Charles H. Rowell, "'Let Me Be with Ole Jazzbo': An Interview with Sterling A. Brown," *Callaloo* 14 (1991): 799–800.

12. Ibid., 806–7.

13. Pero Gaglo Dagbovie, "Black Women Historians from the Late Nineteenth Century to the Dawning of the Civil Rights Movement," *Journal of African American History* 89, no. 3 (Summer 2004): 252–53; Marion Thompson Wright, *The Education of Negroes in New Jersey* (New York: Columbia University Press, 1940); also Margaret E. Hayes and Doris B. Armstrong, "Marion Manola Thompson Wright, 1902–1962," in *Past and Promise: Lives of New Jersey Women*, ed. Joan N. Burstyn (Metuchen, N.J.: Scarecrow Press, 1990); Walter G. Daniel, "A Tribute to Marion Thompson Wright," *JNE* 32, no. 3 (Summer 1963): 308–10.

14. Avril Johnson Madison and Dorothy Porter Wesley, "Dorothy Burnett Porter Wesley: Enterprising Steward of Black Culture," *Public Historian* 17, no. 1 (Winter 1995): 26.

15. Thomas C. Battle, "Dorothy Porter Wesley: Preserver of Black History, Afro-American Librarian," *Black Issues in Higher Education*, January 25, 1996.

16. "Dorothy Porter Wesley: Howard University Librarian, Dies," *Jet*, January 8, 1996; "Dorothy Burnett Porter Wesley, 1905–1995," *Journal of Blacks in Higher Education* 43 (Spring 2004): 1; Dorothy Porter, "Documentation on the Afro-American: Familiar and Less Familiar Sources," *African Studies Bulletin* 12, no. 3 (December 1969); Janette Hoston Harris, "In Memoriam: Charles Harris Wesley," *Journal of Negro History* 83, no. 2 (Spring 1998); Dorothy B. Porter, "First International Congress of Africanists," *JNE* 32, no. 2 (Spring 1963).

17. Charles H. Rowell, "An Interview with Lois Mailou Jones," *Callaloo*, no. 39 (Spring 1989): 359.

18. Tritobia Hayes Benjamin, "Lois Mailou Jones," in Darlene Clark Hine, ed., *Black Women in America: An Historical Encyclopedia*, with associate editors Elsa Barkley Brown and Rosalyn Terborg-Penn (Brooklyn, N.Y.: Carlson Publishers, 1993), 651.

19. Ibid., 652.

20. *Africa and the Afro-American Experience: Eight Essays* (Washington, D.C.: Howard University Press, 1977).

21. Kwame Nkrumah was a Pan-Africanist leader of independent Ghana. He was educated in the United States at another historically black institution, Lincoln University in Pennsylvania.

22. Debra Newman Ham, "'For Such a Time as This': Lorraine A. Williams and the Howard University Department of History," *Negro History Bulletin* (July–December 1998); Winston, *Department of History*.

23. Ham, "For Such a Time as This."

24. Rosalyn Terborg-Penn, "Merze Tate," in Hine, *Black Women in America*. Books by Merze Tate include *The Disarmament Illusion: The Movement for a Limitation of Armaments to 1907* (1942), *The United States and Armaments* (1948), *The United States and the Hawaiian Kingdom: A Political History* (1965), and *Mineral Railways in Africa* (1989).

25. Banks from Dagbovie, "Black Women Historians," 241. He also cites Paula Giddings, *When and Where I Enter: The Impact of Black Women on Race and Sex in America* (New York: Amistad, 1984).

26. Madison and Wesley, "Dorothy Burnett Porter Wesley," 26; Banks, *Black Intellectuals.*

27. Dagbovie, "Black Women Historians," 241–44. To learn more about black women's experience with both racism and sexism in the academy, read Deborah Gray White, ed., *Telling Histories: Black Women Historians in the Ivory Tower* (Chapel Hill: University of North Carolina Press, 2008).

28. Gregory U. Rigsby, "Afro-American Studies at Howard University: One Year Later," *JNE* 39 (1970): 210.

29. Charles H. Thompson, "Race and Equality of Educational Opportunity: Defining the Problem," *JNE* 37 (1968): 191–203, quoted in Lenwood G. Davis and Belinda S. Daniels, "Charles H. Thompson: A Bibliography," *JNE* 50 (1981): 115.

30. Davis and Daniels, "Charles H. Thompson," 117; Kluger, *Simple Justice,* 168.

31. Quotations in this and the following several paragraphs come from Department of History, Howard University, "A Tribute to the Memory of Professor William Leo Hansberry," November 20, 1972, 1–2, Folder 27, Box 166–28, Series E, Rayford Logan Papers, MSRC.

32. Kwame Wes Alford, "The Early Growth and Development of William Leo Hansberry and the Birth of African Studies," *Journal of Black Studies* 30, no. 3 (January 2000); "William Leo Hansberry, 1894–1965," *Africa: Journal of the International African Institute* 36, no. 3 (July 1966): 325; Franz Ansprenger, "Hansberry College Inaugural Seminar on the Emergence of African Political Thought," *Journal of Modern African Studies* 1, no. 4 (December 1963). Another Howard University history professor, Joseph E. Harris, distinguished professor of African history since 1993, took up the Hansberry mantle, pioneering the area of African diaspora history with his important scholarship. See Joseph H. Harris, "African Diaspora Studies: Some International Dimensions," *Issue: A Journal of Opinion* 24, no. 2 (1996); Joseph H. Harris, ed., *Global Dimension of the African Diaspora* (Washington, D.C.: Howard University Press, 1993). Harris also edited two volumes of Hansberry's history notebook. See notebook volume 1, Joseph H. Harris, ed., *Pillars in Ethiopian History* (Washington, D.C.: Howard University Press, 1974, 1981), and notebook volume 2, Joseph H. Harris, ed., *Africa and Africans Seen by Classical Writers* (Washington, D.C.: Howard University Press, 1977).

33. Arthur P. Davis, "E. Franklin Frazier (1894–1962): A Profile," *JNE* 31 (1962): 432–33.

34. Ibid., 433.

35. Arthur P. Davis, "True Scholars Called Hope of Our Civilization," *Baltimore African American,* May 27, 1950, 6. This paper's name has changed several times over its lifetime.

36. Charles H. Wesley, *The History of Alpha Phi Alpha: A Development in College Life* (Baltimore, Md.: Foundation Publishers, 2000).

37. Ibid.

38. Linda M. Perkins, "Lucy Diggs Slowe: Champion of the Self-Determination of African American Women in Higher Education," *Journal of Negro History* 18 (Winter–Autumn 1996): 89–104. To find more information on black sororities, see Paula Giddings, *When and Where I Enter: The Impact of Black Women on Race and Sex in America* (New York: William Morrow, 1984); Paula Giddings, *In Search of Sisterhood: Delta Sigma Theta and the Challenge of the Black Sorority Movement* (New York: William Morrow, 1988); Lawrence C. Ross Jr., *The Divine Nine: The History of African American Fraternities and Sororities* (New York: Kensington Books, 2000).

39. *Baltimore African American,* October 10, 1936, 14. More research must be done on the Morehouse connection among members of the Howard intellectual commu-

nity. Theologian Walter Earl Fluker's Leadership Center at Morehouse College has been pioneering research into the Morehouse connections among Mays, Thurman, and Johnson, especially in regards to the Howard Thurman Papers Project housed there.

40. Joyce A. A. Camper, "Sterling Brown: Maker of Community in Academia," *African American Review* 31 (1997): 441. See also William F. Ryan, "Of Sterling Quality," *American Visions* (1987): 43–49.

41. Camper, "Sterling Brown," 45–48.

42. Rayford Logan, "Howard University," p. 2, undated, Folder 2 (Howard University, 1961–1965), Box 166–13, Series F, Rayford W. Logan Papers, MSRC.

43. Joanne V. Gabbin, *Sterling A. Brown: Building the Black Aesthetic Tradition* (Westport, Conn.: Greenwood Press, 1985), 49; Gabbin, "Sterling Brown: Maker of Community in Academia," *African American Review* 31 (1997).

44. Gabbin, *Sterling A. Brown*, 50.

45. Quotations in this and the next several paragraphs are from Sterling A. Brown, "Frazier Memoriam," pp. 2–4, undated, Folder 5, Box 131–1, E. Franklin Frazier Papers, MSRC.

46. This quotation and those in the following several paragraphs are from Houston A. Baker Jr., "Sterling's Magic: The Scholar and Poet Sterling Brown Stamped American Poetry with the Music of the Black Vernacular," *Black Issues Book Review* 3 (2001): 32–33. See also Michael Ekwueme Thelwell, "The Professor and the Activists: A Memoir of Sterling Brown," *Massachusetts Review* (Winter 1999/2000): 617–38.

47. Quotations in this and the next several paragraphs are from George Clement Bond and John Gibbs St. Clair Drake, "A Social Portrait of John St. Clair Drake: An American Anthropologist," *American Ethnologist* 15 (1988): 767–68.

48. See also Charles Jarmon, "Sociology at Howard University: From E. Franklin Frazier and Beyond," *Teaching Sociology* 31, no. 4 (October 2003); Anthony M. Platt, "The Rebellious Teaching Career of E. Franklin Frazier," *Journal of Blacks in Higher Education*, no. 13 (Autumn 1996); Gaines, *Uplifting the Race;* Kevin Gaines, *American Africans in Ghana: Black Expatriates and the Civil Rights Era* (Chapel Hill: University of North Carolina Press, 2006); Kevin Gaines, "E. Franklin Frazier's Revenge: Anticolonialism, Nonalignment, and the Black Intellectuals' Critiques of Western Culture," *American Literary History* 17, no. 3 (Fall 2005).

49. Charles Johnson chaired the department of social sciences at Fisk beginning in 1928. In 1947 he became the first black president of Fisk University and remained in that capacity until he died of a sudden heart attack in 1956. Horace Mann Bond was the president at Fort Valley State University in Georgia, beginning in 1939.

50. Miles Mark Fisher IV, "The Howard Years," in Lawrence E. Carter, ed., *Walking Integrity: Benjamin Elijah Mays, Mentor to Martin Luther King Jr.* (Macon, Ga.: Mercer University Press, 1998), 132. For more on Benjamin E. Mays, see Barbara Dianne Savage, *Your Spirits beside Us: The Politics of Black Religion* (Cambridge, Mass.: Belknap Press of Harvard University Press, 2008); Barbara Dianne Savage, "Benjamin Mays, Global Ecumenism, and Local Religious Segregation," *American Quarterly* 59, no. 3 (September 2007); Zachery R. Williams, "Prophets of Black Progress: Benjamin E. Mays and Howard W. Thurman, Pioneering Black Religious Intellectuals," *Journal of African American Men* 5, no. 4 (March 2001).

51. Thurman, *Head and Heart*, 87.

52. D. O. W. Holmes, "Kelly Miller the Educator." Remarks at the obsequies of Dean Emeritus Kelly Miller at the Andrew Rankin Chapel, Howard University, on

January 2, 1940, by D. O. W. Holmes, president, Morgan State College, Baltimore, Maryland, Kelly Miller Papers, MSRC.

53. Ibid., 2. Other works on Miller include W. D. Wright, "The Thought and Leadership of Kelly Miller," *Phylon* 39 (1978): 180–92; C. Alvin Hughes, "The Negro Sanhedrin Movement," *Journal of Negro History* 69 (1984): 1–13; August Meier, "The Racial and Educational Philosophy of Kelly Miller, 1895–1915," *JNE* 29 (1960): 121–27.

54. Platt, "Rebellious Teaching Career," 90.

55. For more concerning the intersection of black masculinity and black intellectuals, see Marlon B. Ross, *Manning the Race: Reforming Black Men in the Jim Crow Era* (New York: New York University Press, 2004).

56. The idea of this double consciousness was theorized by Du Bois, though it was experienced by many black scholars both before and after his lifetime. In addition to the Howard intellectuals, other scholars of note who have wrestled with this dual identity include Carter G. Woodson and Charles S. Johnson. Important works on these scholars include David L. Lewis, *W. E. B. Du Bois: Biography of a Race, 1868–1919* (New York: Henry Holt, 1993); David L. Lewis, *W. E. B. Du Bois: The Fight for Equality and the American Century, 1919–1963* (New York: Henry Holt, 2000); Goggin, *Carter G. Woodson;* and Richard Robbins, *Sideline Activist: Charles S. Johnson and the Struggle for Civil Rights* (Jackson: University Press of Mississippi, 1996). Also see Janken, *Rayford W. Logan.*

57. Holloway, *Confronting the Veil.*

58. Janken, *Rayford W. Logan,* 205.

59. McKinney, *Mordecai,* 83; Harold Lewis, from an address given during the symposium celebrating the hundredth anniversary of the birth of Mordecai Wyatt Johnson, January 12, 1990, videotape, Johnson Papers, MSRC; Walter B. Hill Jr., "The Suggestion that Ralph J. Bunch Was a Communist while Teaching at Howard University," *Journal of Blacks in Higher Education,* no. 17 (Autumn 1997): 114–15.

60. Rayford W. Logan, "The Diary of Rayford Logan," Library of Congress, Manuscript Division, 1943, cited in McKinney, *Mordecai,* 82.

61. Hill, "Suggestion that Ralph Bunche Was a Communist," 114.

62. Ibid.

63. Eleanor Lee Yates, "The Quiet Activist: Ralph Bunche," *Black Issues in Higher Education* 19 (2002): 46; Ron Walters, "Dr. Ralph Bunche," *Washington Informer* (1996): 15. There are several other good biographies of Ralph Bunche, including Henry, *Ralph Bunche;* Brian Urquhart, *Ralph Bunche: An American Life* (New York: W. W. Norton, 1993); and Benjamin Rivlin, ed., *Ralph Bunche: The Man and His Times* (New York: Holmes and Meier, 1990); also Charles Henry, "Abram Harris, E. Franklin Frazier, and Ralph Bunche: The Howard School of Thought on the Problem of Race," in Matthew Holden Jr., ed., *The Changing Racial Regime* (New Brunswick, N.J.: Transaction Publishers, 1995). For more on his radical thought and public intellectual activities, see John B. Kirby, "Ralph J. Bunche and Black Radical Thought in the 1930s," *Phylon* 35, no. 2 (1974); Jonathan Scott Holloway, "Ralph Bunche and the Responsibilities of the Public Intellectual," *JNE* 73, no. 2 (Spring 2004): "The Legacy of Ralph Bunche and Education: Celebrating the Centenary Year of His Birth."

64. "Sixteen New Professors Join Howard U. Faculty," *Baltimore African American,* September 20, 1952, 9.

65. Abe to Alaine, May 10, 1947, Folder 2, Box 164–34, Series C, Alain L. Locke Papers, MSRC.

66. The best biographical work on Abram Harris is by economist William A.

Darity Jr., in "Abram Harris: An Odyssey from Howard to Chicago," *Review of Black Political Economy* 15 (1987): 4–40, and in Darity and Ellison, "Abram Harris, Jr.," 611–27.

67. Abe to Alaine, May 12, 1942, Folder 2, Box 164–34, Series C, Alain L. Locke Papers, MSRC; Alain L. Locke, ed., *The New Negro,* 1st Antheneum ed. (New York: Antheneum, 1968). William Parity Jr., "Eric Williams and Slavery: A West Indian Viewpoint?" *Callaloo* 20, no. 4 (Autumn 1997).

68. Hansberry to Logan, May 12, 1953, Folder 10, Box 166–19, Series C, Rayford Logan Papers, MSRC.

69. Rayford W. Logan to Dr. J. St. Clair Price, May 13, 1953, ibid.

70. St. Clair Price to Hansberry, August 5, 1954, and Frank M. Snowden to Hansberry, January 12, 1959, Folder 5, Box 166–12, ibid.; Logan to St. Clair Price, October 2, 1946, Folder 10, Box 166–19, ibid.

71. Franklin to Locke, September 8, 1949, Folder 23, Box 164–30, Alain L. Locke Papers, MSRC.

72. Franklin to My Dear Friend, April 7, 1950, Folder 8, Box 166–11, Series C, Rayford Logan Papers, MSRC.

73. Logan to St. Clair Price, March 15, 1954, Box 166–19, Folder 10, ibid.

74. Nabrit to Logan, December 1, 1961, Folder 23, Box 166–16, ibid.

75. Ibid., January 19, 1962.

76. Ibid., December 1, 1961.

77. The information and quotations in this and the next several paragraphs are from Rayford Logan, "Howard University," undated (believed to be around 1962), Folder 4, Box 166–13, Series F (Writings by Logan), ibid.

78. Michael R. Winston, a writer and the president of the Alfred Harcourt Foundation, taught history at Howard from 1964 to 1990.

79. G. Frederick Stanton to Rayford Logan, September 26, 1966, Folder 20, Box 166–20, Series C, Rayford Logan Papers, MSRC.

80. Logan to Nabrit, September 30, 1966, Folder 23, Box 166–16, Series F, ibid.

81. Stanton L. Wormley to Logan, October 29, and Logan to Wormley, November 7, 1966, Folder 20, Box 166–23, Series C, ibid.

82. Logan to Wormley, November 7, 1966, ibid.

83. Janken, *Rayford W. Logan,* 225–27.

84. Quotations in this and the several following paragraphs are from the "Address by Dr. James M. Nabrit, Jr., President of Howard University, Formal Opening Exercises, September 16, 1963," pp. 1–2, James M. Nabrit Papers, Location unprocessed, MSRC.

85. Mercer Cook, Honor's Day Speech at Howard University, October 11, 1966, Folder 3, Box 157–5, Series D, Mercer Cook Papers, MSRC.

86. Ralph J. Bunche, Speech given at the Howard University Installation of Phi Beta Kappa Chapter of the District of Columbia, Andrew Rankin Chapel, April 8, 1953, Folder 18, Box 166–48, Series I, Rayford Logan Papers, MSRC.

87. Robert L. Harris Jr. to Rayford Logan, 5 November 1978, Folder 11, Box 181–4, ibid.

Chapter Four

1. Quotations in this and several following paragraphs are from Martin Kilson, "Styles of Black Public Intellectuals," *Black Renaissance/Renaissance Noire* 1 (1998): 1–2.

2. For a more contemporary examination of the concept of race men, see Carby's *Race Men.*

3. Kilson, "Black Public Intellectuals," 50.

4. "Dean Mays to Speak at Third Baptist Church," *Washington African American,* October 1, 1938, 18.

5. Mays, *Born to Rebel,* 148; Benjamin E. Mays, "The Color Line around the World," *JNE* 6, no. 2 (April 1937): 134–43.

6. "Friends of West Indies Federation Set in D.C.," *Baltimore African American,* April 12, 1958, 9.

7. Ibid.

8. For more information on the relationship of U.S. presidents with Howard University, see Muse, "Federal Government"; also Clifford L. Muse Jr., "Howard University and U.S. Foreign Affairs during the Franklin D. Roosevelt Administration, 1933–1945," *Journal of African American History* 83 (Autumn 2002).

9. "LBJ Howard Commencement Day Speaker," *Tri-State Defender,* May 20, 1961, 1; Joyce Ann Hanson, *Mary McLeod Bethune and Black Women's Political Activism* (Columbia: University of Missouri Press, 2003); Audrey T. McCluskey and Elaine M. Smith, eds., *Mary McLeod Bethune, Building a Better World: Essays and Selected Documents* (Bloomington: University of Indiana Press, 1999).

10. Arnaud Bontemps was a writer and the librarian of Fisk University beginning in 1943.

11. Marian Minus to Sterling Brown, March 23, 1939, Correspondence, File M, Box 8, Sterling Brown Papers, MSRC; Thomas E. Jones to Brown, February 5, 1941, File J, ibid.; Maurice A. Lawrence to Brown, January 19, 1963, File L, Box 13, ibid.; Lawrence to Nabrit, January 9, 1963, File L, Box 13, ibid.

12. Quotations from this and the several following paragraphs are from "Dr. Du Bois at Howard," Editorial, *Baltimore African American,* April 12, 1958, 5.

13. Logan, "Phylon Profile VI," 320; Logan, "Carter G. Woodson."

14. C. G. Woodson to Sterling Brown, December 11, 1931, Correspondence, Folder W, Box 7, Sterling Brown Papers, MSRC.

15. Clarence G. Contee, "The Encyclopedia Africana Project of W. E. B. Du Bois," *African Historical Studies* 4 (1971): 81–82.

16. *Baltimore Afro-American,* May 30, June 6, 1936.

17. Contee, "Encyclopedia Africana Project," 84–85.

18. Quotations in this and several following paragraphs are from W. E. B. Du Bois, "A Portrait of Carter G. Woodson," *Masses and Mainstream* 3 (June 1950): 24–25.

19. Woodson to Brown, May 8, 1936, Correspondence, Folder W, Box 7, Sterling Brown Papers, MSRC.

20. Ibid.

21. Ibid., November 7, 1936.

22. Patrick J. Gilpin, "Charles S. Johnson and the Race Relations Institutes at Fisk University," *Phylon* 41, no. 3 (1980); Katrina M. Sanders-Cassell, *Intelligent and Effective Direction: The Fisk University Race Relations Institute and the Struggle for Civil Rights, 1944–1969* (New York: Peter Lang, 2005); Patrick J. Gilpin and Marybeth Gasman, *Charles S. Johnson: Leadership beyond the Veil in the Age of Jim Crow* (Albany: State University of New York Press, 2003).

23. Gilpin, "Charles S. Johnson," 308.

24. Charles S. Johnson to Brown, June 19, 1928, File J, Box 6, ibid.

25. Walter White to Frazier, August 7, 1934, and Frazier to White, March 30, 1935, Folder 32, Box 131–16, Series B, E. Franklin Frazier Papers, MSRC.

26. White to Frazier, May 7, 1934, ibid.

27. Ibid.

28. Quotations in this and the several following paragraphs are from Frazier to White, May 17, 1934, ibid.

29. Quotations in this and the several following paragraphs are from "1500 Hear Integration–Non Segregation Debate," *Tri-State Defender,* November 18, 1961, 6.

30. Plummer, *Rising Wind,* 247, 253–54.

31. Ibid.

32. "Howard to Host African Society," *Baltimore African American,* March 30, 1963, 12; "Howard to Host Session on S. African Struggles," *Baltimore African American,* January 26, 1963, 17; "Confab to View Factors in S. African Struggle," *Tri-State Defender,* February 2, 1963, 7. For more information on the American Negro Leadership Conference on Africa, see James H. Meriwether, "The American Negro Leadership Conference on Africa and Its Arden House Conference: Politicizing and Institutionalizing the Relationship with Africa," *Afro-Americans in New York Life and History* 21 (1997): 39–63.

33. Rayford Logan, "The Historical Aspects of Pan-Africanism, 1900–1945," Third Annual AMSAC Conference, Folder 46, Box 166–37, Series F, Rayford Logan Papers, MSRC; "Confab to View Factors in S. Africa Struggle," *Tri-State Defender,* February 2, 1963, 7.

34. Logan, "Historical Aspects of Pan-Africanism," 15–16.

35. Plummer, *Rising Wind;* Brenda Gayle Plummer, "Evolution of a Black Foreign Policy Constituency," *Trans Africa Forum* 6 (Spring–Summer 1989).

36. Alain L. Locke to Nnamdi Azikiwe, November 7, 1945, Folder 42, Box 164–11, Series C, Alain L. Locke Papers, MSRC.

37. Janken, *Rayford W. Logan,* 205.

38. Memo from Eric Williams to Dean St. Clair Price, April 26, 1944, Folder 19, Eric Williams Memorial Collection, University of the West Indies.

39. Williams to Mordecai Johnson, September 21, 1944, Eric Williams Memorial Collection, University of the West Indies.

40. C. L. R. James to Alain Locke, February 2, 1953, Folder 27, Box 164–39, Series C, Alain L. Locke Papers, MSRC.

41. Locke cited from Dantes Bellegarde, *Au Service d'Haiti: appréciations sur un Haitien et son oeuvre* (Port-au-Prince: Théodore, 1962), 184.

42. Ibid.

43. *New York Times,* July 4, 1924; Janken, *Rayford W. Logan,* 74–75.

44. Janken, *Rayford W. Logan,* 74.

45. "Haitian Assails Us at League Meeting," *New York Times,* September 12, 1930.

46. Mercer Cook, "Dantes Bellegarde," *Phylon* 1 (1940): 132.

47. Patrick D. Bellegarde-Smith, "Dantes Bellegarde and Pan-Africanism," *Phylon* 42 (1981): 238–39, 241.

48. Samuel Hopkins, "Ambassador Says Niger Love JFK," *Baltimore African American,* January 19, 1963, 20.

49. Ibid.

50. Quotations in this and the several following paragraphs are from Mercer Cook, "René Maran (1887–1960)," pp. 2–3, undated, Folder 22, Box 157–5, Mercer Cook Papers, MSRC. See also Michel Fabre, "René Maran, the New Negro and Negritude," *Phylon* 36 (1975): 340–51.

51. For the Chicago School of Sociology, see Barbara Ballis Lal, "Black and Blue in Chicago: Robert Park's Perspective on Race Relations in Urban America, 1914–

1944," *British Journal of Sociology* 38, no. 4 (December 1987); Lee D. Baker, *From Savage to Negro: Anthropology and the Construction of Race, 1896–1954* (Berkeley and Los Angeles: University of California Press, 1998); Martin Bulmer, *The Chicago School of Research* (Chicago: University of Chicago Press, 1984); James E. Teele, ed., *E. Franklin Frazier and Black Bourgeoisie* (Columbia: University of Missouri Press, 2002); Ken Plummer, ed., *The Chicago School: Critical Assessments* (New York: Routledge, 1997).

52. R. Fred Wacker, "An American Dilemma: The Racial Theories of Robert E. Park and Gunnar Myrdal," *Phylon* 37, no. 2 (1976): 120.

53. Ibid., 120–25.

Chapter Five

1. Winston, "Through the Back Door," 698.

2. Interview with Ethelbert Miller, summer 2004, Howard University, transcript in author's possession.

3. Joseph E. Harris, "Professor Merze Tate: A Profile, 1905–1996," *Negro History Bulletin* (July–December 1998); Merze Tate, "The War Aims of World War I and World War II and Their Relation to the Darker Peoples of the World," *JNE* 12, no. 3 (Summer 1943): 521–32; Lorraine A. Williams, ed., *Africa and the Afro-American Experience: Eight Essays* (Washington, D.C.: Howard University Press, 1977); Dagbovie, "Black Women Historians," 241–61; Madison and Wesley, "Dorothy Burnett Porter Wesley."

4. Winston, "Through the Back Door," 695, 698.

5. Henry, "Howard School of Thought," 36. For Locke, see ibid., 51, 54. Characterizing the Howard paradigm as "transitional," Henry argued that Bunche, Harris, and Frazier promoted "a class analysis of race relations" favoring black/white worker unity, while pointing out the dysfunctionality of black culture. Ibid., 54. Jonathan Holloway expressed similar views in *Confronting the Veil*, 45–50. See also Winston, "Through the Back Door."

6. Jennifer Jordan, "Sterling Brown: A Race Man in the 1960s," *Callaloo* 21, no. 4 (Autumn 1998): 888–94.

7. Ralph J. Bunche, "A Critique of New Deal Social Planning as It Affects Negroes," *JNE* 5, no. 1 (January 1936); Ralph J. Bunche, "A Critical Analysis of the Tactics and Programs of Minority Groups," *JNE* 4, no. 3 (July 1935); Ralph J. Bunche, "The Negro in the Political Life of the United States," *JNE* 10, no. 3 (July 1941); Abram L. Harris, "A White and Black World in American Labor and Politics," *Social Forces* 4, no. 2 (December 1925); Abram L. Harris, "Economic Foundations of American Race Division," *Social Forces* 5, no. 3 (March 1927); E. Franklin Frazier, "The Status of the Negro in the American Social Order," *JNE* 4, no. 3 (July 1935); E. Franklin Frazier, "The Present Status of the Negro Family in the United States," *JNE* 8, no. 3 (July 1939).

8. E. Franklin Frazier, "The Role of Negro Schools in the Post-War World," *JNE* 13, no. 4 (Autumn 1944); E. Franklin Frazier, "The Negro Community, a Cultural Phenomenon," *Social Forces* 7, no. 3 (March 1924); E. Franklin Frazier, "The Negro Middle Class and Desegregation," *Social Problems* 4, no. 4 (April 1957); E. Franklin Frazier, "The Negro Family and Negro Youth," *JNE* 9, no. 3 (July 1940).

9. For more information on the Institute of the Black World, see Stephen Ward, "Scholarship in the Context of Struggle: Activist Intellectuals, the Institute of the Black World (IBW), and the Contours of Black Power Radicalism," *Black Scholar* 31, no. 4 (2001): 42–53.

10. Interview with Dr. James B. Stewart, January 6, 2004, transcript in possession of author.

11. Alain L. Locke and Bernhard J. Stern, eds., *When Peoples Meet: A Study in Race and Culture Contacts* (New York: Hayden and Eldredge, 1946).

12. *Baltimore African American*, May 23, 1931, 1.

13. Dr. Anna Julia Cooper was a noted black author, educator, and leading member of the talented tenth community in Washington, D.C. See Anna Julia Cooper, *A Voice from the South, by a Black Woman of the South* (Xenia, Ohio: Aldine Printing House, 1892).

14. Otto Klineberg to Sterling Brown, April 8, 1941, Correspondence, Folder K, Box 9, Sterling Brown Papers, MSRC.

15. Mia Bay, *The White Image in the Black Mind: African American Ideas about White People, 1865–1925* (New York: Oxford University Press, 2000); George M. Fredrickson, *The Black Image in the White Mind: The Debate on Afro-American Character and Destiny, 1817–1914* (New York: Harper and Row, 1971).

16. John Edgar Tidwell, "Double Conscious Brother in the Veil: Toward an Intellectual Biography of Sterling A. Brown," *Callaloo* 21, no. 4 (Autumn 1998): 937. See also John Edgar Tidwell, John S. Wright, and Sterling A. Brown, "'Steady and Unaccusing': An Interview with Sterling A. Brown," *Callaloo* 21, no. 4 (Autumn 1998).

17. Otto Klineberg to Sterling Brown, April 8, 1941, Correspondence, Folder K, Box 9, Sterling Brown Papers, MSRC; Fahamisha Patricia Brown, "And I Owe It All to Sterling Brown: The Theory and Practice of Black Literary Studies," *African American Review* 31, no. 3 (Autumn 1997); Houston Baker and Patricia Redmond, eds., *Afro-American Literary Study in the 1990s* (Chicago: University of Chicago Press, 1989); John Edgar Tidwell, John S. Wright, and Sterling A. Brown, "'Steady and Unaccusing': An Interview with Sterling A. Brown," *Callaloo* 21, no. 4 (Autumn 1998).

18. Robert L. Harris Jr., "Segregation and Scholarship: The American Council of Learned Societies' Committee on Negro Studies, 1941–1950," *Journal of Black Studies* 12 (1982): 315, 317.

19. Ibid., 318–19.

20. Ibid., 319–21.

21. Gilpin, "Charles S. Johnson," 300.

22. "Cuban Heads New Racial Study Body," *Baltimore African American*, December 4, 1943, 12.

23. Melville Herskovits to Committee on Negro Studies, November 14, 1944, Correspondence, Folder H, Box 8, Sterling Brown Papers, MSRC (enclosing Jorge A. Vivó to Melville Herskovits, October 24, 1944, ibid.).

24. Ibid.

25. "Cuban Heads New Racial Study Body," *Baltimore African American*, December 4, 1943, 12.

26. "Black History Museum," *Sun Reporter*, February 15, 1979, 4.

27. Ibid.

28. "The Origin of the Idea," Folder 13, Box 71–1, Series C, Kelly Miller Papers, MSRC.

29. Ibid., 28–29.

30. Ibid., 29–30.

31. Ibid., 32; Mordecai Johnson to Professor Miller, July 28, August 19, 1938, Folder 25, ibid.; Minutes of the Meeting of the Committee on the National Negro Library and Museum, September 13, 1938, Folder 14, ibid.

32. "The Origin of the Idea," p. 32, Folder 13, Box 71–1, Series C, Kelly Miller

Papers, MSRC; Mordecai Johnson to Professor Miller, July 28, August 19, 1938, Folder 25, ibid.; Minutes of the Meeting of the Committee on the National Negro Library and Museum, September 13, 1938, Folder 14, ibid.

33. Miller to Guy B. Johnson, November 11, 1938, Folder 25, ibid.

34. Miller to Johnson, May 3, 1939, ibid.

35. Brawley to Miller, September 7, August 11, August 15, 1938, Folder B, ibid.

36. "Gloomy VA Dean Assailed for V.T. Doctrine: Prof. Rayford Logan Raps Dean Hancock's Columbia Speech," *Baltimore African American*, May 23, 1931, 1.

37. Logan to Dr. Charles H. Thompson, July 20, 1940, Folder 4, Box 166–21, Series C, Rayford Logan Papers, MSRC.

38. "African Research Academy Started," *Baltimore African American*, November 20, 1943, 11.

39. Nabrit to Logan, July 1, 1965, Folder 23, Box 166–16, Series C, Rayford Logan Papers, MSRC.

40. Horace Mann Bond, "C. H. Thompson Urges Legal Steps to Get Better Schools," *Pittsburgh Courier*, August 4, 1934, 7. Education professor Charles H. Thompson wrote a number of articles for the *Journal of Negro Education* and other scholarly journals on the condition of black colleges and the question of segregation. See, for example, Charles H. Thompson, "The Control and Administration of the Negro College," *Journal of Educational Sociology* 19 (1946): 484–95; "The Present Status of the Negro Private and Church-Related College," *JNE* 29 (1960): 227–44; "The Prospect of Negro Higher Education," *Journal of Educational Sociology* 32 (1959): 309–16; "The Higher Education of Negro Americans: Prospects and Program, a Critical Summary," *JNE* 36 (1967): 295–314.

41. "H.U. Launches Adult Education Program," *Baltimore African American*, September 27, 1952, 20.

42. Eugene C. Holmes, "Alain L. Locke and the Adult Education Movement," *JNE* 34 (1965): 5, 6.

43. Ibid., 7. Among the articles written by Alain Locke that detail his educational philosophy and that contributed to the field of adult education, see "Moral Training in Elementary Schools," *Teacher* 8 (1904): 95–101; "The Role of the Talented Tenth," *Howard University Record* 12 (1918): 15–18; "Negro Education Bids for Par," *Survey* 54 (1925): 567–70; "Minorities and the Social Mind," *Progressive Education* (1935): 141–50; "Types of Adult Education: The Intellectual Interests of Negroes," *Journal of Adult Education* 8 (1935–1936): 352; "Education for Adulthood," *Adult Education Journal* 6 (1947): 104–11. Also see Rudolph A. Cain, "Alain Leroy Locke: Crusader and Advocate for the Education of African American Adults," *JNE* 64 (1995): 87–99.

44. "H.U. Launches Adult Education Program," *Baltimore African American*, September 27, 1952, 20.

45. Francille Rusan Wilson, "Racial Consciousness and Black Scholarship: Charles H. Wesley and the Construction of Negro Labor in the United States," *Journal of Negro History* 81 (1996): 72, 75, 84.

46. Davis and Daniels, "Charles H. Thompson," 111–12; Kluger, *Simple Justice*, 168–72, 221–22, 257, 280, 292, 331, 534.

47. Kluger, *Simple Justice*, 168–72, 221–22, 257, 280, 292, 331, 534 (168); Winston, "Through the Back Door," 695, 698.

48. Winston, "Through the Back Door." Regarding the *Brown* case, see also Ronald Roach, "The Scholar-Activists of Brown," *Black Issues in Higher Education*, May 20, 2004, 26–31; Earl Calloway, "Dr. Mordecai Johnson Laid the Foundation for *Brown v. Board of Education*," *Chicago Defender*, January 31, 2004, 23.

49. Muse, "Howard University and the Federal Government," 1–20; Babaloa Cole, "Appropriation Politics and Black Schools: Howard University in the U.S. Congress, 1879–1928," *JNE* 46 (1977): 7–23.

50. Eleanor W. Traylor, R. Victoria Arana, and John M. Reilly, "Runnin' Space: The Continuing Legacy of Sterling Brown," *African American Review* 31 (1997): 389–92. A good recent biography of Amiri Baraka is Komozi Woodard's *A Nation within a Nation: Amiri Baraka (Leroi Jones) and the Black Power Politics* (Chapel Hill: University of North Carolina Press, 1999).

51. A good treatment of the historical evolution and development of African studies in the United States and abroad during the Cold War era is William G. Martin and Michael O. West, eds., *Out of One, Many Africas: Reconstructing the Study and Meaning of Africa* (Urbana: University of Illinois Press, 1999).

52. Benjamin Mays, *The Negro's God as Reflected in His Literature* (Boston: Chapman and Grimes, 1930). This work was one of the first twentieth-century theological examinations of African American interpretations of God.

53. Mark L. Chapman, *Christianity on Trial: African American Religious Thought Before and After Black Power* (Maryknoll, N.Y.: Orbis Books, 1996); Mark L. Chapman, "'Of One Blood': Mays and the Theology of Race Relations," in Carter, *Walking Integrity.* See also William Stuart Nelson, ed., *The Christian Way in Race Relations* (Freeport, N.Y.: Books for Libraries Press, 1971; reprint, New York: Harper, 1948); "School of Religion at Howard," *Pittsburgh Courier,* November 1, 1965, 10.

54. For example, see Bunche, *World View of Race;* Frazier, *Black Bourgeoisie.*

55. For more on the New York Intellectuals, see Jumonville, *Critical Crossings.*

56. Harold Cruse was an American academic, an outspoken social and cultural critic, and professor of history and Afro-American studies at the University of Michigan. He was one of the very first African Americans to become a professor without possessing a college degree. He helped create the Center for Afro-American and African Studies. See also Harold Cruse, *The Crisis of the Negro Intellectual* (1967; New York: Quill, 1984); William Jelanie Cobb, ed., *The Essential Harold Cruse: A Reader* (New York: Palgrave, 2002); Jerry Watts, ed., *The Crisis of the Negro Intellectual Reconsidered* (New York: Routledge, 2004).

57. E. Franklin Frazier, "Failure of the Negro Intellectual," in G. Franklin Edwards, ed., *E. Franklin Frazier on Race Relations* (Chicago: University of Chicago Press, 1968), 268–69.

58. Ibid., 272–73; Clovis E. Semmes, "The Sociological tradition of E. Franklin Frazier: Implications for Black Studies," *JNE* 55, no. 4 (Autumn 1986): 493.

59. Frazier, "Failure of the Negro Intellectual," 269–70.

60. Frazier, *Black Bourgeoisie.*

61. Frazier, "Failure of the Negro Intellectual," 272–73.

62. Ibid., 279.

63. Teele, *Frazier and Black Bourgeoisie.*

64. Michael R. Winston, "E. Franklin Frazier's Role in African Studies," in James E. Teele, ed., *E. Franklin Frazier and Black Bourgeoisie* (Columbia: University of Missouri, 2002), 139. See also Platt, "Rebellious Teaching Career," 86–90; Platt, *Frazier Reconsidered.*

65. Winston, "Frazier's Role," 139–40.

66. The Council on African Affairs was a leading Pan-Africanist and anticolonization organization founded in 1937. Like historically black colleges and universities and their scholars, the CAA was heavily impacted by Cold War McCarthyism, dissolving by the 1950s, however not before having energized the links between the struggles of African Americans and other colonized populations in Africa and

Asia. See Plummer, *Rising Wind;* also Penny von Escher, *Race against Empire: Black America and Anticolonialism, 1937–1957* (Ithaca, N.Y.: Cornell University Press, 1997).

67. Ibid., 140. For a more detailed discussion of the activities of the global black intellectual community, see Plummer, *Rising Wind.*

68. For a thorough treatment of Alioune Diop and *Présence Africaine,* see Salah D. Hassan, "Inaugural Issues: The Cultural Politics of the Early *Présence Africaine,* 1947–1955," *Research in African Literatures* 30 (1999): 194–221.

69. Teele, *Black Bourgeoisie,* 142.

70. Juan Williams, *The Joint Center: Portrait of a Black Think Tank* (Washington, D.C.: Joint Center for Political and Economic Studies, 1995), 5.

71. Ibid., 11.

72. Ibid., 8, 6.

73. Clark was also on the board of trustees at Howard University. At its inception, the Joint Center "was intentionally attached to Howard University," so that it could "achieve solid academic footing." Williams, *Joint Center,* 6.

74. Williams, *Joint Center,* 8.

75. Ibid., 6. See also John H. Britton Jr., "Fueling the Black Political Participation Movement: The Joint Center for Political Studies," *PS: Political Science and Politics* 7, no. 1 (Winter 1974): 6–8.

76. Williams, *Joint Center,* 11. The success of the Joint Center came, ironically, as the civil rights movement and the breakdown of segregation began to deplete the Howard community. During the late 1960s, black issues and race became "trendy" and attracted the support of large foundations and white universities that had traditionally marginalized the study of Africa and African Americans.

77. Williams, *Joint Center,* 8.

78. Alex Poinsett, *Walking with Presidents: Louis Martin and the Rise of Black Political Power* (Lanham, Md.: Madison Books, 1997), 177.

79. The board of governors in 1974 included social psychologist Kenneth Clark; Howard University president James Cheek; vice president for academic affairs at Howard University, Andrew Billingsley; vice president of Chicago's Sengstacke newspaper chain and adviser to presidents, Louis Martin; the Honorable Edward W. Brooke, U.S. senator from Massachusetts; and Pittsburgh lawyer Wendell Freeland. Scholars with whom the Joint Center established close professional relationships were political scientists Matthew Holden of the University of Wisconsin–Madison; Ronald Walters of Howard University; Mack Jones of Atlanta University; Charles Hamilton of Columbia University; Robert Weaver of Hunter College; government professor Martin Kilson; and Tom Pettigrew of Harvard University.

80. Britton, "Fueling the Black Political Participation Movement"; Poinsett, *Walking with Presidents,* 176–77.

Conclusion

1. Courtland Milloy, "D.C. Should Find Ways to Attract Black Scholars," *Washington Post,* January 9, 2002, B1.

2. Cornel West, "The Dilemma of the Black Intellectual," *Journal of Blacks in Higher Education* 2 (1993/1994): 59.

3. Franklin, "Dilemma of the American Negro Scholar," 297.

4. Quotations in this and the next several paragraphs are from Jerry G. Watts,

"Dilemmas of Black Intellectuals: What Role Should We Play?" *Dissent* (1989): 501.

5. Abram Harris was heading the economics department at Howard from 1936 to 1945, when he went to the University of Chicago. He stayed there until his death in 1963. John Hope Franklin went from Howard to Brooklyn College in 1956.

6. Sophia F. McDowell, Gilbert A. Lowe Jr., and Doris A. Dockett, "Howard University's Student Protest Movement," *Public Opinion Quarterly* 343, no. 3 (autumn 1970). See also Rojas, *From Black Power to Black Studies;* Turner, *The Next Decade.*

7. Robert Bruce Slater, "The First Black Faculty Members at the Nation's Highest-Ranked Universities," *Journal of Blacks in Higher Education* (1998–1999): 97.

8. Ibid.

9. Jumonville, *Critical Crossings.*

10. Fluker and Tumber, *Strange Freedom,* 5.

11. Interview with Dr. James B. Stewart, January 6, 2004, transcript in author's possession. See also Collins, "Black Public Intellectuals."

12. Baker, *Betrayal.*

SELECTED BIBLIOGRAPHY

PRIMARY SOURCES

Manuscript Collections

Manuscript Division, Moorland-Spingarn Research Center, Howard University, Washington, D.C.
  Sterling A. Brown Papers
  Mercer Cook Papers
  E. Franklin Frazier Papers
  Mordecai Wyatt Johnson Papers
  Alain L. Locke Papers
  Rayford W. Logan Papers
  Kelly Miller Papers
  James M. Nabrit Papers
Manuscript Division, Library of Congress, Washington, D.C.
  Rayford W. Logan Papers
Eric Williams Memorial Collection, University of the West Indies
  Eric Williams Papers

Newspapers

Baltimore Afro-American (also known as the *African American*)
Chicago Defender
Dallas Express
Messenger
New Pittsburgh Courier
New York Age
New York Times

Opportunity
Pittsburgh Courier
Sun Reporter
Tri-State Defender
Washington Daily American
Washington Post
Washington Tribune

Autobiographies, Biographies, and Memoirs

Mays, Benjamin E. *Born to Rebel: An Autobiography.* Athens: University of Georgia Press, 1971, 1987.

Thurman, Howard. *With Head and Heart: The Autobiography of Howard Thurman.* New York: Harcourt Brace Jovanovich, 1979.

Contemporary Books, Periodicals, and Miscellaneous Items

Aley, Robert J. "College Salaries." *Educational Review* 59 (1920): 244–49.

Bunche, Ralph J. *A World View of Race.* Washington, D.C.: Associates in Negro Folk Education, 1936.

Bunche, Ralph, Y. H. Krikorian, William Stuart Nelson, Stanley Braithwaite, Benjamin Karpman, and W. E. B. Du Bois. "The Passing of Alain Leroy Locke." *Phylon* 15 (1954): 243–52.

Cook, Mercer. "Dantes Bellegarde." *Phylon* 1 (1940): 125–35.

_____. "Phylon Profile, XVIII: Ralph Johnson Bunche, Statesman." *Phylon* 9 (1948): 303–9.

Davis, Arthur P. "E. Franklin Frazier (1894–1962): A Profile." *Journal of Negro Education* 31 (1962): 429–35.

Du Bois, W. E. B. *The Souls of Black Folk.* 1903. Centenary edition, edited by Henry Louis Gates Jr. and Terri Hume Oliver. New York: W. W. Norton, 1999.

_____. "Howard and Lincoln." *Crisis* 32 (1926): 7–8.

Dyson, Walter. *Howard University, the Capstone of Negro Education: A History, 1867–1940.* Washington, D.C.: Graduate School of Howard University, 1941.

Edwards, G. Franklin. *E. Franklin Frazier on Race Relations.* Chicago: University of Chicago Press, 1968.

Franklin, John Hope. "Courses Concerning the Negro in Negro Colleges." *Quarterly Review of Higher Education among Negroes* 8 (1940): 138–44.

Frazier, E. Franklin. *Black Bourgeoisie: The Rise of a New Middle Class in the*

United States. London: Collier-Macmillan, 1957; New York: Collier Books, 1962.

Holmes, Eugene C. "Alain L. Locke and the Adult Education Movement." *Journal of Negro Education* 34 (1965): 1, 5–10.

Kempner, Aubrey J. "How Professors Live." *School and Society* 12 (1920): 436–41.

Locke, Alain L. "Moral Training in Elementary Schools." *Teacher* 8 (1904): 95–101.

_____. "The Role of the Talented Tenth." *Howard University Record* 12 (1918): 15–18.

_____. "Negro Education Bids for Par." *Survey* 54 (1925): 567–70.

_____. "Minorities and the Social Mind." *Progressive Education* (1935): 141–50.

_____. "The Intellectual Interests of Negroes." *Journal of Adult Education* 8 (1935–1936): 352.

_____. "Education for Adulthood." *Adult Education Journal* 6 (1947): 104–11.

Logan, Rayford W. "Phylon Profile VI: Carter G. Woodson." *Phylon* 6, no. 4 (1945): 315–21.

_____. "Howard University." Undated, Folder 2, Howard University: 1961–1965, Box 166–13, Series E, Rayford W. Logan Papers, MSRC.

_____. *History of Howard University: The First Hundred Years, 1867–1967*. New York: New York University Press, 1969.

_____. "Carter G. Woodson: Mirror and Molder of His Times, 1875–1950." *Journal of Negro History* 58, no. 1 (January 1973).

Nelson, William Stuart. *The Christian Way in Race Relations*. Reprint. Freeport, N.Y.: Books for Libraries Press, 1971.

"A New Course in History at Howard University." *Howard University Record* 17 (1923): 237–39.

Rigsby, Gregory U. "Afro-American Studies at Howard University: One Year Later." *Journal of Negro Education* 39 (1970): 209–13.

Thompson, Charles H. "The Control and Administration of the Negro College." *Journal of Educational Sociology* 19 (1946): 484–96.

_____. "The Prospect of Negro Higher Education." *Journal of Educational Sociology* 32 (1959): 309–16.

_____. "The Present Status of the Negro Private and Church-Related College." *Journal of Negro Education* 29 (1960): 227–44.

_____. "The Higher Education of Negro Americans: Prospects and Program—A Critical Summary." *Journal of Negro Education* 36 (1967): 295–314.

_____. "Race and Equality of Educational Opportunity: Defining the Problem." *Journal of Negro Education* 37 (1968): 191–203.

Veblen, Thorstein. *The Higher Learning in America.* New York: B. W. Huebsch, 1918.

Wechsler, James A. *Revolt on the Campus.* New York: Covic, Friede, 1935.

Wesley, Charles H. "Carter G. Woodson—as a Scholar." *Journal of Negro History* 36, no. 1 (January 1951): 12–24.

Woodson, Carter G., ed. *The Works of Francis J. Grimké.* 4 vols. Washington, D.C.: Associated Publishers, 1942.

Official Federal Published Reports

Congressional Record: Sixty-Ninth Congress, First Session. Washington, D.C.: U.S. Government Printing Office.

Congressional Record: Seventieth Congress, Second Session. Washington, D.C.: U.S. Government Printing Office.

SECONDARY SOURCES

Books

Baker, Houston. *Betrayal: How Black Intellectuals Have Abandoned the Ideals of the Civil Rights Era.* New York: Columbia University Press, 2008.

Banks, William M. *Black Intellectuals: Race and Responsibility in American Life.* New York: W. W. Norton, 1996.

Bellegarde, Dantes. *Au Service d'Haiti: appréciations sur un Haitien et son oeuvre.* Port-au-Prince: Théodore, 1962.

Bender, Thomas H. *Intellect and Public Culture: Essays on the Social History of Academic Intellectuals in the United States.* Baltimore: Johns Hopkins University Press, 1993.

Bloom, Alexander. *Prodigal Sons: The New York Intellectuals and Their World.* New York: Oxford University Press, 1986.

Carby, Hazel. *Race Men.* Cambridge, Mass.: Harvard University Press, 1998.

Carter, Lawrence E., ed. *Walking Integrity: Benjamin Elijah Mays, Mentor to Martin Luther King Jr.* Macon, Ga.: Mercer University Press, 1998.

Cruse, Harold. *The Crisis of the Negro Intellectual.* New York: William Morrow, 1967.

Fluker, Walter Earl, and Catherine Tumber, eds. *A Strange Freedom: The Best of Howard Thurman on Religious Experience and Public Life.* Boston: Beacon Press, 1998.

Franklin, John Hope. "Dilemma of the American Negro Scholar." In *Race and History: Selected Essays, 1938–1988*, ed. John Hope Franklin. Baton Rouge: Louisiana State University Press, 1989.

Gabbin, Joanne V. *Sterling A. Brown: Building the Black Aesthetic Tradition.* Westport, Conn.: Greenwood Press, 1985.

Goggin, Jacqueline. *Carter G. Woodson: A Life in Black History.* Baton Rouge: Louisiana State University Press, 1993.

Green, Constance. *The Secret City: A History of Race Relations in the Nation's Capital.* Princeton, N.J.: Princeton University Press, 1967.

Henry, Charles P. *Ralph Bunche: Model Negro or American Other?* New York: New York University Press, 1999.

Hine, Darlene Clark, ed. *Black Women in America: An Historical Encyclopedia.* Associate editors Elsa Barkley Brown and Rosalyn Terborg-Penn. Brooklyn, N.Y.: Carlson Publishers, 1993.

Holloway, Jonathan Scott. *Confronting the Veil: Abram Harris Jr., E. Franklin Frazier, and Ralph Bunche, 1919–1941.* Chapel Hill: University of North Carolina Press, 2002.

Janken, Kenneth. *Rayford W. Logan and the Dilemma of the African American Intellectual.* Amherst: University of Massachusetts Press, 1993.

Jumonville, Neil. *Critical Crossings: The New York Intellectuals in Postwar America.* Berkeley and Los Angeles: University of California Press, 1991.

Kluger, Richard. *Simple Justice: The History of* Brown v. Board of Education *and Black America's Struggle for Equality.* New York: Alfred A. Knopf, 1976.

Lewis, David L. *W. E. B. Du Bois: Biography of a Race, 1868–1919.* New York: Henry Holt, 1993.

_____. *W .E. B. Du Bois: The Fight for Equality and the American Century, 1919–1963.* New York: Henry Holt, 2000.

Lipset, Seymour Martin. *Rebellion in the University.* Boston: Little, Brown, 1971.

Luker, Ralph E. *The Social Gospel in Black and White: American Racial Reform, 1885–1912.* Chapel Hill: University of North Carolina Press, 1991.

Martin, William G., and Michael O. West, eds. *Out of One, Many Africas: Reconstructing the Study and Meaning of Africa.* Urbana: University of Illinois Press, 1999.

McKinney, Richard I. *Mordecai, the Man and His Message: The Story of Mordecai Wyatt Johnson.* Washington, D.C.: Howard University Press, 1997.

McNeil, Genna Rae. *Groundwork: Charles Hamilton Houston and the Struggle for Civil Rights.* Philadelphia: University of Pennsylvania Press, 1983.

Meier, August. *Negro Thought in America, 1880–1915: Racial Ideologies in the*

Age of Booker T. Washington. Ann Arbor: University of Michigan Press, 1963.

Moses, Wilson Jeremiah. *Alexander Crummell: A Study of Civilization and Discontent.* Amherst: University of Massachusetts Press, 1989.

Moss, Alfred. *The American Negro Academy: Voice of the Talented Tenth.* Baton Rouge: Louisiana State University Press, 1981.

Platt, Anthony M. *E. Franklin Frazier Reconsidered.* New Brunswick, N.J.: Rutgers University Press, 1991.

Plummer, Brenda Gayle. *Rising Wind: Black Americans and U.S. Foreign Affairs, 1935–1960.* Chapel Hill: University of North Carolina Press, 1996.

Rivlin, Benjamin, ed. *Ralph Bunche: The Man and His Times.* New York: Holmes and Meier, 1990.

Robbins, Richard. *Sideline Activist: Charles S. Johnson and the Struggle for Civil Rights.* Jackson: University of Mississippi Press, 1996.

Rojas, Fabio. *From Black Power to Black Studies: How a Radical Social Movement Became an Academic Discipline.* Baltimore: Johns Hopkins University Press, 2007.

Teele, James E., ed. *E. Franklin Frazier and the Black Bourgeoisie.* Columbia: University of Missouri Press, 2002.

Thorpe, Earl. *The Mind of the Negro: An Intellectual History of Afro-Americans.* Westport, Conn.: Negro Universities Press, 1970.

Turner, James E. *The Next Decade: Theoretical and Research Issues in Africana Studies.* Ithaca, N.Y.: Africana Studies and Research Center, 1984.

Urquhart, Brian. *Ralph Bunche: An American Life.* New York: W. W. Norton, 1993.

Wesley, Charles H. *The History of Alpha Phi Alpha: A Development in College Life.* Washington, D.C.: Howard University Press, 1929; reprint, Baltimore: Foundation Publishers, 2000.

Wilford, Hugh. *The New York Intellectuals: From Vanguard to Institution.* Manchester, England: Manchester University Press, 1995.

Williams, Juan. *The Joint Center: A Portrait of a Black Think Tank.* Washington, D.C.: Joint Center for Political and Economic Studies, 1995.

Wolters, Raymond. *The New Negro on Campus: Black College Rebellions of the 1920s.* Princeton, N.J.: Princeton University Press, 1975.

Woodard, Komozi. *A Nation within a Nation: Amiri Baraka (Leroi Jones) and Black Power Politics.* Chapel Hill: University of North Carolina Press, 1999.

Articles

Baker, Houston A. "Sterling's Magic: The Scholar and Poet Sterling Brown Stamped American Poetry with the Music of the Black Vernacular." *Black Issues Book Review* 3 (2001): 32.

Bellegarde-Smith, Patrick D. "Dantes Bellegarde and Pan-Africanism." *Phylon* 42 (1981): 233–44.

Benjamin, Tritobia Hayes. "Lois Mailou Jones." In *Black Women in America: An Historical Encyclopedia,* ed. Darlene Clark Hine, associate eds. Elsa Barkley Brown and Rosalyn Terborg-Penn. Brooklyn, N.Y.: Carlson Publishers, 1993.

Bond, George Clement, and John Gibbs St. Clair Drake. "A Social Portrait of John Gibbs St. Clair Drake: An American Anthropologist." *American Ethnologist* 15 (1988): 762–81.

Cain, Rudolph A. "Alain Leroy Locke: Crusader and Advocate for the Education of African American Adults." *Journal of Negro Education* 64 (1995): 87–99.

Cole, Babaloa. "Appropriation Politics and Black Schools: Howard University in the U.S. Congress, 1879–1928." *Journal of Negro Education* 46 (1977): 7–23.

Collins, Patricia Hill. "Black Public Intellectuals: From Du Bois to the Present," *Contexts* 4, no. 4 (Fall 2005): 22–27.

Contee, Clarence G. "The Encyclopedia Africana Project of W. E. B. Du Bois." *African Historical Studies* 4 (1971): 77–91.

Dagbovie, Pero Gaglo. "Black Women Historians from the Late Nineteenth Century to the Dawning of the Civil Rights Movement." *Journal of African American History* 89, no. 3 (Summer 2004): 241–61.

Darity, William A., Jr., and Julian Ellison. "Abram Harris, Jr.: The Economics of Race and Social Reform." *History of Political Economy* 22 (1990): 611–27.

Darity, William J. "Abram Harris: An Odyssey from Howard to Chicago." *Review of Black Political Economy* 15 (1987): 4–40.

Davis, Lenwood G., and Belinda S. Daniels. "Charles H. Thompson: A Bibliography." *Journal of Negro Education* 50 (1981): 111–21.

Fabre, Michel. "Rene Maran, the New Negro and Negritude." *Phylon* 36 (1975): 340–51.

Gilpin, Patrick J. "Charles S. Johnson and the Race Relations Institutes at Fisk University." *Phylon* 41, no. 3 (1980): 300–311.

Harris, Janette Hoston. "Woodson and Wesley: A Partnership in Building the Association for the Study of Afro-American Life and History." *Journal of Negro History* 83, no. 2 (Spring 1998): 109–19.

Harris, Robert L., Jr. "Segregation and Scholarship: The American Council of Learned Societies' Committee on Negro Studies, 1941–1950." *Journal of Black Studies* 12 (1982): 315–31.

Hassan, Salah D. "Inaugural Issues: The Cultural Politics of the Early Presence Africaine, 1947–1955." *Research in African Literatures* 30 (1999): 194–221.

Henry, Charles P. "Abram Harris, E. Franklin Frazier, and Ralph Bunche: The Howard School of Thought on the Problem of Race." In *The Changing Racial Regime,* ed. Matthew Holden Jr. New Brunswick, N.J.: Transaction Publishers, 1995.

Hill, Walter B. "The Suggestion that Ralph Bunche Was a Communist while Teaching at Howard University." *Journal of Blacks in Higher Education* (1997): 114–15.

Hughes, C. Alvin. "The Negro Sanhedrin Movement." *Journal of Negro History* 69 (1984): 1–13.

Jennings, Willie James. "The Burden of the Black Leader." *Books and Culture: A Christian Review* (March/April 1998): 1–10.

Kilson, Martin. "Styles of Black Public Intellectuals." *Black Renaissance/Renaissance Noire* 1 (1998): 1–17.

Madison, Avril Johnson, and Dorothy Porter Wesley. "Dorothy Burnett Porter Wesley: Enterprising Steward of Black Culture." *Public Historian* 17, no. 1 (Winter 1995): 26.

Meier, August. "The Racial and Educational Philosophy of Kelly Miller, 1895–1915." *Journal of Negro Education* 29 (1960): 121–27.

Meriwether, James H. "The American Negro Leadership Conference on Africa and Its Arden House Conference: Politicizing and Institutionalizing the Relationship with Africa." *Afro-Americans in New York Life and History* 21, no. 2 (1997): 39–63.

Moses, Wilson J. "The Lost World of the Negro, 1895–1919: Black Literary and Intellectual Life before the Renaissance." *Black American Literature Forum* 21 (1987): 61–84.

Muse, Clifford. "Howard University and the Federal Government during the Presidential Administrations of Herbert Hoover and Franklin D. Roosevelt, 1928–1945." *Journal of Negro History* 76 (1991): 1–20.

Platt, Anthony M. "The Rebellious Teaching Career of E. Franklin Frazier." *Journal of Blacks in Higher Education,* no. 13 (Autumn 1996): 86–90.

Rowell, Charles H. "Let Me Be with Ole Jazzbo: An Interview with Sterling A. Brown." *Callaloo* 14 (1991): 795–815.

Slater, Robert Bruce. "The First Black Faculty Members at the Nation's Highest-Ranked Universities." *Journal of Blacks in Higher Education* (1998–1999): 97.

Spencer, Jon Michael. "The Black Church and the Harlem Renaissance." *African American Review* 30 (1996): 453–60.

Thelwell, Michael Ekwueme. "The Professor and the Activists: A Memoir of Sterling Brown." *Massachusetts Review* (Winter 1999/2000): 617–38.

Traylor, Eleanor W., R. Victoria Arana, and John M. Reilly. "Runnin' Space: The Continuing Legacy of Sterling Brown." *African American Review* 31 (1997): 382–92.

Wacker, R. Fred. "An American Dilemma: The Theories of Robert Park and Gunnar Myrdal." *Phylon* 37 (1976): 117–25.

Watts, Jerry G. "Dilemmas of Black Intellectuals: What Role Should We Play?" *Dissent* (1989): 501–7.

West, Cornel. "The Dilemma of the Black Intellectual." *Journal of Blacks in Higher Education* 2 (1993/1994): 59–67.

Williams, Yohuru R. "John Hope Franklin's Troubled Tenure at Howard University, 1947–1956: Professor of History." *Negro History Bulletin* (July–December 1998).

Wilson, Francille Rusan. "Racial Consciousness and Black Scholarship: Charles H. Wesley and the Construction of Negro Labor in the United States." *Journal of Negro History* 81 (1996): 72–88.

Winston, Michael R. "Through the Back Door: Academic Racism and the Negro Scholar in Historical Perspective." *Daedalus* 100 (1971): 671–701.

———. *The Howard University Department of History, 1913–1973.* Washington, D.C.: Howard University Press, 1973.

———. "Carter Godwin Woodson: Prophet of a Black Tradition." *Journal of History* 60, no. 4 (October 1975): 459–63.

———. "E. Franklin Frazier's Role in African Studies." In *E. Franklin Frazier and the Black Bourgeoisie,* ed. James E. Teele. Columbia: University of Missouri Press, 2002.

Wright, W. D. "The Thought and Leadership of Kelly Miller." *Phylon* 39 (1978): 180–92.

Yates, Eleanor Lee. "The Quiet Activist: Ralph Bunche." *Black Issues in Higher Education* 19 (2002): 46.

INDEX

Academia. *See* Education, higher
Academic freedom: Durkee not respecting, 24, 33; Johnson's support for, 51, 59, 66–67; Red Scare and, 112; in writing of centennial history of Howard, 119–22
Accommodationism, 22
Accreditation, 32, 59; in Johnson's goals, 46, 54, 67
Activism: of black intellectuals, 2–3; global, 150; by Howard faculty, 12–13; by Howard graduates, 4–5; by Howard intellectuals, 8, 80–81, 95, 158–59; scholarship and, 184–85, 197; scholarship *vs.*, 126–28, 132–33; Thurman's, 58
Administration: Johnson's, 62–63, 67, 69; Johnson's lack of experience in, 61, 63; salaries compared to faculty's, 44–45
Africa, 137, 160; American Society for the Study of African Culture and, 146–48; in black public sphere, 126–27; diaspora and, 168, 198; Frazier's expertise on, 184–86; Hansberry's work in, 96, 206n26; history of, 62, 96; Howard intellectuals and, 62, 96, 151, 153, 184–86, 206n26; independence movements in, 146–47, 185; relations with United States and Britain, 147–48; research in, 91–93, 183–84
Africa-America Institute (AAI), in New York, 9, 180
Africa and the Afro-American Experience (Williams), 92
African Academy of Arts and Research, 173

African-American Institute, 206n26
African American policy studies, 95
African American religious studies, 162
African American studies, 167, 181
African American studies, at Howard, 5, 22, 95, 198
African diaspora studies, 168–69
African history department, Hansberry in, 61
African policy studies, 95, 198
African studies: Frazier in, 60, 184, 186; Hansberry in, 61, 96–97, 116–17; Howard intellectuals' involvement in, 157–58, 167, 180
African Studies Association, 184
African studies department, Howard's, 95, 186
Africana encyclopedia project, 18, 136–39
Africana policy studies, 6, 95, 160, 175, 178; Howard pioneering, 9, 142, 157–59, 177, 181
Africana Research Center, at Cornell University, 179
Africana studies, 169, 181
Afro-Americans and Africans (Williams), 92
Afro-Americans and the United Nations (Harris), 125
Afro-Asian Conference, 146
Afrocentrism, and Hansberry, 96–97
Agency, African American, 111–12
Algood, Miles C., 30
Alumni, Howard, 20, 36, 150, 179; dissatisfaction with Durkee, 11, 23–24, 28–29, 31–33; as epitome of black public intellectuals, 3–4; on selection of president, 34–35; trustees' relationship

intellectuals' involvement in, 166, 168

Congress, U.S., 30, 32, 93; Howard's appropriations from (*See* Appropriations); interference at Howard, 59, 112

Conkling Bruce, Roscoe, 24

Cook, George William, 18–19, 22

Cook, W. Mercer, 77, 114, 152, 211n3; AMSAC and, 146–47; on intellectual community at Howard, 83–85, 123–24; Maran and, 153–54

Cooper, Anna Julia, 163, 220n13

Cornell University, Africana Research Center at, 179

Council on African Affairs, 184–85, 222n66

Cramton, Louis C., 32, 47, 50

Cramton Bill, appropriation to Howard in, 39

Crisis, 35, 96; censorship of Du Bois in, 142–43; *Journal of Negro Education* compared to, 178; as outlet for black intellectuals, 84, 128, 142

Crisis of the Negro Intellectual, The (Cruse), 14–15, 182

Crummell, Alexander, 11, 14–15, 28, 161

Cruse, Harold, 14–15, 182, 222n56

Cuba, collection of works by authors from, 169

Cullen, Countee, 133

Cultural pluralism, 159, 160–61, 164–65

Culture, African, 173

Culture, black, 13, 23, 164, 176; Frazier's critiques of, 181; integration of, 182–83; music in, 160–61; research on, 106–7, 160; in Washington, 12, 14

Curriculum, faculty criticisms of Howard's, 22–23

Curry School of Expression, in Boston, 33

Dagbovie, Pero, 8, 16, 89, 94

Davis, Arthur P., 61, 97, 107, 119, 121

Davis, John A., 143, 146–47, 193

Davis, W. Allison, 85, 107, 140

Dawson, William L., 131

Deans, 22, 54; of college of education, 60; of law school, 55–56; of school of religion, 57–59; Triumvirate, 18–19; vs. Durkee, 19, 28–29

Diggs, Charles C., 130–31

"Dilemma of the American Negro Scholar, The" (Franklin), 190–91

"Dilemma of the Black Intellectual, The" (West), 190

"Dilemmas of Black Intellectuals" (Watts), 191–92

Diop, Alioune, 146, 185

Discrimination, 47, 64; effects in education, 95–96; gender, 93–94; research on, 159–60; in status of black intellectuals, 126, 128, 191, 193; theology of race relations used against, 57. *See also* Racism

Doctors, Howard training, 60

Dollard, John, 165

Double consciousness, 6, 18, 67, 215n56; of black male intellectuals, 111–12; of black scholars, 82, 128–29, 132; reconciliation of, 183–86; secular vs. sacred, 69

Douglass, Frederick, 99

Drake, St. Clair, 107, 193

"Dream Team," at Harvard University, 7, 157–58, 189–90, 203n12

Drew, Charles, 60, 79, 189

Dreyfus, Alfred, 196

Du Bois, W. E. B., 204n8; Africana encyclopedia project and, 136–39; *Crisis*, 96; criticisms of, 18; Crummell's influence on, 14–15; on double consciousness, 6, 215n56; in fraternity, 99; harassed during Red Scare, 16; Howard intellectuals' relationship with, 8, 132; on Howard's selection of president, 35; Howard University as heirs to legacy of, 1, 3; influence of color line idea of, 17; influence of talented tenth idea of, 17; influence on Howard's Black Africana studies policy institute, 4; interactions with Howard intellectuals, 196; *Journal of the International Institute of Afro-American Studies* and, 168; Locke's report to Johnson on, 65; on next president to be black, 34; position on segregation: censorship in *Crisis*, 142–44; praise for Locke, 85, 87–88; reputation of, 17; speaking at Howard, 70, 112, 162; social science department

ABOUT THE AUTHOR

Zachery R. Williams is the Director of the African Cultures and Policy Studies Institute and the editor of *Africana Cultures and Policy Studies: Scholarship and the Transformation of Public Policy.*